Pacific Destiny

Related books by Edwin P. Hoyt

The Mutiny on the Globe

War in the Deep

The Lonely Ships

How They Won the War in the Pacific

Blue Skies and Blood:
The Battle of the Coral Sea

The Battle of Leyte Gulf

The American Attitude

Storm over the Gilberts

To the Marianas

The Boxer Rebellion

Pacific Destiny

The Story of America in the Western Sea
from the Early 1800s to the 1980s

by Edwin P. Hoyt

W. W. Norton & Company

New York   London

Copyright © 1981 by Edwin P. Hoyt

Published simultaneously in Canada by George J. McLeod Limited, Toronto.

Printed in the United States of America

All Rights Reserved

First Edition

Library of Congress Cataloging in Publication Data

Hoyt, Edwin Palmer.
   Pacific destiny.

   Bibliography: p.
   Includes index.
   1. East Asia—Foreign relations—United States.
2. United States—Foreign relations—East Asia.
3. Asia, Southeastern—Foreign relations—United
States. 4. United States—Foreign relations—
Asia, Southeastern. 5. World War, 1939-1945—
Pacific Ocean. I. Title.
DS518.8.H64 1981   327.7305   81-2709
ISBN 0-393-01472-X   AACR2

W. W. Norton & Company, Inc. 500 Fifth Avenue, New York, N.Y. 10110
W. W. Norton & Company, Ltd. 25 New Street Square, London EC4A 3NT

1 2 3 4 5 6 7 8 9 0

For Olga Gruhzit Hoyt

who has suffered through all the years of research and writing
that led up to this book.

Contents

Contents

Contents

Pacific Destiny

1

Beginnings

~~~~~~~~~~

ON THE AFTERNOON OF MARCH 28, 1814, an offshore wind began blowing up from the south through the bare ravines of the hills that enclose Valparaiso's shallow harbor. In an hour the breeze had become a gale. This was precisely the weather Captain David Porter had prayed against, for Valparaiso Bay is scarcely worthy of the name; as he had feared, the cable to his port anchor parted and the starboard anchor began dragging out to sea as the usually quiet waves of the bay turned white with spray. Off at the point on the western end of the bay Captain Porter could see his enemies: Captain James Hillyar's frigate *Phoebe* and her sloop of war, *HMS Cherub*. For a month and a half the 36-gun British frigate and her attendant ships had blockaded the American 32-gun frigate *Essex* in Valparaiso harbor, and although these gun ratings for both ships are understated, the *Phoebe* was a far stronger vessel. Captain Porter was not afraid of a fight, but since the British forces were more powerful his only chance to survive lay in escaping to the open sea.

In this wind he was sailing with topsails close reefed; even the topgallant sails were immediately taken in as the wind drove the *Essex* across the bay. The men on the main topgallant yard were finishing the lashing when a squall struck just as the ship rounded the point. The *Essex* heeled over, nearly gunwale down, and her main topmast broke off and crashed into the sea carrying to death the four men on the topgallant yard.

There was nothing to do but turn and run back for the slender protection of the anchorage. Porter gave the order but the British, who for two months had observed the laws of neutrality that set the limitation for warfare at Chile's three-mile limit, now saw a chance to pursue and conquer a wounded

1

enemy and the laws of war were cast to the gale. The *Phoebe* and the *Cherub* ran in and prevented Porter from reaching his destination. Instead, the American ship had to anchor in a tiny bay a quarter mile offshore. It was obvious to all aboard the American frigate that the enemy was going to attack even before the battle flags were raised.

In answer, Porter ordered flags to every mast to show his willingness to meet the challenge, illegal though it was. Cautiously the *Phoebe* came up until she was under the stern of the anchored *Essex* and the *Cherub* moved in on her port bow. These two positions were relatively safe from the guns of the American ship. She carried forty 32-pound carronades, fine for broadsides but short of range and not trainable. She also had six 12-pound long guns fore and aft and there was nothing the British could do to avoid fire from these. But in a contest of gunnery, the *Phoebe* had all the advantages for she carried thirty 18-pound long guns, sixteen 32-pound carronades, eight 24-pound long guns, and six long 12-pounders. As long as she could stay away from the *Essex* broadsides she outgunned the American ship ten to one.

At six minutes before four o'clock in the afternoon Captain Hillyar opened fire. For half an hour the *Phoebe* ranged back and forth behind the *Essex,* firing one broadside and then the other. In front the *Cherub* did the same, using her eighteen 32-pound carronades, eight 24-pounders, and two long 9-pound guns. The damage to the American frigate was enormous. Captain Porter's one hope was to manage to attach a spring to his single anchor cable. This spring would make it possible to turn the *Essex* even at anchor, and thus let Porter bring those deadly carronades to bear in broadside attack. Three times the springs were attached, and three times the British shot them away before Porter could fire his big guns. The sails were soon riddled. The ensign at the gaff was shot down and so was the ship's motto flag at the mizzen. Soon only one flag remained. It was the banner that symbolized the young American Navy's defiance of Britannia: *Free Trade and Sailor's Rights*. That was what the war was all about.

The Americans in the bow trained their three long 12-pound guns on the *Cherub,* and in the first fifteen minutes of the battle holed her sails repeatedly and put a number of shots into her hull, then set to firing grape to rake the decks. When one man fell dead and three others were wounded, the captain of the *Cherub* found his position too uncomfortable and moved around behind the *Essex* to join the *Phoebe*. The *Essex* had only three long 12-pounders to bear on both ships at the stern, but even so, after half an hour Captain Hillyar retired from the battle and moved away to repair damage to masts and sails.

The Americans ran up more flags and did what they could to bring more guns to bear. But 12-pound long guns could not be dragged the 140 feet from stem to stern in a few minutes, and that was all they had. In half an hour the British were back again, taking position on the starboard quarter of the *Essex,* out of range of the carronades. Now, even the long guns at the stern could not be brought to bear.

In such a desperate position, Captain Porter gave the order to get under way; he would try to move up and board the *Phoebe*. But when the men turned to bring up the sails, they discovered that all lines had been shot away except one and that they could hoist only the flying jib. They did, Captain Porter ordered the anchor cable cut, and the *Essex* turned, bringing her broadsides to bear as she moved toward her enemies. The British immediately retired again, having the advantage of relatively undamaged rigging, and they continued to pour shot into the *Essex* from out of her range.

In the first phase of the battle, Captain Porter's crew had been hit hard, but now the killing became slaughter. Midshipman David Glasgow Farragut was on the gundeck, and he later wrote of the men around him falling like grass in a hurricane. A boatswain's mate standing beside him was struck squarely in the abdomen by a roundshot, his whole belly was taken out, leaving a great hole, and then he fell dead. Farragut went up to the main deck to stand near the captain, and as he came up he saw a round shot ricochet off the scuppers and kill four men at the long gun there.

Porter was keeping count. Fifteen men were killed manning one of the long guns, and that was how it was going all over the ship. He decided to run the ship ashore and destroy her, saving the crew to take refuge in neutral Chile. But the wind shifted and turned the *Essex* again toward the *Phoebe*. The destruction continued.

Finally Captain Porter called his officers to assemble and report on the condition of ship and crew. He found that only one officer, Lieutenant Stephen Decatur McKnight, was still on his feet. The cockpit, the steerage, the wardroom and the berth deck were filled to overflowing with the wounded. The ship had so many holes in her bottom that she was sinking.

Having heard this unhappy report, at 5:40 in the afternoon Captain Porter surrendered to his enemies. He had come into battle with a crew of 255 men and 155 of them were killed, dying, or wounded, and 31 were missing. Of these, 7 led by Quarter Gunner Adam Roche, had deserted in the face of the enemy, taking the ship's only remaining boat to shore. All the rest had fought bravely to the very end. Because the British ships could stand off the anchored *Essex* out of range, the *Phoebe* reported only 4 men killed and 7 wounded and the *Cherub* only 1 dead and 3 wounded. Captain Porter and his men were captured and sent to the United States under parole aboard one of Porter's own captives, the ship *Atlantic*. Parole meant Captain Porter agreed to refrain from fighting the British again. It was a gentlemanly solution to the problem of prisoners of war, which no ships in foreign waters were prepared to accommodate. The *Phoebe* and the *Cherub* having ended this serious threat to British commerce, then went about His Majesty's other business. Thus came to

3

an end the remarkable career of the first American commerce raider ever to harry the enemy in Pacific waters.

IN THE 13 MONTHS before the battle of Valparaiso the *Essex* had come to the Pacific through a series of accidents, not because of any design on the part of the American administration or naval strategists. While travelling to India, Captain Porter had learned of the presence of a large number of British ships off South America, a fact generally unknown or at least ignored in Washington.

In the beginnings of English domination of North America, England's eyes were on the Atlantic Ocean. To England at that time the Pacific Ocean was a vast and largely unexplored waste. Even by the time of the Revolution, only a handful of American vessels had ventured into the Pacific, rounding Cape Horn; and except for the China trade and whaling the area seemed to have little to offer. Even the handful of whalers who went into the Pacific were considered foolish for there still were plenty of whales to be taken in the Atlantic south of the Azores and along the South American coast. Thus, serious American involvement in the Pacific did not occur until the War of 1812.

Captain Porter, commander of the *Essex,* was the first American naval figure to explore the Pacific. When the call to arms came on June 18, 1812, the frigates *President, United States, Congress,* and the smaller vessels *Hornet* and *Argus* set sail almost immediately from New York. *Essex* was to follow them south and join up to harry British shipping in the Caribbean. A fleet of a hundred Jamaican merchant ships was set to pass near the coast of the United States just about the time they would arrive off Florida.

By the time *Essex* sailed, nearly two weeks after the others, the authorities in Washington had new orders for Captain Porter. He was to search for the British 36-gun frigate *Thetis,* which was supposedly carrying gold and silver to South America. Porter sailed south, did not find the *Thetis,* but did capture a number of British vessels. Midshipman David Glasgow Farragut, who was not yet twelve years old, made his reputation on this voyage for bravery in the face of the enemy.

After all his seniors had been assigned to man captured vessels and there were no spare lieutenants left aboard the frigate, twelve-year-old Midshipman Farragut was made prize captain of a whaling merchantman, in charge of a small prize crew. The whaling captain believed he could overcome this mere boy and tried to retake his ship, whereupon Mr. Midshipman Farragut drew his cutlass, ordered his men to fire for effect if necessary, and put down the attempt. He told the captain if he made another move he would be put in irons.

4

Later the British crew was taken off ship and an even smaller prize crew sailed her away to neutral waters while Midshipman Farragut rejoined the *Essex* on her raiding.

The *Essex* was to be part of a squadron that would be sent to the Indian ocean to draw British warships away from the American blockade. *Essex* failed to make contact with the other ships off South America. The orders gave Captain Porter the latitude to choose his own course in case of such failure, so he decided to head into the Pacific because he had heard that British whalers had come to the area in great numbers. On February 14, 1813, the *Essex* sailed around the Horn. She met a dreadful gale; for three days the small ship tossed and plunged in the heaviest seas her crew had ever seen; the gun deck portholes were stove from bow to stern; boats were lost. At one point it seemed certain the *Essex* would capsize, but at the end of the first week of March she reached calm water and ten days later put in at Valparaiso for provisions.

Captain Porter learned that British men-of-war as well as many British whaling vessels were cruising off the Pacific coast of South America. Since whale oil was the standard fuel for lighting, and the South American fleet was Britain's major supplier, he decided to destroy the British whaling fleet, knowing that this action would bring considerable pain to London. During the next six months the *Essex* captured more than a dozen whalers, merchantmen and privateers sailing for the British. One new enemy whaleship, christened *Atlantic,* was found to be so sound and so fast that she was equipped with twenty guns and turned into an American warship. Porter named her *Essex Junior,* and sent her off under an American crew to hunt alone.

By midsummer the name *Essex* was so well known and feared that the hunting grew sparse. Captain Porter brought the *Essex* to James Island off the Peruvian coast, and the men repainted her to change her appearance. She was disguised as a whaler, with an imitation trypot aft and the gunports concealed. At the same time the crew painted a prize named the *Seringapatam* to look like the *Essex.* Another prize was disguised as a sloop of war. These ships were sent off north to dupe the enemy while the *Essex,* to all appearances now a whaler, set out south to continue her captures. On September 15, 1813, Captain Porter captured the privateer *Sir Andrew Hammond,* and a few days later Porter made rendezvous with *Essex Junior.* Lieutenant John Downes, captain of the *Essex Junior,* sailed to Valparaiso to learn news of the war. There he heard that the British had sent a squadron out to try to catch the *Essex.* When Captain Porter had that information, he decided it would be a good idea to leave this region for a while.

Besides the obvious threat posed by a superior British naval force, the Captain foresaw other troubles. The *Essex* had been many months at sea and the ship was full of rats. These rats had grown so hungry that they came out

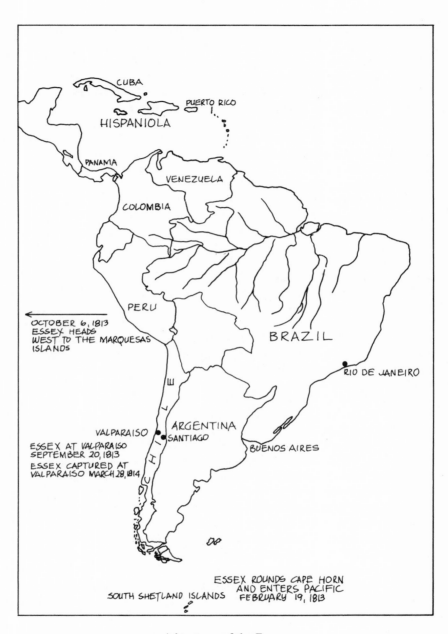

Adventures of the *Essex*

at night and attacked the crew. There had been no chance to repair properly the damage suffered by the ship in the voyage around Cape Horn.

Captain Porter looked over his charts: Westward lay the virtually unknown Marquesas Islands. Behind, to the east, lay civilized Peruvian and Chilean ports, but these must be expected to draw British warships. Captain Porter knew that to go inside one of these harbors was to court disaster. He decided to sail west to the islands where his enemies would scarcely expect to find him, and there to clean his ships and make repairs. For that reason, early in October, the *Essex* and her entourage of captured vessels sailed for the South Pacific, and on October 23, they arrived at Nukuhiva, one of the largest of the Marquesas, where they found a deep harbor. Captain Porter went ashore, claimed the islands for the United States, and set his men to building a fort. The Marquesas were now American territory.

Like most Polynesians, the Marquesans were belligerent and for years had been almost exclusively engaged in fighting one another. At the time that the Americans arrived, the Marquesan tribes had reached a standoff; but the coming of the ships to Nukuhiva brought an enormous advantage to the islanders who lived around this bay. The Americans gave them iron cooking pots, steel knives, and bullets that made jewelry. Learning of these riches, the other tribes decided to take all and launched several attacks on the village and the fort. The Americans took in the villagers and defended the fort, but after a few weeks the matter grew so serious that Captain Porter sent out a punitive expedition. The American sailors engaged in several skirmishes and killed a number of Marquesans with their firearms. The muskets cowed the other tribes and reluctantly they withdrew. Peace came to the island temporarily.

When the *Essex* and her flotilla had anchored, Captain Porter demanded the parole (guarantee that they would not try to escape) of his many British captives from the whaling ships. They agreed, and he freed the British to live on the island during their stay. Most of the American seamen also went ashore to live. Soon all the white men were feasting and drinking and the seamen were becoming familiar with their officers. Porter saw that this familiarity meant trouble. The Polynesian way of life created disciplinary problems. The chaplain said he was horrified by the aggressiveness of the women. He pleaded with Captain Porter to set sail, but Captain Porter said he had to get the *Essex* in shape for another cruise. He had a responsibility to Congress and the Navy department that transcended his responsibility to God. He did agree, however, to the chaplain's demand that at least the young midshipmen should be preserved from such arrant wickedness, so twelve-year-old Midshipman David Farragut and the other pubescent crewmen were sent aboard ship—one of the whalers—where the chaplain was in command. Instead of disporting themselves with native girls, as did their elders, the youngsters studied navigation, ethics, English, and arithmetic.

Two of the captured British whalers were sent to America with full loads of whale oil, under United States naval crews. This departure so decreased the size of the American garrison that the British captives decided it was worth while to try to rebel and seize the fort. But the plot was betrayed by a native to Captain Porter, and the British captives were then confined, fenced in on one small peninsula of the island.

During this interregnum, the *Essex*'s guns were taken down and overhauled thoroughly; the stores were taken ashore and the ship was sealed up and smoked to kill the rats.

The de-ratting completed, the stores were moved back aboard ship, augmented by smoked fish and pork acquired on the island. At the end of November the chaplain reported that the amoral life of the Polynesians was destroying the morale as well as the morals of Porter's men. His complaint was redundant since Captain Porter had already decided it was high time to put to sea.

When the men had the news that the ships were ready, the grumbling began. They were being told to leave a luxury they had never before known for duty. Some of the most independent sailors began talking of mutiny. When Captain Porter issued his sailing orders, the sounds of discontent grew louder. The center of the conspiracy was an English seaman named Robert White, a member of the crew of one of the British vessels who had elected to join the American Navy.

White wanted to remain in Nukuhiva with his *wahine*. He would be king of the island. Robert White gathered about him a cadre of mutineers. A few days before the announced sailing date, Seaman White assembled his group aboard the *Essex Junior,* which was being reprovisioned after ratting. He outlined his desperate program for mutiny—and then a life of total abandon in the islands. But within hours Captain Porter learned of the plot. He advanced the sailing date to put the mutineers off balance. At dawn on the morning of December 10, 1813, Captain Porter ordered every man to board ship. Along the shore armed marines stood guard to be sure the order was obeyed.

Aboard the *Essex* the captain walked to the capstan on the main deck. This was the point at which the crew was normally gathered. Captain Porter was red-faced, shaking with anger. He drew his cutlass with a slash in the air and laid it on the capstan as the boatswains mustered the men on the port side. When the crew was quiet, standing at attention, Porter spoke.

"All of you who are in favor of weighing the anchor when I give the order, pass over to the starboard side. . . ."

"In favor of?"

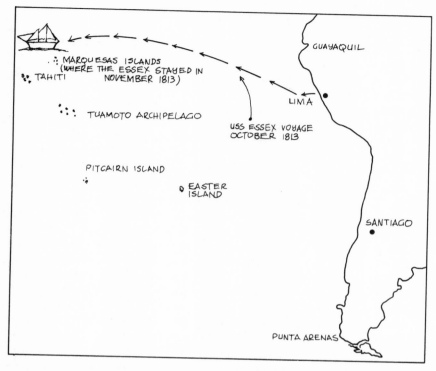

The *Essex* moves up the west coast of South America during the War of 1812

This was not a normal order. They saw every officer, armed with pistols and a cutlass, the marines ringed about the deck, muskets ready. The seamen were surrounded by weapons and grim faces. One by one the men passed over and stood on the starboard deck.

Captain Porter looked at the men bleakly.

"Robert White, step forward."

White stepped up.

"Did you not tell them aboard *Essex Junior* that the crew of this ship would refuse to weigh anchor?"

White trembled.

"No sir," he said.

"You lie, you scoundrel!"

Captain Porter turned.

"Where is the list of men who visited the *Essex Junior* on Sunday?"

A midshipman handed the list to him, and he began to call names.

9

"Able Seaman Hatchett, step forward."

The man stepped up.

"Did you or did you not hear of this thing on board the *Essex Junior?*"

"Yes sir."

"Seaman Blodgett, did you or did you not hear. . . ."

"Yes sir."

"Seaman Allen, did you or did you not . . . ?"

"Yes sir."

Every man testified that he heard of the mutiny aboard the *Essex Junior*. The captain picked up his cutlass. He turned to Seaman White.

"There you are, you scoundrel. Run! Run for your life."

White leaped up, looked over his shoulder as the captain took a step toward him, and then threw himself over the starboard rail and began swimming for shore. Porter stepped back and sheathed the cutlass. He turned to the men.

He praised their virtues under fire during the past months. The pleasure of the tropic shore had been good, he said, but now this was all behind them. They were American seamen duty-bound once more. Porter said he would blow up the ship, rather than see the success of any mutiny. Let them be sure they understood that.

Finishing on that grim note he swung around, and the fiddler stepped up on the capstan and began to saw out the notes of "The Girl I Left Behind Me." The men grasped the bars and began moving clockwise, chain rattled, and the anchor came up out of the coral sand. Men moved into the rigging and set the sails. In half an hour they were out of the harbor. The *Essex* sailed east and north, back into battle. After several more adventures the *Essex* was trapped in Valparaiso harbor by the British warships, the *Phoebe* and the *Cherub*. After that most unequal fight on the edge of the harbor and Captain Porter's surrender to save what was left of his crew, the saga of the first American warship in the Pacific was nearly ended, but not quite. Captain Porter had left a garrison behind at Nukuhiva under Lieutenant John M. Gamble to watch over the fort and the three prizes not deemed suitable for battle. He intended to return or send for them. But, almost as soon as the warships sailed, natives from the inland villages attacked the fort, the friendly Marquesans were killed or fled, and the Americans had to move back to the ships in the harbor.

It was an uncomfortable life, but bearable, until one man tried to swim ashore and was drowned. A few weeks later four men stole a longboat and deserted. By April John Gamble's force was down to seventeen officers and men aboard three ships, the *Seringapatam,* the *Sir Andrew Hammond,* and the *Greenwich.* One day in May when Lieutenant Gamble boarded the *Seringapatam,* he was attacked by mutinous sailors. But even in mutiny they were not totally heartless. They put Gamble into a canoe and sailed away with the ship. He survived and rejoined the other Americans.

By May 1, 1814, the number of Americans was reduced to eight. On May 9, 1814, Marquesans attacked the ships and in repelling them, one sailor was killed and three others were wounded. So the effective force was cut to four men. The next night Lieutenant Gamble abandoned the *Greenwich* and sailed in the *Sir Andrew Hammond,* leaving the new American territorial acquisition unguarded. Lieutenant Gamble had the only firearm, a pistol, with six cartridges. After seventeen days his ship reached the Sandwich Islands (as Hawaii was then called), and she was unfortunate enough to encounter the British *Cherub,* which had been involved in the destruction of their mother ship the *Essex.* Lieutenant Gamble and his men were taken aboard the British warship but were freed finally when the *Cherub* called at Rio de Janeiro. Lieutenant Gamble and company arrived in New York in August, 1815; by this time America was firmly blockaded and the government had neither time nor resources to consider the treatment of new "colony" in the Pacific, so Nukuhiva was forgotten in Washington. The islands were "discovered" by the French a few years later and became part of their colonies in the Pacific.

2

Stirrings

~~~~~

WHEN THE WAR OF 1812 ENDED (despite the battle of Valparaiso Bay of 1814), the American adventure in the Marquesas was forgotten because the United States of America was oriented eastward. This orientation was quite natural given the racial origins of the people who settled the Eastern American colonies: English, French, Dutch, Swedish, Irish, German, and Spanish. The continent was vast and few men penetrated its breadth to the Pacific side until Lewis and Clark had made the journey in 1803 to prove the feasibility of an overland route to the far west. John Jacob Astor had established a fur trading post at the mouth of the Columbia River in 1811, but American awareness of the Pacific was slow in coming although at least four European nations had early recognized the potential of the Pacific basin and had established colonies in Asia and the Pacific islands where the spice trade had flourished. Indeed that was one of the reasons for the discontent of England's American colonies in 1775, because the London government insisted that Americans "buy British" and sternly discouraged the establishment of direct American trade with the Far East.

For five years after the war the nation was bemused by internal affairs. Such attention as was given to the navy and trade focused on the Mediterranean where Stephen Decatur finally put an end to the depredations of the Barbary Pirates. So it was not until 1820 that the first United States warship visited Canton for goodwill; she was the USS *Congress*, one of the big frigates that had been built during the Quasi-War with France and the Barbary Wars. Her Captain was J. D. Henley. Merchant ships, however, had preceded the United States Navy. Almost as soon as the British were driven from

13

American shores merchants of the eastern seaboard set out to look for business and joined with alacrity in the spice, ivory, and opium trade of China. Before the turn of the nineteenth century, too, American sailors visited Japan. They were surprised to learn that the Japanese disliked white foreigners and would not let them land. When some U.S. merchant-ship crews defiantly tried to go ashore, they found themselves driven off by angry *samurai*. So the Americans retreated from Japan, baffled, as were the English and the French, but they did not abandon the Pacific.

The American navy, far more than the American government, seemed to appreciate the potential of "the other ocean" which sprawled halfway across the world. Three years after President James Monroe cemented George Washington's policy of isolationism with the Monroe Doctrine, Captain W. B. Finch took the USS *Vincennes* on a voyage to China and other countries. But the first real United States naval involvement in the Pacific came in 1824, shortly after President James Monroe had laid a claim to a protectorate over the Western hemisphere. In 1824, Commodore Isaac Hull was sent with a squadron of ships down to Callao, the port of Lima, on the Pacific side of South America, to guard against foreign influences and protect American fisheries.

In the summer of 1824, Commodore Hull received a letter from U.S. Consul Michael Hogan at Valparaiso, informing him of a mutiny aboard the American whaler *Globe* from Nantucket. The *Globe*'s captain and mates had been killed, and the mutineers had sailed to some undetermined Pacific islands and planned to burn the ship and live on the islands. But half a dozen men had escaped with the ship and sailed it back to Valparaiso. They had been arrested by the U.S. Consul, Michael Hogan, suspected of mutiny, and sent back to Nantucket to face trial. Now the other mutineers had to be found and brought to punishment.

The Hogan letter was advisory and Commodore Hull had too many official duties to pay much attention to it. But in May, 1825, Hull had orders from Secretary of the Navy S. L. Southard to conduct a search of the Pacific islands for the *Globe* mutineers, and if he could find them, to bring them home. These orders coincided with other commands to show the flag in the Pacific, call at as many ports as possible and ascertain the possibilities of fishing and trade, and chart the unknown seas.

Commodore Hull chose Lieutenant John Percival for this task. "Mad Jack" Percival was known throughout the navy for his exploits in the Barbary Wars and in the squadron for his bravery and determination. There could not have been a better man for the job. His ship, the USS *Dolphin,* was a topsail schooner, ideal for the task of island hopping because of her fore and aft rig, and small enough so that her absence from the squadron for many months would not be critical.

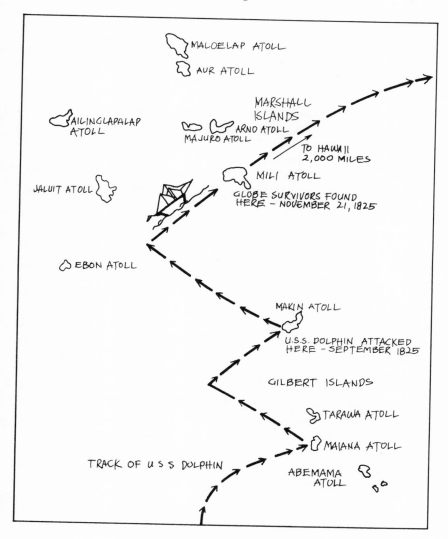

Track of USS *Dolphin*

In September the *Dolphin* was deep in the Pacific. She visited the Caroline islands but found nothing there. Lieutenant Percival then began searching for landfalls at various positions reported by American ships—mostly whalers—where they had sighted land. But the whaling captains' navigation often was not accurate and Lieutenant Percival found no land where land should have been.

In September, 1825, the *Dolphin* put in at the Kingsmill Group of the Gilbert Islands. Lieutenant Percival learned that the *Globe* had been there. He also ran into trouble.

The islanders were very wild. They came aboard the anchored ship in grass skirts and shark tooth necklaces, with spears and clubs. They wanted to trade. They stole a few pieces of equipment when Lieutenant Percival would not trade them and refused to return the equipment. At dark the sailors hustled them off the ship, but that night fires burned around the beach and drums beat. Next day, about noon, canoes moved in on the *Dolphin* from all directions. It did not take long for the Americans to see that their occupants were belligerent.

Lieutenant Hiram Paulding, the officer of the watch, was challenged by an islander wearing shell necklaces, anklets, and wristlets, and carrying a shark-tooth spear, who boarded the ship. Lieutenant Paulding raised his pistol. The warrior raised his spear. Lieutenant Paulding gestured him overboard. The spearman made a threatening move, and Lieutenant Paulding shot him in the legs and the spearman dropped his weapon. Paulding had been using bird shot so the islander was not badly hurt.

He went away. But others were not to be driven off, it appeared. The canoes circled the ship for an hour. Finally, as the Americans showed no signs of letting them board, they dispersed to shore.

Lieutenant Jack Percival had been ordered to explore all the islands he found, so he took a boat and went to the shore. The islanders surrounded the boat as it came in. One jumped into the boat, seized a musket from a marine, jumped back over the side and disappeared in the brush. Lieutenant Percival went in to investigate. He told his executive officer to be ready to fire the ship's guns on signal at a hut on the hill.

Percival came back without the musket and gave the order. Soon the hut was riddled. This brought about a parley; an old chief came up with a green branch in his hand. Percival demanded the musket and got it back. But as evening came on, and the drums began to beat, the atmosphere ashore grew menacing. Percival toured the island, found it almost waterless and not very valuable to an American eye, and finally made it back to his ship under the angry glares of the islanders. Then the lieutenant lost no time in weighing anchor, to clear the island before darkness lowered.

The *Dolphin* stopped at several other islands but found nothing of interest nor any traces of the *Globe* mutineers. Finally on November 19, 1825, the topsail schooner reached the Marshall chain. The first two days were spent finding and taking on fresh water. In the process one shore party discovered a whaler's lance. But when the islanders were asked about it, they said they did not know where it had come from. After three days of search, during which they found a few rotted bits of canvas, Lieutenant Percival moved to the atoll of Mili. And here, while the islanders admitted nothing, Mad Jack found evidence of American sailors. The platforms of several canoes were made from sailors' wooden chests. He found pieces of ash spars on islands where ash did not grow.

After two days the Americans began to move along the islands and on one found a leather mitten with the name Rowland Coffin on it. Lieutenant Percival had a list of the names of the crew of the *Globe*. Rowland Coffin was a son of one of the owners. The *Globe* had been here, no doubt about it.

Poking about the islands of Mili, the searchers came across a cache. They found a skeleton and a box of Spanish silver pieces and other debris of western sailors. And finally they found two young men who spoke English although they were as dark as the people with whom they lived.

These were William Lay and Cyrus Hussey, the only two survivors of the *Globe* crew. The others had been killed a year before by the natives after Samuel Comstock, the leader, had stolen an islander's wife. These two young boys had alone been spared. Now they were saved. Lieutenant Percival called all of the chiefs of the atoll together and warned them to respect American ships in the future on pain of extermination; he found the place where the *Globe* mutineers had lived and died and dug up the bones of the mutineers to bring home.

On the way they stopped at the Hawaiian Islands, where Lieutenant Percival quarreled with the Reverend Hiram Bingham over sailors' rights (to women and rum ashore), and Bingham persuaded King Kamehameha to put a *kapu* on the women of Honolulu so that they would not consort with the sailors. The furious sailors set fire to Mr. Bingham's house, which must have pleased a number of Hawaiians. But they also tried to burn down the house of a local chief. The soldiers of the King restrained them, there was a fight, and Lieutenant Percival had some explaining to do when he returned to Valparaiso. But so great was his exploit otherwise, and so pleased was Commodore Hull with the outcome, that the Reverend Mr. Bingham's plaints produced no lasting scars.

THE NEXT IMPORTANT UNITED STATES NAVAL ADVENTURE in the Pacific came in 1831 when President Andrew Jackson sent Captain John Downes in the 44-gun frigate *Potomac* to suppress pirates who were interfering with the American spice trade in Sumatra. It was a matter of national honor and, more than that, of trade; Andy Jackson was not about to let a "gang of natives" push American merchant crews around.

The incident had begun on February 7 of that year, when a captain named Endicott anchored his ship, the *Friendship*, off Qualla Battoo on the northwest coast of Sumatra and began loading a cargo of pepper for his firm's warehouses in Salem, Massachusetts. Qualla Battoo, by a seaman's standards, was a thoroughly miserable hole, only four degrees above the equator, and so hot that the planks of the deck warped in the sun, oil came oozing out of the rope rigging, and tar dripped from the ship's seams. From a seaman's point of view, the place was equally obnoxious: there was no harbor, and the *Friendship* was forced to lay offshore half a mile in what was no better than open sea and bring all the cargo out in the ship's boats. Captain Endicott had kept the first mate and eight of the men of the crew aboard the ship, but he sent Second Mate John Barry ashore with four men to supervise the loading, and later the captain went ashore himself.

Before he left the ship, Captain Endicott cautioned the mate: the Malays who inhabited this shore were notoriously slippery and ferocious, and many a Massachusetts captain had a tale to tell of a narrow escape from murder in these waters. But the mate said he would be alert, he was not afraid, and all seemed well.

It was normal practice to turn the ships' boats over to Malay crews when loading. The American merchant ships did not burden themselves with crew so the extra hands were welcome, and besides, the Malays were skilful at negotiating the rough surf off their island. The captain went up the river that led to the high plateau where the pepper was grown and stopped about two miles from the beach where Mate Barry was supervising the loading at the trading station. The Malay crew took out the first load, and all was well. But when the boat went on the next trip to the ship, Captain Endicott saw the Malays pull up on the shore instead of going directly out of the river. He ordered two of the *Friendship*'s crew to stop weighing pepper and watch the Malays, but he was only mildly suspicious. He supposed the Malays had decided they needed more men to get the next load through the surf, which did seem especially rough that day.

In fact, the porters had exchanged places with armed warriors, twice as many as the usual crew. The Malays came alongside the ship, concealing short swords under their clothes. The first mate looked them over, but the language barrier let the Malays pretend to misunderstand his order that only a few of them board the ship, and soon the whole boatload had clambered onto the deck of the *Friendship*. The mate and his crewmen were armed but when the Malays moved all about the ship, jabbering and showing interest mostly in the rigging, they put their guns down, and began to stow the boatload of pepper casks in the hold. As soon as the Americans turned their backs, the Malays attacked the mate; three of them drove their krises into his back, and he died on the spot. His men rushed to help, but two of them were killed, three captured, and the rest barely managed to leap over the side and swim out to a small point that was cut off by steep cliffs from the land. There the Malays could not get them, except by boat.

When Captain Endicott's two lookouts saw the surge of action on the *Friendship,* they hurried to tell the captain, and all those ashore got into the second boat and pulled for the open sea, even as the Malays aboard the ship were finishing their grisly murders and beginning to signal their companions ashore. As the second boat came down the river, Malays tried to intercept it, but the captain and his men ducked the shower of spears that came at them and reached the surf. As they moved out into deeper water, a brown figure came swimming up and seized the gunwale of the boat. The captain recognized the man, Po Adam, a Malay trader who owned a coasting schooner. He had left his vessel and come swimming to them because he feared that since he had traded with the white men, the furious natives of Qualla Battoo might kill him too. The Americans took Po Adam aboard. They were chased by several canoes full of armed warriors, and the only weapon they had was Po Adam's sword. He flourished the sword to keep the Malay warriors away, the Americans rowed for their lives, and they soon outdistanced the Malays. They saw the four men who had managed to make the protected promontory, picked them up, and headed southeast. Twenty miles down the coast they came to another trading settlement, Muckie, where three other American vessels were loading spices. When Captain Endicott told his story the American captains were outraged. They knew that if the behavior at Qualla Battoo went unpunished their own ships might be endangered. So by morning all three vessels were standing off Qualla Battoo. They sent an emissary ashore to the "rajah" of Qualla Battoo. The messenger demanded return of the ship and compensation for the deaths of the American crew men. The "rajah" sneered and told them to take the ship if they could and ordered his men to aim their shore cannon at the American vessels. The three American merchantmen then opened fire on the shore installations and on the *Friendship,* and the Malays returned the cannoning. But finally the Americans sent out boats and the boarding parties had not reached the ship before the Malays panicked and jumped overboard to swim for shore. The boarders regained possession for Captain Endicott, but possession of what was almost a wreck. The ship had been ransacked and rifled of everything of value, from blocks and tackle to the $12,000 in gold in the safe in the captain's cabin. So though Captain Endicott got his ship back, and one load of pepper that had been stowed below, he had lost his capital and had to return to Salem to report failure to his owners.

Salem merchants were close-fisted men, and the loss on this voyage, figuring the profits that might have been, was $40,000. So Salem protested with all its might to Washington, where President Jackson was just then showing himself extremely conscious of the needs of American trade because of quarrels with the British in the Caribbean and a long campaign of suppressing piracy there. Jackson acted quickly. The 44-gun frigate *Potomac* was lying in New York harbor, waiting to take Martin Van Buren to London where he would become the new American minister to the English court. When Jackson heard of the Sumatra affair, he delayed Van Buren's voyage and had orders sent to Captain Downes of the *Potomac* to sail posthaste to the Pacific, carrying Mate Barry from the *Friendship,* who came aboard the *Potomac* as a master's mate, to guide them to the culprits. The ship arrived at Sumatra in February, 1832, with orders to punish the murderers of Qualla Battoo.

Captain Downes knew that if he came in flying the Stars and Stripes, with half of the 44 guns exposed, that the Malays would either disappear or try to cover their tracks. So as the frigate came up on the shore, the captain ordered the gunports closed and rigging laid—apparently carelessly—to hide the neat line of gunports. The sails were slacked off, the lines were loosened, gear was scattered about the decks, and the Danish flag was run up. Captain Downes wanted to give the appearance of a sloppy and very neutral merchant-man come to trade. He succeeded almost too well. Before they reached Qualla Battoo, a coastal schooner came up and friendly natives from another tribe boarded to say that they had a boatload of fresh fish to trade. Once aboard, they saw that they were on a man of war, and so Captain Downes felt he must detain them until after his attack. The schooner was lashed on the seaward side of the *Potomac*. She anchored at the river's mouth and the whaleboat was sent ashore. Lieutenant Irvine Shubrick and the men of his expedition were dressed in the blue jackets and white trousers of merchant seamen. They went in toward shore at 2:30 in the afternoon. As they approached, the Malays began to line the banks, flourishing guns and swords. They made it quite clear that they were hostile. This was the confirmation of enmity that Captain Downes sought. He planned an attack on the place for midnight. The boat crews were assembled then, they went over the seaward side of the ship, armed with guns and cutlasses, and when every boat was manned, the flotilla rounded the ship and headed in toward the surf and the river. Mate Barry guided them. Lieutenant Edson and Lieutenant Tennet led the company of marines, Lieutenant Ingersoll led the first division of seamen, Lieutenant Shubrick led the second division, and Lieutenant Hoff led the third division. Acting Sailing Master Totten was in charge of a six-pound gun brought ashore which the men had named "Betsy Baker."

The settlement of Qualla Battoo consisted of a small town protected on the north from land enemies by a wooden stockade fort. Lieutenant Hoff and several men attacked the fort and drove the Malays back into the "citadel" behind. The Malay commander, Rajah Maley Mohammed, exhorted his men to die bravely for Allah, and they did: within an hour the Americans had taken the citadel and killed a dozen warriors (including one fierce woman) and

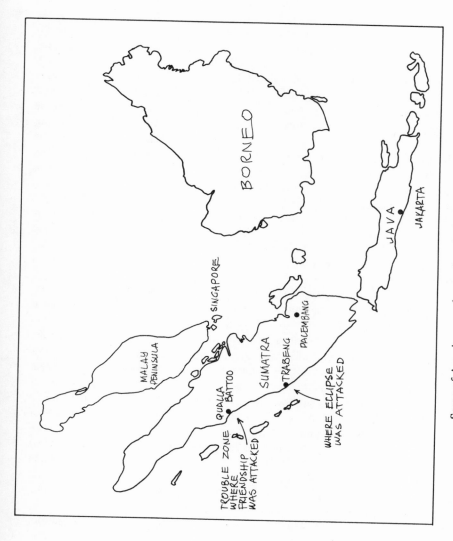

Scene of American naval operations in the Dutch East Indies

wounded forty or fifty other Malays who were then captured. Lieutenants Edson, Tennet, and Ingersoll attacked another fort in the center of the town, and after a hard fight cleared that fort of the Malays. Most of this fighting had been done around dawn. Lieutenant Shubrick led the other force with the six-pound gun in the attack against the third and strongest fort, overlooking the bank of the river. Here the Malays said that every man would fight to the death; and they did. At first the gunfire from the stockade was effective enough to keep the Americans back, but Lieutenant Shubrick took the six-pound gun and a number of men around the side to flank the fort. There he happened to encounter a number of Malays in sailing craft who were waiting there for a signal to attack the ship out beyond the breakers. He surprised the Malays, killed a number of them with the six-pounder and the fire of his musketeers, and routed the others so that they jumped into the water, swam for shore, and disappeared in the thick jungle behind the town. Shubrick then led the attack on the river fort, and after a fierce fight, it, too, was subdued. The Americans burned the forts, the town blazed up, and those Malay warriors who were not killed escaped into the bush. When the Americans heard the sound of "retreat" and assembled on the beach, they discovered they had lost two men and eleven were wounded. They estimated the Malay dead at one hundred and the wounded at two hundred.

They were still assembling when Captain Endicott's friend, Po Adam, appeared to tell the Americans that the Malays had already begun to reappear from the jungle on the landward side of the town. Captain Downes decided to give them a show of the guns of a frigate in action, and for an hour the *Potomac* threw one broadside after another against the town and the remains of the forts. At the end of the bombardment, white flags began to appear along the beach, and as dusk fell, a boat came toward the frigate, its occupants waving a flag. They said they were emissaries of the Malays, who wanted to talk peace with the Americans. Captain Downes let them wait for a time, then had them brought before him. They fell on their knees and asked that he stop the firing of the terrible big guns (32-pounders). He told them they had committed a dreadful crime against America in attacking Captain Endicott's vessel and this was their punishment. If there were any more attacks on American ships, he warned, the punishment would be far worse. Not one stick of one village would be left standing.

The Malays promised to behave, so peace was restored to Qualla Battoo, or what was left of it, and when the Americans came along this coast, after this punishment of 1832, they were allowed to trade in peace. Rajah Po Mohamet, the leader of the tribe, had been killed in this battle in the forests, and his successor did not quickly forget Po Mohamet's fate.

But down the coast, the Malay rajah of the village of Trabang said he would not knuckle under to the Americans the way the Qualla Battooans had done, and within the next year or two he had so shamed the warriors of Qualla Battoo that they began to talk about the old ways. One August day in 1838, when the American ship *Eclipse* was loading pepper at Trabang her crew was attacked, one man was mortally wounded, and the captain was killed. The Malays escaped with $18,000, and the Malay rajah went boastfully to Qualla Battoo and Muckie, showing off his money. In a burst of generosity (enforced by need for allies) he gave the rajahs of Muckie and Qualla Battoo a share of the plunder. They then prepared for the coming of the Americans, but not very quickly, because last time it had taken a year for the Americans to avenge the *Friendship*. But this time, the American 44-gun frigate *Columbia* and the corvette *John Adams* were in the Pacific, making a cruise around the world. When Commodore George C. Reid had word of the outrage at Sumatra, he changed course, and in December, 1839, the two warships reached the scene. They came straight to Qualla Battoo and discovered that the new rajah, Po Chute Abdullah, had taken a portion of the loot, and they destroyed the town. Commodore Reid sent a landing force of 360 men ashore to be sure the job was completed this time. Then they moved to Muckie and discovered that its rajah had also shared in the loot, so they destroyed that town. By this time, the Malays were immensely impressed by the speed with which retribution had arrived. This time the peace they signed was lasting, and piracy in the spice islands came to an end.

3

Expanding

~~~~~~~

THE LUCRATIVE SPICE TRADE and a growing American awareness of European colonial expansion in the Pacific brought Congress a new appreciation of the Pacific. In the spring of 1836, Congress had authorized a scientific and exploratory expedition by the Navy into uncharted waters. Two years later, Lieutenant Charles Wilkes led a six-ship flotilla across the Atlantic to the Antarctic Ocean to explore the "unknown continent." (Wilkesland, Antarctica, is named for the lieutenant.) In 1840, the expedition moved north to the islands of the South Pacific, and in July the 18-gun flagship *Vincennes* was sailing in the waters around Fiji. A detachment of sailors went ashore on one of the Fiji Islands where islanders attacked and forced the Americans to abandon one of the *Vincennes*'s boats. The next day Lieutenant Wilkes led a punitive expedition ashore and burned the village near the site of the attack.

A few days later another shore party was attacked and Midshipmen Joseph Underwood and Henry Wilkes were killed. This brought sterner action: Lieutenant Cadwalader Ringgold led a party of seventy men against a fortified village nearby. They attacked in hand-to-hand combat and burned the fort and the village, killing the chief and six warriors. Then the expedition sailed on a visit to the Gilbert Islands which brought a similar experience: more fighting, the kidnaping of one sailor, and another punitive expedition in which a dozen natives were killed.

This same surge of expansion took Commodore Lawrence Kearney to Canton in 1843, and in December of that year his ships, the USS *Constellation* and the USS *Boston* lay in the Pearl River. Kearney persuaded the representatives of the Chinese Empire to sign a treaty opening several ports to

25

Japan and China

American ships for trade. That was what the Americans wanted—trade, not territory—but they had more than a little difficulty in securing the trade. The Chinese were not pleased with the coming of foreigners in large numbers. Before the 1840s, trade had been strictly controlled by the Manchu government in Peking. In 1841 the British had forced the Chinese to open their ports and cede Hongkong to Britain, but the reaction throughout China was severe, and in June, 1844, the Chinese began destroying foreign property. In July, the United States sent marines to Canton "to protect American property."

26

Expanding

Through this show of force the United States secured "extraterritorrial rights" which meant Americans were not subject to Chinese law.

Success in opening the China trade led Congress to further excursions. In 1845, Congress announced that Japan and Korea should both be opened to Americans. No one seemed to care how the Japanese and Koreans felt about the matter. The former, in particular, objected strongly. The Japanese experience with westerners had not been to the liking of the country's rulers. The Spanish and Portuguese had come to Japan in the sixteenth century and brought the Jesuits who tried to convert the Japanese from Shintoism and Buddhaism to Christianity. After thirty years the foreigners were expelled; thereafter the only Europeans allowed to come to Japan were the Dutch, who had exhibited no presumptuous attempts to "civilize" a highly civilized people, and even the Dutch were confined to an island in Nagasaki harbor. Even in the middle of the nineteenth century, other foreigners were not allowed to land. This anti-western attitude, although forgotten by the west a few years later, was not forgotten by the Japanese, and would be revived again in the twentieth century.

Because Congress had decided in 1845 to open Japan, the Navy sent Captain James Biddle west with two ships; but the authorities refused to see him, and when he left the islands without incident because he had been told not to arouse any enmity, the Japanese considered his going a great victory for them. The next year it was learned in Washington that the whaling ship *Lawrence* had been sunk and that eighteen survivors of her crew had reached Japan and were confined there. This gave the United States a new excuse to send warships to Japan, and Commander James Glynn in the *Preble* went to Nagasaki to secure the release of the whalers. Congress and the administration took a much more positive view of the need for freedom of the Pacific these days. The Atlantic whaling grounds had been heavily worked, and even the South Pacific waters were beginning to yield poorly. When new whaling grounds were discovered within sight of the Japanese archipelago, the American ships had begun to flock there: in one year the Japanese counted eighty-six American whaling ships offshore. United States property and the lives of the whalers must be protected off Japan, said the United States government. Captain Biddle did secure the release of his countrymen, the men of the *Lawrence*, seized in 1846, but no guarantee for the future was promised. Congress was not happy with the result, and in 1852 sent Captain Matthew Calbraith Perry to Japan with orders that he was not to accept a refusal to sign a treaty that would open trade and protect Americans in Japan. With two steam warships and three sailing vessels, Perry appeared off Uraga in Yedo Bay (Tokyo Bay). His ships were immediately surrounded by a horde of small craft. Over the years, the Japanese had learned that the westerners would do almost anything to make a profit, and the commonest of people came out to the ships

27

when they arrived to trade for western goods. The imperial court and the nobility had little but contempt for the westerners and their materialism. From some of the former prisoners of the Japanese, Perry had learned of the Japanese attitude. He decided to greet arrogance with arrogance. As the Japanese tried to board the American ships, they were thrust back at bayonet point, and Perry announced that he would deal with no one but the official representative of the emperor. After much discussion, the vice governor of Uraga was allowed to come on board, but not to see Perry; no indeed, the meeting was with a young lieutenant, John Contee. The embarrassed vice governor promised to send a higher official to call on Perry the next day. When morning came more boats scurried about the harbor, and the Japanese made a great show of sending troops to march up and down the shore. But in the afternoon the governor of Uraga came to the *Mississippi,* Perry's flagship. He, too, was granted audience only by Lieutenant Contee. The day before his assistant had insisted that the Americans go to Nagasaki, which was the only port open for foreigners. Perry had refused then, and through Contee he refused again. The talk was carried out through interpreters, since Contee did not understand Japanese. He did notice that the governor used different words when he referred to the president of the United States and to the emperor of Japan and concluded properly that the title given the president was not a very noble one. Thereafter Perry insisted that the same words be used to refer to both national chiefs of state. The governor was taken aback. No foreigner had ever before shown such intelligence. And so the point was won.

The negotiations bogged down. The governor insisted that he had to send to Tokyo for instructions and said this would take four days. Three days, said Perry, that was all he would wait. Then he would steam into Tokyo Bay. That threat upset the governor, for it was just what the Japanese did not want. He was also upset by the activity of surveying and sounding parties that Perry sent out to make observations for charts of the bay and the surrounding waters. Perry ignored the protest. For three days the Americans waited, and the survey boats went out.

At the end of the third day the word came from Tokyo. The letter from President James Buchanan to the emperor would be received by an official from the Tokyo court. He would meet the Americans in a special building on the beach near Uraga, but the Americans must go to Nagasaki, the port of foreigners, to receive the reply.

Captain Perry said he would do nothing of the sort. He expected a reply here, at Uraga, and if he did not get one he would regard the Japanese act as unfriendly. The implied threat was not lost on the Japanese. They said they would transmit the American demand to Tokyo.

While the parleying continued, the Japanese were erecting the tent where a member of the Heavenly Court would receive the Americans. Finally the hour came. Captain Perry appeared in his best dress blues, white gloves, and sword, with a huge black American sailor on each side of him, guarded by a procession of a hundred marines, with two ships' boys carrying rosewood boxes with golden hinges and mountings. These boxes contained the documents from Washington. The letter and the other papers were inscribed on vellum in a fine Spencerian hand, bound in blue silk velvet, and sealed with the official seal of the United States of America in red wax, with golden tassels hanging down from the seals.

The Japanese sent a large retinue from Tokyo to accompany two princes of the realm. Perry delivered the letter and was told he must return to Nagasaki for the answer. Again he refused. He was going away, but he would be back in nine or ten months, he said, and would expect the answer, and he would bring many, many more ships. The threat hung in the air as the meeting broke up.

Perry went to China. In November while in Macao he learned that the French and the Russians were apparently making moves to open Japan, and he hurried back to Tokyo Bay with nine ships. He anchored near Yokohama, and after some protest the Japanese accepted his presence there and built "a treaty house" on the shore. But the reception was still extremely cool, and, in fact, a number of *samurai* pledged themselves to kill Perry. But he persevered, and in the end won recognition by the Japanese government. A State Department representative, Townsend Harris, remained in Japan as consul general, and the Japanese sent an ambassador to Washington in 1860. Japan was formally opened to American trade a few years after China.

Even after the official road had been opened, the way was not easy, and the American navy was often involved in military action in Asia and the Pacific. In the spring of 1855, United States marines landed at Shanghai to protect American businessmen. That same summer the USS *Powhatan* was engaged in fighting pirates in the bay near Hongkong. A month later another United States navy force landed at Viti Levu in Fiji to burn several villages and capture the local king, to stop harassment of American traders.

In October, 1855, three American navy ships entered the Pearl River, again to protect Americans caught up in the British opium wars. This time Chinese forts outside Canton fired on the USS *Portsmouth,* and Commander Andrew Foote landed a large force of marines and sailors, and bombarded the forts. The landing force captured four forts in a battle that lasted three days, and killed four hundred Chinese soldiers. The American military involvement continued that year and the next.

When the Civil War began in 1861, the Union Navy's attention shifted from the Pacific for the most part, but there remained the problem of protecting traders who were not always welcome in various parts of the region. During these years the most serious incident in Pacific waters was created by the Prince of Nagoya, who had no use for foreigners. On July 15, 1863, the USS *Wyoming* was attacked by several Japanese warships and the guns of seven forts, as she passed through the Strait of Shimonoseki. She returned the fire, sank two of the men of war, disabled a third, and destroyed the batteries of one of the forts.

The civil war at sea was fought almost entirely in the Atlantic and the Gulf of Mexico. Rear Admiral Charles H. Bell commanded the Pacific Squadron, but its major duty was to protect the California steamer lanes, which ran to Central America. The Confederate raider *Shenandoah* sailed around Cape Horn from England and captured some ships off the west coast but when the war ended in the summer of 1865 and her captain learned of the surrender of the Confederacy, he sailed back around the Horn to England to avoid turning over his ship to the Yankees.

The war ended, and the United States again turned attention to foreign trade, a matter of increasing interest since the war had brought an enormous growth to industry in the northern part of the United States.

In Japan a new dynasty came to power in 1868 (Meiji) and the United States sent a naval expedition to impress the new rulers. The naval officers came home to recommend that the Japanese be encouraged to send students to the American service academies. The first Japanese cadet, Junjo Matsamura, was enrolled at the Naval Academy in 1868, and he completed the course in 1873. So the United States was to have a hand in the training of a modern Japanese navy, a matter that would affect the course of events in the coming century.

In 1880, American attention turned also to Korea, and a fleet under Rear Admiral John Rodgers sailed to the mouth of the Han river to do what Perry had done in Tokyo Bay. The treaty was signed in 1882. A period of "restlessness" followed, and marines had to be landed to "protect American interests" as long as six years later. The United States was still undetermined about its attitude toward colonialism, but although that was true in Congress, it was not true in the Department of the Navy, where there was no doubt about what should be done. The navy wanted bases across the Pacific, from Pearl Harbor, to the kingdom of the Hawaiian Islands, to China. After much negotiation over a number of years the Pearl Harbor base was secured. Then the navy turned its attention further west.

Lieutenant Charles Wilkes had visited the Samoan Islands in 1839 on one of his survey missions, and from time to time American ships called at the harbor of Apia on the island of Upolu. In the 1870s, when the United States was beginning to build a steam navy, the Navy Department became extremely interested in the possibilities of Pago Pago as a coaling station. A treaty was signed with the Samoan government and Congress appropriated $100,000 to build the coaling station. The Germans and the British secured similar concessions, much to the United States Navy's distress. The British backed away, trading their Samoan interests for tacit United States acceptance of a special British position in Tonga and the Solomon Islands, but the Germans and Americans continued to compete for influence and the copra trade until in 1889 the two nations nearly went to war.

In March of that year, a hostile American squadron faced an equally hostile German squadron in Apia harbor. A battle was imminent when a typhoon blew up on the morning of March 15 and wrecked both squadrons in the harbor. The Apia incident made one fact clear: the United States Navy was leading the nation on an imperialist path in the interest of "national security." For while most Americans still considered the Atlantic and Pacific oceans as walls against foreign incursions; the navy, converting to steam-driven vessels, had a different view. No navy could be effective in the days of coal without coaling stations in the middle of the oceans. The only way to get coaling stations was by annexation of territory or establishment of bases by treaty, and both courses involved an imperialist position. So by the beginning of the last quarter of the nineteenth century, Americans were more committed than they knew to the maintenance of an American imperialism in the Pacific Ocean.

4

"A piece of land at this port, sufficient for a wharf...."

IN THE WINTER OF 1863–64, the United States government was too fully occupied with the prosecution of the war against the Confederacy to devote serious thought to problems in the Pacific Ocean. Yet the idea of securing a base for the navy in Hawaii did come up then, advanced by Secretary of State William Seward. The occasion was an attempt by the Hawaiian government to secure a "reciprocity treaty," eliminating tariffs and assuring the future of the growing sugar industry in the island kingdom. King Kamehameha V sent a minister to Washington to pursue the matter of the treaty, but Seward told him bluntly that any treaty of that sort would be possible only if the United States were to secure something truly valuable, such as a naval coaling station. At that time, the idea of a treaty did not take hold, but when the Civil War ended the Navy Department did not forget about the need for that coaling station. Rear Admiral George F. Pearson, commander of the Pacific squadron, went to Honolulu to "cultivate" American relations with the Hawaiians.

The idea of an American naval base was appealing to the American businessmen who had settled in the islands. Admiral Pearson's arrival in the steam frigate *Lancaster* was greeted warmly by the American community, and in 1866 so was the addition of a North Pacific Squadron to the United States Navy. Hawaiian acceptance of the United States naval presence increased after Queen Emma, the widow of Kamehameha IV, made a trip to Britain and on her way home was given passage aboard the USS *Vanderbilt,* flagship of the commander of the squadron. Thereafter, to fulfill the North Pacific Squadron's duty to watch over American interests in the Hawaiian Islands,

33

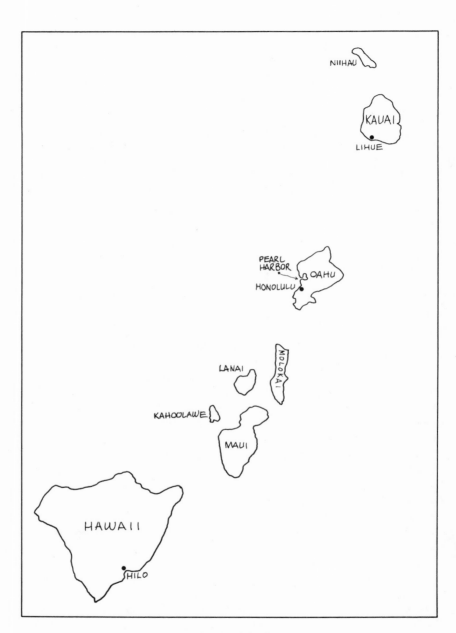

Hawaiian Islands

the cruiser *Lackawanna* was assigned to Honolulu—an American action typical of the "battleship diplomacy" of the times.

Relations between the United States and Hawaii were threatened by American political activity in the islands. Captain William Reynolds, commander of the *Lackawanna,* had earlier spent a number of years as naval representative on Kauai and as a naval storekeeper in Honolulu. He was infamous at the Hawaiian Court for his advocacy of annexation of Hawaii to the United States, and his presence in the islands was regarded by many as an indication of official American policy.

The presence of the *Lackawanna* was resented by British interests in Hawaii and by the new King, Kamehameha V, to such a degree that in 1867 when the matter of the treaty of reciprocity came up again, the king said he would never sign a treaty until the American warship left Hawaiian waters. Fortunately, however, the United States had just decided to take over Midway Island, and Captain Reynolds and the *Lackawanna* were sent there in the summer of 1867 with no loss of face.

The *Lackawanna* was replaced on the Hawaii station by the *Mohongo* whose captain was a genial man named Simpson. Since the Hawaii cabinet had been fretting for months about Reynolds, the change in naval representatives was regarded officially and unofficially in Honolulu as a positive sign of American friendship.

After the election of Republican Ulysses S. Grant to the American presidency in 1868, Henry A. Peirce came to Hawaii as American minister. Immediately—he had hardly settled into his house—he began a campaign to secure a U.S. naval base in the islands. It was evident at Court that he was a proponent of annexation of the kingdom to the United States. He wrote home to the secretary of state that the establishment of a base would further the aim.

As long as Kamehameha V lived, there was no hope for an American base in Hawaii; but that king died in 1872, and since he was the last of the Kamehameha line, a new king was chosen by election. Coincidentally, just a week after the election, Admiral A. M. Pennock, commander of the United States North Pacific Squadron, arrived in Honolulu aboard his flagship, the *California*. It really *was* coincidence, but no one could so persuade the British and the Hawaiians of that fact. They saw a campaign to make of Hawaii an American colony. But even the British were aware of the difficulty of Hawaii's position as a small, impotent monarchy in the middle of the Pacific. Further, the most prominent British businessman in Hawaii, Theo H. Davies, had seen in the boom years of the Civil War that the economic future of the islands was closely tied to that of America. The Hawaiian sugar traders, no matter what their nationality, wanted the reciprocity treaty more than ever, particularly when the high American tariff on sugar made it difficult to sell sugar in the American market. When the treaty came under discussion again at the Court of the new king, Lunalilo, it was generally accepted that the Americans would demand a *quid pro quo,* and the American *quid* (naval base) in exchange for the Hawaiian *quo* (treaty) would assure the renewed profitability of the sugar industry. On February 8, 1873, the pro-American Honolulu newspaper, *The Pacific Commercial Advertiser* brought the matter into the open in an editorial which suggested that the Americans be given a base on the Pearl River. Theo H. Davies and other non-American businessmen opposed the idea of ceding any territory, but it was apparent from the beginning that they were fighting a losing battle. What Davies feared, Minister Peirce in 1873 advocated openly: the ultimate annexation of Hawaii as a United States colony.

Lunalilo died early in 1874 and David Kalakaua was elected king, establishing another new royal line. The confusion and unrest of so many changes in government had persuaded America and Britain into the custom of keeping a warship or two in the islands. The Americans maintained two such ships in Hawaii, the *Tuscarora* and the *Portsmouth,* and the British stationed one, the *Tenedos*. There was good reason for the concern of Washington and London, it appeared. On Kalakaua's election day rioting by opposing political factions broke out in Honolulu, and marines and sailors were landed from both the American and British ships to "protect" British and American property. The real effect of such landings was to overpower physical opposition to the duly constituted authority as recognized in the Crown.

Unexpectedly, King Kalakaua turned out to be opposed to the cession of any territory to the Americans, so the idea of the reciprocity treaty was again put aside. But the Panic of 1876 brought a depression to the sugar industry and even the opponents of the naval base began to agitate for a treaty.

They were in luck, because American commercial instinct had overcome military policy. Two groups of Americans on the Pacific coast were eager to establish a major shipping industry to trade with Australia and the Far East, and the Hawaii stopping point was important to them. So Hawaii got its reciprocal trade treaty in 1876 the way Hawaii wanted it, with the question of the naval base put aside. The treaty worked admirably (for Hawaii) for eight years. Then beet sugar interests in the west of America and cane sugar growers in the south began agitation to dump "reciprocity," and this time Congress became adamant about the naval base. The expansion of Britain and Germany in the Pacific had persuaded the senators. The treaty would be renewed, said the foreign relations committee of the United States Senate, only if the United States was given an exclusive right to use Pearl Harbor.

In the beginning, the Pearl Harbor concession was "temporary." It was tied to the reciprocity treaty and would end if that treaty ended. But by 1890, many people in Hawaii, particularly those of American heritage, were agitating for a permanent cession of the land to the United States, hoping that the

Americans would then spend a large amount of money to build a base, which in turn would help the economy of the islands. The pro-Americans believed that the United States would take a far greater interest in the islands if this occurred, but the matter was not really resolved during the life of the kingdom.

The future of Pearl Harbor was still in doubt, and although the Navy had title to the place, no effort had even been made to dredge the harbor or remove the reef that prevented entrance of deepwater ships.

Under President Benjamin Harrison's Republican administration, the forces of "manifest destiny"—which meant colonial expansion—were in power in Washington and the American-oriented revolutionaries expected support from the United States. They got it, although possibly to a greater degree than the government in Washington had planned. The *bete noir* in the case was John Leavitt Stevens, the United States minister to Hawaii. Stevens, a Republican and a religious minister as well as a diplomat, was one of the most ardent believers in manifest destiny. Since his arrival in Hawaii in September, 1889, his dispatches to Washington had continually urged the United States to move Hawaii under the American umbrella. He was sufficiently vague about this in Hawaii to avoid outright castigation by the anti-annexation party, but he was equally open in announcing that his policy, and that of the Blaine administration, was to "foster Hawaii as an American dependency."

On the death of King Kalakaua in January, 1891, the succession to the throne passed to his sister Queen Liliuokalani. The queen had been educated by American missionaries and might be expected to be pro-American. But the fact was that Liliuokalani had seen the corruption of the missionaries. (Her teacher, the Reverend Amos Cooke, left the ministry to found the firm of Castle & Cooke, which rapidly became one of the most important trading companies in the islands.) As she saw the Americans pressing constantly for more power and more economic control, she rebelled and set a course to regain much of the royal power that had been abdicated over the years to the elected legislature. On January 14, 1893, she proposed to hand Hawaii a new constitution, which restored royal power; the "Reform" (annexation) Party rebelled. Just at this moment, the United States warship *Boston* with Minister Stevens aboard was on a trip to Hilo on the island of Hawaii. Captain G. C. Wiltse of the *Boston* had been informed of the developments while the ship lay in Lahaina on the island of Maui, and Wiltse had made arrangements for the landing of a military force at Honolulu, once again "to protect American lives and property from the mob." So when the *Boston* came into port about 11 o'clock in the morning, she was ready for action. Minister Stevens went to the American legation, and then called on British Minister James Wodehouse. They agreed that the queen must not promulgate her new constitution (so far had foreign manipulation of the Hawaiian kingdom come that they saw nothing amiss in making such a decision). But the queen was adamant and announced that day to her cabinet that she was going ahead. The cabinet officials began to argue and bullied the queen into waiting for a few days. In all this, the queen's support came from the Hawaiian nationalist movement, and as the discussion raged in Iolani Palace a crowd of Hawaiians stood outside. This was the "mob" that Captain Wiltse feared. The queen announced that she had been prevented from giving them the new constitution that would have restored their privileges at the expense of the foreigners who had come in and accepted Hawaiian citizenship; the crowd was not pleased, but in time it dispersed. But the new citizens, and some who were not citizens, began to talk of taking matters into their own hands. They were sure of American Minister Stevens' support and to a lesser degree of that of Minister Wodehouse. They formed a "Committee of Public Safety" that same day.

Earlier a number of Hawaiian citizens and others had formed an "Annexation Club." The leaders of this club now took over the Committee of Public Safety, and they argued that the committee had to take matters into its own hands because the queen was clearly bent on "revolutionary" activity. The term, of course, was a misnomer. The queen was bent on restoring the power of the monarchy, which had been decreased generation after generation largely by American influence. But it was clear that these men, most of them Americans or Hawaiian citizens of American descent, were not at that point interested in political debate about rights or wrongs but in seizing power. They appointed a special committee, consisting of Lorrin Thurston, W. C. Wilder, and H. F. Glade, to call on American Minister Stevens and ascertain his attitude toward immediate seizure of power. This was all masked as a request for American military aid to "protect property."

In the past, as various groups had tried to wrest power from the kingdom, Minister Stevens had always promised support to the kingdom. This time, he would not for he too regarded the queen's attitude as "revolutionary." Thurston came away from the meeting to tell the Committee of Public Safety that Minister Stevens had pledged the support of the marines and sailors aboard the *Boston*. If the rebels got control of the government buildings, Stevens said, he would recognize the *de facto* government.

The rebels hoped to secure the support of the queen's cabinet in their revolution, but when Foreign Minister Samuel Parker and the other ministers of the cabinet heard of the plans, they flatly refused to consider treason against the queen. They had recently become extremely concerned about the growing power of the Americans and the Japanese. The planters of Hawaii had imported Japanese laborers into the islands and by 1893 more than fifteen percent of the population of Hawaii was Japanese. The Japanese government insisted that these people, as long as they were resident in Hawaii, should have all rights of Hawaiian citizens (including that of the vote), and the

Hawaiians resented this attitude almost as much as they feared the Americans. In their proclamation the ministers of the queen tried to take the edge off the rebellious spirit of the annexation party. They began to realize that the political situation was desperate when Minister Parker and Attorney General Arthur P. Peterson called on American Minister Stevens and received evasive answers to most of their questions.

At that moment, the queen's government had the power to resist any attempt to take over the government buildings, if the foreign ships and their troops stayed out of the fray. The rebels—the annexionists—had organized a military club, "The Honolulu Rifles," but they were short of rifles. The queen's military force had guns in the armory on the grounds of Iolani Palace. But on January 16, 1893, Captain Wiltse of the *Boston* landed American troops and this action turned the tide. With the American minister and the American troops behind them, the revolutionaries declared a Provisional Government. They began moving small arms into the streets and were challenged by a policeman on King Street, the main thoroughfare. John Good, the "ordnance officer" of the revolutionaries, had most of their guns in his wagon when Police Officer Leialoha grabbed the reins of his horses. Good shot the policeman in the shoulder and felled him, then went on. The armed revolutionaries then seized the government building and Minister Stevens immediately recognized the Provisional Government as the true government of Hawaii. The American flag was raised over the government building, and the troops from the *Boston* remained ashore to protect the flag.

In the years that followed many investigations and accounts of the revolution were published, and the Americans sent a special commission to find out what had actually happened. The queen, deposed, claimed that she had yielded to the "superior force of the United States" and never abandoned that position. Even in 1981, as the Hawaiians sought reparations in Congress for the seizure of their land by the revolutionaries and the eventual annexation to the United States, the facts of the rebellion were still in dispute, and Congressman Daniel Akaka, a Hawaiian, demanded a new investigation, eighty-eight years after the fact. But one thing seems quite beyond doubt: the United States Navy ship *Boston* and American marines and sailors made the Hawaiian revolution possible. It was the first successful imperialistic move of the United States in the Pacific, and it guaranteed the naval base the United States Navy and the expansionists wanted.

5

Gridley Fired
When He Was Ready

~~~~~~~~

IT WAS NO ACCIDENT that American ships happened to be on hand in Honolulu harbor in times of trouble, culminating in the American naval interference in Hawaiian affairs that made the revolution possible. A dozen years before that rebellion in the islands, American naval policy had taken a new turn. In 1881, President Chester A. Arthur had urged Congress to rebuild the American navy along modern lines. The first American steel warship was built in 1884 and mounted with modern guns with rifled barrels, which added immeasurably to the accuracy of bombardment. It was the cruiser *Chicago* (of the same class as the famous *Boston*). William C. Whitney, secretary of the navy in Grover Cleveland's first administration, began the reorganization of the navy, and Captain Alfred Thayer Mahan established an entirely new principle of naval strategy for the United States: creation of a powerful fleet. At that time the United States ranked twelfth among the world's naval powers—after Britain, France, Russia, Germany, Holland, Spain, Italy, Turkey, China, Norway-Sweden, and Austria-Hungary. The policy was continued under President Benjamin Harrison. The claim was that the United States must have a powerful fleet as a "guaranty of perpetual peace." In fact, Tracy wanted two fleets, a twelve-ship fleet of armored battleships in the Atlantic, and a fleet of eight in the Pacific. Since the Panama Canal was still a dream, the ships, once committed, could not be transferred easily from one ocean to the other.

Before 1890, the United States Navy showed yearnings for a new imperialism in a nation that professed no imperialistic ambitions. This ambition (as noted) nearly led to war with Germany in 1889 over Samoa. After the typhoon intervened in Apia harbor, wrecking the German warships *Eber*,

Adler, and *Olga,* and the American *Trenton, Vandalia,* and *Nipsic,* outstanding issues were settled by a compromise that split Samoa between the United States and Germany. Thus fuelled, the yearnings of the naval party increased. Secretary Tracy and President Harrison were the prime advocates of "Manifest Destiny," as this policy became known.

After the Hawaiian revolution had become a *fait accomplis,* Secretary Tracy asked Rear Admiral J. S. Skerret, commander of the Pacific Squadron, to make a report on the new government. Skerret studied the political situation and reported to Washington that the new Hawaiian government was unstable and unpopular and undemocratic and could never survive a general election in the islands. This was not exactly what the secretary wanted to hear, and he was no happier a few months later when the United States Senate refused to ratify the annexation of Hawaii to the United States. In 1892, Grover Cleveland recovered the presidency from Harrison, and the naval expansion policy went begging because Cleveland despised imperialism. Cleveland did come around to endorsing a bigger navy because of a national depression that began in 1893. Secretary of the Navy Hilary Herbert persuaded Cleveland that a shipbuilding program would help solve the country's economic ills, so Cleveland endorsed the building of three 10,000-ton battleships and a dozen new torpedo boats at a cost of $12 million. Thus in 1896, the navy was ready to flex its muscles after the Republicans came back to office.

President William McKinley made much of the Monroe Doctrine; he pointedly indicated that he wanted Spain to get out of the western hemisphere. The Democrats were lukewarm, particularly to the extended contention that Hawaii and the Danish West Indies must be brought under American control. At this time, two powerful newspaper publishers, Joseph Pulitzer and William Randolph Hearst were fighting for circulation in a New York City newspaper war. They seized upon a revolution that had begun in Cuba as proof of the need for American intervention to throw Spain out of Cuba.

In the Pacific this new imperialism showed itself in the strengthening of the American Asiatic Squadron with an eye cast always at the Spanish in the Philippine Islands. After Theodore Roosevelt was appointed assistant secretary of the navy, he began agitating for annexation of Hawaii, employing the Pacific fleet for the purpose, if necessary. It seemed that the fleet might be needed for Japan had decided that it did not like the idea of Americans taking over the Philippines or Hawaii or any other part of the Pacific. The fact was that after the Sino-Japanese war of 1894, the Japanese had emerged as a Pacific power and were feeling their strength. In 1897, Japan made strong representations against American annexation of Hawaii and appeared to be about to send several warships to Honolulu. The excuse was a growing anti-Japanese tension in the islands for which Japan blamed the Americans. The American-descended residents, as they saw the Japanese become the largest racial group in the islands, finally stopped Japanese immigration.

Gridley Fired When He Was Ready

For the first time in history Japan appeared here as a potential enemy of the United States, and the United States Navy Department responded with a plan for war with Japan. In the summer of 1897 Secretary of the Navy John Davis Long gave secret orders to the commander of the Pacific Squadron at Pearl Harbor to hoist the Stars and Stripes and proclaim a protectorate over Hawaii if the Japanese became troublesome. The battleship *Oregon,* newest in the fleet and one of the most powerful in the world, was put on orders to be ready at any moment to sail from Puget Sound to Pearl Harbor. The crisis was ended in June by outside factors: Russia and Germany froze Japan out of the China trade and turned Japanese resentments elsewhere. Under the influence of Captain Mahan and Assistant Secretary Roosevelt, the navy made plans for the seizure of the Philippines in case of war with Spain. Roosevelt was responsible for the selection of Commodore George Dewey as chief of the Asiatic Squadron in spite of Dewey's low ranking as an officer; Roosevelt told Secretary Long that Dewey was the only man aggressive enough to handle a war job.

"War fever" seemed to permeate most of American society and was certainly not lessened by the activities of the "yellow" press. Secretary Roosevelt, on February 25, 1898, cabled Dewey to order the Asiatic Squadron down to Hongkong from Nagasaki and to keep the ships filled with coal. "In the event of declaration of war on Spain, your duty will be to see that the Spanish squadron does not leave the Asiatic coast and then begin offensive operations in the Philippines. . . ."

This was done by Roosevelt over a weekend when Secretary Long was away from the Navy Department. When war did come, in April, Dewey said that only Roosevelt's early actions had given him the time necessary to prepare for battle.

War was decided on by Spain on April 21, 1898. Immediately, the British in Hongkong politely asked Commodore Dewey to remove his ships from the neutral harbor of Hongkong. Anticipating this, Dewey had arranged for use of a temporary base at Mirs Bay on the China coast, thirty miles east of Hongkong, but the Navy Department had sent extra ammunition via the *Baltimore,* which arrived in Hongkong on April 22 with her bottom too foul to go into battle. Dewey lost no time in getting her into drydock and stalled the port authorities. She came out just as the British port officials boarded Dewey's flagship, the *Olympia,* to announce that the squadron would have to leave Hongkong immediately.

The British had let him stall because they liked him and felt sorry for him. The Spanish squadron in Manila, commanded by Rear Admiral Don Patricio Montojo y Pasaron, consisted of five "protected cruisers," one wooden cruiser, and three gunboats. A protected cruiser was a ship with some armor, but not total armor plate. Dewey's ships, six of them, had even less armor, but the slowest of his ships was almost as fast as the fastest Spanish ship. Nevertheless, the British naval officers in Hongkong predicted that Dewey would sail away to disaster. ". . . a fine set of fellows," remarked one Royal Navy officer about his American counterparts, "but unhappily we shall never see them again." The naval analyst, F. T. Jane, said much the same from London. He expected the Spanish to soon be bombarding American cities along the coasts.

"The patriotic citizens of the United States may rue the day when the muddling finger of Uncle Sam was thrust into the hornet's nest of Cuba," said Mr. Jane. And even Captain Mahan had some reservations about the chances of America to win a victory.

On April 24, Dewey got his orders at Mirs Bay: he was to move to the Philippines and begin operations at once against the Spanish. He sailed, and then stopped because he had been given last-minute information that the American consul stationed at Manila had left the Philippines to come to Hongkong to see him. The consul arrived at Mirs Bay at 11 on the morning of April 27, and three hours later the squadron sailed. As they moved toward the Philippines, the consul told all he knew: the Spanish had laid mines in the entrance to Manila Bay; he also had collected detailed information about the forts around the bay and the disposition of the Spanish ships.

The squadron reached Bolinao Point, Luzon, where it stopped to land a Filipino revolutionary. There the ships stripped for action. The panelling in the wardroom was thrown overboard—it might catch fire in battle. Chairs, tables, and chests all went over the side, and all the wooden bulkheads put up to make life at sea more comfortable were now taken down and stowed below. The *Boston* (the ship from the Hawaiian revolution) was sent forward with the *Concord* to look over Subic Bay where the Spanish squadron was expected to be. But the Americans did not find the enemy there; Admiral Montojo had moved to Manila Bay.

The ships returned and the commodore called a meeting aboard the *Olympia* where he issued his battle order: they were going in to Manila Bay to find the enemy.

The ships set out at night at six knots without lights except for one single lamp on the taffrail of each ship so that the one behind could follow. At 11 P.M. the ships went to General Quarters just before they entered Manila Bay. The Spanish, who had lookouts posted, did not worry much, for they expected the Americans to be blasted by the mines as they came in. But the Spanish minelayers did not know their jobs very well; they had laid contact mines below the depth that Dewey's ships drew.

For months the Spanish had been talking about the "impregnability" of the defenses of Manila, which included sixty coastal guns in fortified positions around the bay. If the Americans managed to get some ships through the mine field—this was the story being told at Hongkong that very minute by a steamer captain who had the word direct from the Spanish mouths a few days earlier—why the foolish Yanks would be blown out of the water by the coastal guns. "No, there was not a chance for the poor devils. . . ."

It was remarkable how most of the world believed that the Spanish navy was a tiger. Chief among the disbelievers were the Spanish naval officers and particularly Admiral Montojo, who knew how old and ineffectual his ships were. He chose to fight in Manila Bay rather than Subic Bay because the water close inshore at Subic Bay was so deep he was afraid his sailors would drown after they escaped their sinking ships.

Commodore Dewey, having studied his enemy, was confident that the Spanish navy was unequal to the task ahead. He might have been fearful of the mines and the announced potential of the shore guns, but he steamed directly into Manila Bay, ignoring both. It was, once again, the illustration of the value of audacity. Had Dewey been wrong, even one of his ships sunk by a mine, even one destroyed by a fortress, history might have put him down as a fool. But no mine was struck, no shore gun found the range, and he did not run aground in strange waters by entering at night.

He did take the precaution of entering through the bay's southern entrance, whereas the traditional channel was north, two miles from the coast of Luzon, past Corregidor island. Dewey's ships moved through the 3.5 mile wide channel between Caballo and El Fraile islands, south of Corregidor at about 11:30 that night. When they were opposite El Fraile Island, the Spanish gunners discovered them and fired several rounds from the guns on the island, hitting nothing. Then the ships were past, and heading up the bay toward Manila, 22 miles away.

At 5:15 on the morning of May 1, the squadron was discovered off Manila in the gathering light. A shot came from one of the Manila batteries, then came another from a battery at Cavite, but the range was too great and the projectiles dropped into the sea. Dewey did not bother with the batteries but headed toward Cavite, where he could see the Spanish squadron.

Admiral Montojo's depression about the outcome of the battle was so great that he did not consider trying to fight while under steam. Instead, he anchored near shallow water in Bakor Bay (the swim to shore kept nagging him). In theory it was not a bad position: the Malate battery at Manila could fire on ships coming in at the Spanish squadron; at Sangley Point, north of Cavite, the Spanish had mounted two 5.9-inch guns and three heavy muzzle loaders; and a mile southwest of Sangley Point was a modern 4.7-inch rifled gun. But, the 4.7-inch gun could not be brought to the angle of approach of the Americans, and only one of the muzzle loaders could bear, so the situation was not bright.

Furthermore, as Dewey suspected, the Spanish squadron in a naval sense was a floating disaster. The largest ship was the cruiser *Castilla*. Her hull

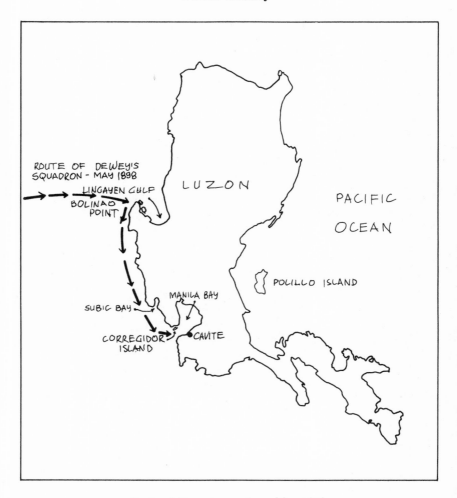

Route of Dewey's squadron, May 1898

leaked, her boilers were full of holes, and she could barely move; in fact she had nearly gone "dead" on a trip to Subic Bay a few days earlier. The men who manned her had so little confidence in her ability to survive that they sandbagged the hull on the side toward the sea and brought sand-filled lighters alongside to protect her.

The second Spanish ship, the *Ulloa*, was a hulk—her machinery was ashore under repair so she could not steam out to fight. The 4.7-inch gun south of Sangley Point was one of hers, taken off to a place where it might do some good. The *Velasco,* moored off Cavite Arsenal, was also an anchored hulk, carrying neither guns nor any of her boilers. Admiral Montojo's flagship, the *Reina Cristina,* was the best ship of the squadron, but she had no armor except shields around some of her guns, and those guns were all inferior to those of the American ships. *Reina Cristina* had six 6-inch guns, and everything else aboard was on the same comparative scale. The rest of the Spanish squadron was too small, and the ships too light, to make an appreciable difference in the outcome of the battle. The Spanish had nothing to compare with the American flagship *Olympia,* whose 5,800-ton displacement was almost twice as great as *Reina Cristina*'s. The *Olympia* carried four 8-inch guns, ten 5-inch, and twenty smaller guns, and also torpedo tubes. How Mr. Jane and all the other armchair strategists could become so enthusiastic about the Spanish prospects is a mystery veiled by more than three quarters of a century. But of course they could not have known the military secrets: for example, Admiral Montojo's ships had torpedo tubes, but they did not have torpedoes to fit them.

As the naval experts said—after the battle—the sensible approach of the Spanish squadron would have been to land all the men and guns and scuttle the ships. That way the Americans would have to try to make a landing if they wanted Manila, and ashore the Spanish sailors could indeed fight well. Admiral Montojo wanted to do just this, but he was strangled by his own country's bureaucracy. He was under the orders of the Military Governor of the Philippines, who knew nothing of naval warfare and was only concerned with saving face; if Montojo lost the naval action, well then, what could the world expect the governor to do? So Montojo was forced to fight at sea without the means to do so. Some of Montojo's officers suggested that Montojo might launch a surprise attack with his few seaworthy vessels and do some damage to the Americans. Perhaps that was a possibility, if the Spanish ships could get up steam and if ramming the American ships did not sink the Spaniards instead. But success was so very improbable that Montojo wisely did not even give serious consideration to those courses that could end in disaster. Somehow, from where he was, a lucky shot might be fired which would blow up an American magazine or two. If that was hoping for a miracle, then he knew only a miracle would suffice.

When the Americans arrived off Cavite, Admiral Montojo was as ready for them as he could be. He had learned of their coming on the evening of April 30 and had heard the gunfire at the entrance to Manila Bay. As the Americans came in, the Spanish batteries at Cavite opened fire long before the ships were in range. The noise was tremendous but the effects were nil, except on the morale of the Americans. It was unnerving to rush into a harbor and watch the waterspouts of falling shells coming closer, closer, closer. At 5:41 P.M. the *Olympia* fired one forward 8-inch gun. The shell did not hit anything. The other American ships got into action and their firing was just as inaccurate. When they came within range, the American ships turned and passed down the Spanish line, bringing their broadsides to bear. Shot followed shot, without effect, until one of the *Olympia*'s 8-inch projectiles hit the *Reina Cristina*'s forecastle, where it killed and wounded a number of sailors manning the small guns there and sent splinters as far back as the bridge.

But if the American gunnery was below average, the Spanish gunnery failed the course. The Spanish gunnery officers should have plotted out the ranges precisely; they must have been ashore at their clubs instead, for as ships and forts fired, the shells went short or long. It was a remarkable display of incompetence, as the Americans paraded back and forth five times along the Spanish line.

On the last pass, Admiral Montojo decided to act, no matter the consequences. He ordered Captain Cadarso of the *Reina Cristina* to slip cables and steam out and ram the Americans. The *Reina Cristina* was followed by a pair of yellow launches, which came speeding out ahead. The Americans turned the full power of their fleet on the launches and the flagship. When one launch reached a point 800 yards from the fleet, a whole cluster of six-pound shells seemed to strike at once, and the boat simply disintegrated. The second was destroyed less spectacularly; she stopped and then turned and started back for shore, riddled and sinking as she moved. The Americans were well-satisfied with the results. They had destroyed two torpedo boats, they said. (Later, newspaper correspondents with the fleet identified the two boats as "innocent market boats.")

But there was no question about the activity of the *Reina Cristina*. She came bravely out into a storm of shells. High explosives struck the decks, setting fires and smashing equipment. One shell hit the bridge, knocked out the starboard searchlight, and wrecked the bridge steering. A shell killed nine men aft, another struck in the wardroom where the wounded from the first part of the action had been brought and killed nearly all of them. A shell amidships below the main deck burst a steam pipe and the steam scalded many men. Fires broke out near the magazines and they had to be flooded. The ship lost way and soon only two men were standing to fight the guns. She could not ram even a Staten Island ferryboat in this condition, and so Admiral Montojo ordered her turned back toward shore and abandoned because she was sinking. Of a total crew of 409 officers and men, 206 were wounded or killed and among the wounded were the admiral and his flag lieutenant. Captain Cadarso, true to tradition, was determined to be the last man off the ship and stood by supervising the abandonment. Just before the last boat left a shell killed him.

The other Spanish ships were also in trouble. The *Ulloa* had taken many shells and was down to two guns firing when a shell hit at the water line and blew through the ship, killing the captain and half the men still alive. The *Castilla* was afire and all her guns were out of action; she was abandoned as the *Reina Cristina* was sinking. By 9:30 that morning the only ships capable of resistance were the *Cuba, Luzon, Ulloa, Duero,* and the cruiser *Austria*. The *Austria* was on fire and all the others were in dreadful condition. Admiral Montojo, then, was quite surprised when the Americans suddenly turned and went away, out of range. He was no fool, so he ordered all ships to retire to Bakor Bay and there to resist to the end.

Why had Commodore Dewey suddenly backed away? The reason was an error which left the Americans looking extremely foolish. Dewey had asked, at about 9:30 A.M., how much ammunition the ships had left. The firing had been so intense that information was essential.

"Fifteen percent," was the response, whereupon Dewey signalled the retreat. He was worried about the quality of the American shooting—he saw those shells missing the enemy and splashing. He was concerned about the Spanish gunnery, for the Spanish guns shot so furiously that he was sure the damage to his ships must be considerable. Also the *Boston* was hit and had started to burn appreciably while the fires he saw aboard the Spanish vessels seemed insignificant. In other words, Commodore Dewey had a fright. He had done little damage to the enemy it seemed, one of his ships was hit, and he was running out of ammunition. Retirement seemed the best answer. So he gave the order and the Americans moved back, in an atmosphere of gloom, aboard the flagship. The officers did not have the heart to tell the men the truth, so they said the retreat was to let them all have time for breakfast.

Not before the ships had drawn off several miles and the captains went aboard the *Olympia* did the commodore learn that his judgment had been precipitous and unwarranted. Had the Spanish been more capable of battle the course of the action might well have changed, for inshore Admiral Montojo began to believe that the miracle had occurred and he had driven away the Americans. While the Americans were explaining to Dewey that *only* fifteen percent of the ammunition had been expended, they were heartened to hear explosions aboard the Spanish ships. Magazines aboard the *Reina Cristina* and the *Castilla* went up very close together.

So at 11 o'clock the Americans went back to do battle. This time they split up. The *Baltimore* attacked the *Ulloa* and soon sank her. The *Olympia* fired on the Spanish shore installations at Cavite. The *Boston* fired on anything that moved in her vicinity, and the smaller vessels chose targets of their own. In about an hour the battle ended with eleven Spanish ships sunk or burned and two captured. Admiral Montojo said his casualties were 381 men killed and wounded. The Americans soon appeared before Manila and demanded the surrender of the city; the Spanish, who knew Dewey had no landing forces, laughed at them. But when the news of this unequal battle reached America the newspapers claimed it to be the greatest naval victory of the age and compared Commodore Dewey to Lord Nelson. Perhaps such hyperbole could be forgiven; the Americans were extremely self-conscious and wanted badly to become known as a great naval power so they created a myth about the battle of Manila Bay. But what the battle really proved was that a force of modern ships matched against a force of antiques would win every time, and that was certainly nothing new. In terms of naval development, the battle also proved that just because a vessel was built of iron or steel did not mean it was adequately protected against the new guns of the 1890s. In future the ships would be needing armor of at least four inches of belt steel against the hulls. Luckily for the Americans, the Spanish guns were as old as their ships and the squadron suffered virtually no damage. The *Baltimore* had been hit by one shell that ricocheted around the upper deck, wounded two officers and six men and stunned a man who was leaning against a ventilator. The *Boston* was hit a few times but suffered no real damage. The *Olympia* was hit three times but the concussion from her own 8-inch guns did more damage aboard by far than the enemy did. Indeed, the most important casualty of the whole affair was Captain Gridley, who had been ill before the battle began, and died on the passage home. His family at least had one consolation, he would go down in history, for so empty of glory was this unequal struggle that the reporters, searching for catch phrases to stun their readers could come up with nothing better than the low key statement by the commodore at the beginning of the battle: "You may fire when you are ready, Gridley."

And all the rest is history, although it took a good fifty years before the true import of the battle emerged in the annals of America.

6

The Philippine Quagmire

~~~~~

AFTER THE BATTLE OF MANILA BAY, the war dragged on. The American fleet in the bay kept the Spanish from receiving supplies. The Filipino revolutionaries came forward to surround Manila after the battle, and the Americans brought the revolutionary leader Aguinaldo over from Hongkong to organize the army and help the Americans win the war.

Oddly, the people and government of the United States first learned about the battle of Manila Bay from Madrid. Commodore Dewey had cut the cable from Manila and there was no way for him to send a message. The Spanish sent a ship out in the middle of the battle, it reached Hongkong and reported that the Americans had been repelled with heavy losses (that was the "breakfast break" at ten o'clock on the day of the battle). A few hours later another Spanish ship was sent off to Hongkong and gave details of the sinking of enough Spanish ships for the Americans to realize that Dewey had somehow won. An official American dispatch via Hongkong had to wait until May 5 for the *McCulloch,* a small ship that had to coal before she could leave. It was hot in Manila and it took a long time for the Americans to coal.

This leisurely reporting typified the situation: the American squadron sat in the harbor and the Spanish garrison sat on land and neither could take action against the other. On May 18, the USS *Charleston* left San Francisco carrying more ammunition, which Dewey did not need. It was just as well he did not, the ship broke down and had to turn back the next day. It was May 28, 1898, then, before the Americans managed to send out an expeditionary force of twenty-five hundred troops on board three transports, the *City of Pekin,* the *City of Sydney,* and the *Australia.* Had the Spanish been not nearly

51

supine, there was opportunity for them to have organized a resistance that might have made matters very difficult. But most important was the futility of the Spanish effort. On June 15, 1898, a second American expedition was sent off, thirty-five hundred more troops. On June 20 the first expedition stopped off at Guam and attacked, giving the Navy another of those coveted coaling stations. There was virtually no resistance, the governor of Guam had not even learned that there was a war on.

When the expeditionary forces reached Manila on June 30 they found a German squadron had arrived to fish in the troubled waters and was still there, although Commodore Dewey had sent for the *Monterey,* a monitor or heavy-gunned and heavy-armored ship that could deal with anything the Germans had to offer. Meanwhile the Spanish reserve squadron in Cadiz had sailed to the Pacific, gotten as far as Suez, and sailed home again, to meet a "threat" of American ships against the Spanish coast. Finally, after a voyage of misadventure, the *Monterey* arrived in Manila Bay early in August. The Germans were still on hand but their presence did not deter Dewey from deciding on a landing on August 13, 1898. So occurred one of the worst-planned amphibious operations in the history of warfare.

From the beginning it had been a circus; the army troops had been assembled at the Presidio in San Francisco and loaded aboard the transports. The navy had no authority over the transports and the army knew nothing about life at sea. The troops created filth below decks and lice soon took over the troop quarters. The men spat and defecated on deck and urinated over the side, often into the wind. Water ran short, which gave them an excuse not to wash. The marvel that there was no epidemic aboard was attributed by at least one contemporary historian to "the splendid patriotism of the soldiers and volunteers" and only secondarily to strong constitutions.

The United States expeditionary force was lucky not to run into even a Spanish gunboat on the way to Manila, for the captains of the ships paid no attention to one another's signals. It was every ship for itself all the way across.

The troop ships arrived in Manila Bay and sat, surrounded by the American squadron and British and French ships that had joined the Germans to kibitz.

Commodore Dewey and General Merritt, the troop commander, consulted on the best means of getting the Americans ashore. Some of those troops had been aboard ship for more than a month, and to say they were restive would be to put it mildly. Each day the maintenance of discipline became harder, but still the commanders made no decision. On August 7, General Merritt and the commodore sent an ultimatum to the governor, Don Fermin Jaudenes y Alvarez. He would have forty-eight hours in which to remove noncombatants from Manila, they said; then they would attack the city. The governor replied that he had no place to send the women and children since the Filipinos surrounded the capital. That was a stunner. For two days Dewey and Merritt debated. On August 9, they again demanded the surrender of the city. The governor said he had to consult Madrid, but he could not consult Madrid because Dewey had cut the Hongkong cable.

Finally Governor Jaudenes came up with a peculiarly Spanish solution: there must be resistance, otherwise the governor would be in trouble with Madrid. But he would tell his troops to offer only token resistance.

So a "battle" was planned. To a large extent, this battle was staged for the many war correspondents who had come along to record the passage of events. Joseph Pulitzer's New York *World* and William Randolph Hearst's New York *Journal* have been given (by history) a very large share in the fomenting of the Spanish-American war in the first place. No correspondents had accompanied the Dewey Squadron in the beginning because Dewey had been in Hongkong, far from the United States. Joseph L. Stickney, an editorial writer from the New York *Herald,* was on assignment in Japan then and he joined Dewey at Hongkong before the battle. Edward Harden of the New York *World* and an artist named John McCutcheon of the Chicago *Record* had been making a trip around the world aboard the revenue cutter *Hugh McCulloch,* when it was suddenly assigned to the Dewey squadron. So these newspapermen saw the initial action and their stories, although rudely delayed by the Commodore's thoughtlessness in cutting the Hongkong cable, did get through to America. This report whetted the competitive appetites of publishers across the land and scores of correspondents came with the troop ships. For them this "battle" was staged.

The plan called for the Americans to storm ashore in boats and fire a few shots, whereupon the Spanish troops were to surrender. The navy would move in at nine o'clock in the morning, and the ships would bombard the fort at Malate, a mile and a quarter south of Manila. Then Dewey would run up a flag demanding "surrender." The Spanish would run up a white flag and the action would be over. Just in case the weather was not fine, the whole show would be postponed until the sun came out.

The weather obliged and all went well. At nine o'clock the warships were in place. They passed the British squadron's flagship *Immortalite,* and the *Immortalité*'s band struck up "See, the Conquering Hero Comes!" and then segued into the "Star Spangled Banner," and closed with the "El Capitan" march. It was a stirring performance and it aroused the patriotic juices of the newspapermen.

The navy bombarded. The army landed and the troops began firing and advancing. No one was quite sure what they were shooting at because there were no Spaniards in sight. After this became clear, the shooting stopped and the troops marched into Manila. Suddenly someone saw a white flag and

53

General Greene, commander of the shore force, galloped forward on his horse followed by his staff and the newspaper correspondents. Just outside the city they met a Spanish officer and one soldier.

"Have you surrendered?" demanded the general.

"Quien sabe." shrugged the officer. "Someone told me to run up the white flag, so I ran up the white flag."

But the Spanish flag still flew above Manila. Dewey and Merritt sent officers to the city with the Belgian consul to demand an answer: Why was not the scenario being followed?

The Spanish commander replied that he was afraid to surrender until the American troops arrived to be surrendered to. Otherwise, the Filipinos, who were lurking on the edge of town, would charge in and really make a surrender of it. This situation continued until two o'clock in the afternoon, when Dewey's flag lieutenant finally returned to the *Olympia*.

"Well," he said, "they've surrendered."

"Why don't they haul down the flag?" demanded Dewey.

"They're still waiting for somebody to surrender to," said the flag lieutenant. And it was nearly six o'clock before General Greene marched his troops into the fortress; the Spanish flag came slowly down the staff, and the protective force of Americans ran up Old Glory. The war in the Philippines against Spain had ended.

That night Aguinaldo's rebels insisted that they be given a part of the responsibility for holding and governing Manila. The Americans refused. So the Filipinos put up trenches around Manila and declared that the Americans were now the enemy. By the time the newspaper correspondents' stories of the heroic assault were received in the newsrooms back home, the real war in the Philippines had begun. It was to last not for days, but for years, and to cost the Americans far more in lives than the whole Spanish-American war. Eventually one result of the struggle would be the creation of a permanent Asiatic Squadron on the model of the British, French, and German squadrons, and finally the United States would establish the Asiatic Fleet. The advocates of Manifest Destiny had their destiny for certain. The United States was irrevocably committed to the Western Pacific.

7

Into the Suluan Soup

~~~~~~~~

THE AMERICAN OCCUPATION OF MANILA was a big disappointment to two
different groups lurking on the perimeter. The German squadron under Rear
Admiral Diederichs had been sitting on the sidelines hoping for an American
disaster so Germany could pick up the pieces. The kaiser wanted an empire
and his navy was trying to carve it out of the remaining free territories and
lost colonies of the Pacific. But when not one but two American heavy monitors arrived, Diederichs knew he was outclassed. With the American army in
occupation of the land, he saw that if Germany wanted the Philippines she
would have to fight America for them, and he kept offshore. The other disappointed group was that of the rebel leader Emilio Aguinaldo. Commodore
Dewey had brought the rebel chief to the islands from Hongkong, and this
assistance gave Aguinaldo the idea that the Americans, true to their own revolutionary past, were going to help him secure Filipino independence. But
Dewey, knowing the temper of the Congress and the Republican administration, with its sense of the inevitability of becoming a colonial power and
shouldering America's part of the "white man's burden," played his cards
like a politician. He let the Filipinos believe he was all for them. He let the
Spanish believe the Americans would do anything rather than let the Filipinos
have their own country back. He waited, then, for indications from Washington as to which way he should jump. Meanwhile, as Dewey also waited for
troops, Aguinaldo began moving without any American assistance. Even
before the Americans came ashore Aguinaldo had captured all of Subic Bay
except the Isla Grande, where the Spanish had held out that summer. The
Germans sent the ship *Irene* to Subic Bay to keep the insurgents from taking

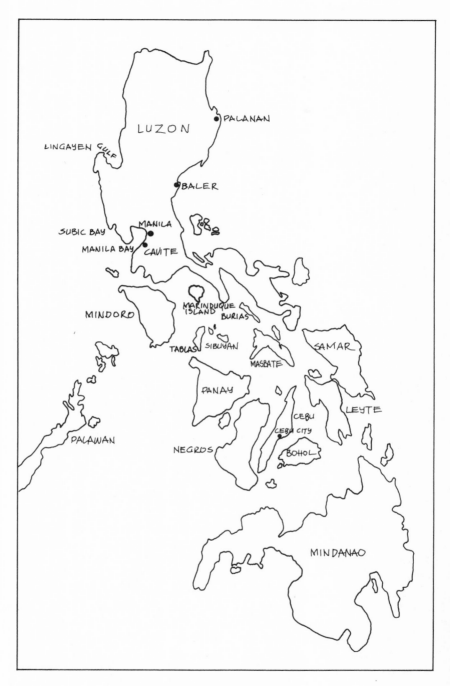

The Philippine Islands

the island. Hearing this, Dewey sent two warships to Isla Grande, whereupon the Germans left, and Aguinaldo captured the place, under the impression that he had been helped by the Americans.

But whatever Aguinaldo believed, and however skilful Dewey was as a politician, the truth soon became apparent. Aguinaldo might have known when the Americans kept on sitting on his land, waiting. He did know when the bitter news came that on November 28, 1898, the United States and Spain had signed a treaty of peace which gave the Philippine Islands and Puerto Rico to the Americans.

Even the peace treaty did not entirely discourage the Germans. In February, 1899, Dewey learned that Admiral Diederichs was meddling at Cebu, which was held by the insurgent forces. Dewey sent a ship down to Cebu, and it landed a detachment of sailors. The town was full of British and German flags and anti-American sentiment; Diederichs had convinced the Filipinos that if the Americans came they would massacre everyone. The Americans were annoyed and spoke sharply to the Germans; finally, the Germans were pushed out of the Philippines.

But from the outset the United States military situation was impossible. The American soldiers held the towns, but they soon learned that Aguinaldo held the hearts of the people, and his forces moved around the edges of the cities, conducting a highly effective guerilla warfare. The situation was not only impossible, Dewey discovered, but dangerous. Early in the spring of 1899 Dewey learned that a small Spanish garrison was still holding out at the port of Baler on Luzon, north of Manila. He sent the warship *Yorktown* there, and the *Yorktown*'s captain sent Lieutenant James Clarkson Gillmore with fourteen men in a boat to sound out the depth of the water near shore, there being virtually no charts of Philippine waters. The boat was attacked, four sailors were killed, and the others were captured. They were marched about from place to place, usually blindfolded, and held captive for months. Finally, they were led into the wilderness and abandoned, either to starve or be killed by the wild tribesmen of the mountains. Since Lieutenant Gillmore was a resourceful man he led his men out of the wilderness to a river that he knew would take them to the sea. They built a raft and floated downstream. On the third day they were rescued by a detachment of American soldiers after they had been captive and abandoned for eight months.

By this time, the end of 1899, the pattern of the American occupation of the Philippines was set. Dewey was long gone; in May he had sailed home triumphantly to be greeted as a conquering hero. Congress, which had in its usual spirit of peacetime pusillanimity abandoned the rank of admiral on the death of David Farragut, the hero of the Civil War, revived the rank, bestowed it on Dewey, and thanked him by Act of Congress for the conquest of Manila. Misunderstanding the nature of the problem in the islands, the navy sent a captain, Albert Smith Barker, to command the forces on the Asiatic station. The naval mission was to support the army troops in the pacification of the islands so a proper civil government could be installed. But the insurgents would not pacify. They kept insisting it was their country and they wanted it. Consequently, in the summer of 1899, Captain Barker found himself forced to employ thirty-five ships, including the mighty *Oregon*. It was quickly apparent to Congress that something was amiss when it took six times as many ships to "pacify" the islands as it had to conquer them. Congressmen began turning up in the islands on investigative trips. What they discovered led them to send higher authority. Rear Admiral John Crittenden Watson came to replace Barker that fall, and a new plan for pacification was worked out. The American navy bought thirteen small gunboats from Spain and began distributing them around the islands. So the Filipinos had come full circle: they were back under martial law. The only difference was that the troops and ships were American.

Since more authority was needed in addition to a new admiral, General Henry W. Lawton was put in charge of the army's forces, and army, marines, and navy combined operations against the guerillas. General Lawton began an offensive against the rebels south of Manila. The Americans captured all the area around Cavite. Soon they also had taken Subic Bay. By late autumn three American divisions were in operation under General Arthur MacArthur, General Lawton, and General Wheaton. Many of the military operations called for amphibious landings, so the navy was constantly supporting the army. For example, on November 7, 1899, the Americans assaulted San Fabian in Lingayen Gulf. The ships of the fleet bombarded the area and then boats landed soldiers and marines. In a matter of hours, the rebel forces had scattered but the trouble was that scattering did not stop the fighting. By the end of 1899 "the spirit of the insurrection had been broken," said the Americans, but apparently the Filipinos did not know it. Their "armies," never particularly well organized, had been overwhelmed, but the armies dissolved into the rain forest and the guerillas fought on. For more than a year the difficult battle continued. It was resolved finally, by a daring military action. Aguinaldo, the president of the Philippine Republic, was driven into the hills, and one by one, his lieutenants were captured and sent into exile. In the spring of 1901, a messenger carrying important documents from Aguinaldo to General Urbano Lacuna was captured by the troops of General Funston, who decided on a bold plan to capture the Filipino leader. Aguinaldo's message had called upon General Lacuna to send reinforcements to the president's camp. Funston decided that his men would impersonate the reinforcements. In Manila bay one night in March, Funston, four American officers, and a Spaniard named Lazaro Segovia boarded the warship *Vicksburg*. The key to success was a troop of Macabebe scouts, an organization of Filipinos who

58

had accepted the American occupation of their country. This unit was led by Hilario Tal Placido.

The *Vicksburg* took the General and his men to Siguran Bay, near the village of Palanan, where Aguinaldo was living. Funston and the other Americans pretended to be prisoners of war who had been captured by the Filipinos, and they were marched into the village by the Macabebe column. Tal Placido and the Spaniard then entered the house where Aguinaldo was living and he welcomed them as allies. Just then firing began outside the house. Aguinaldo rushed to the window, thinking his own men were making a noisy salute to the newcomers. "Stop firing," he shouted. "You. . . ."

That was all he could get out. From behind he was seized by Tal Placido and Segovia. His arms were pinioned and a pistol was pointed at his head. In a moment General Funston arrived and arrested Aguinaldo in the name of the United States government.

The Filipinos at Palanan were disarmed and Aguinaldo was taken aboard the *Vicksburg* and transported back to Manila. With unusual courtesy he was ushered into the office of General Arthur MacArthur, supreme commander of the war against the rebels. MacArthur told Aguinaldo that the revolution had failed. Aguinaldo's people would now begin to surrender, but the bloodshed could be stopped only if the Filipino leader would give the word.

Since MacArthur spoke persuasively Aguinaldo considered the matter. MacArthur gave details, hoping to convince Aguinaldo that his generals were losing heart and surrendering. Further, said the United States general, the Americans were taking city after city and holding them. Aguinaldo was not convinced and so he was held in confinement; but as each American victory came, General MacArthur announced it to his captive. Panay fell in March. After that came Marinduque, another strong rebel place. General Teodoro Sandiko surrendered on April 6, 1901, and that was the last straw. On April 19, Aguinaldo agreed that MacArthur had won. When the general promised civil government and ultimate independence, he took the oath of allegiance to the United States and issued a proclamation to the Filipinos: "Let the stream of blood cease to flow," he said, "and let there be an end to tears and desolation."

The Filipinos had lost much, millions of dollars in property and 16,000 men killed. As for the Americans, they had lost 4,000 men in action and many more from disease. The army had employed 70,000 troops in the pacification of the Philippines; the navy had employed the enormous "squadron" that had really become a fleet; and the United States had spent $185,000,000 in the process. In 1900, the squadron was renamed the Asiatic Fleet. By 1901, then, the American hold on the Philippines was secure, and so was the American naval presence, which had been the driving force in the acquisition of this territory.

Pacific Destiny

The public was told that the Spanish-American war was a struggle to give freedom to the oppressed colonial peoples of the dying Spanish empire. But the actuality was quite different.

In the summer of 1898, after the victory at Manila Bay, when the Republican "manifest destiny" crowd, led by Senator Henry Cabot Lodge of Massachusetts, was demanding the retention of the Philippines as a colony, President McKinley favored independence. He was convinced otherwise by the eagerness of Germany to pick up any leavings and a similar interest shown in the Philippines by Japan. Some British leaders privately urged the United States to take the Philippines lest they fall into hands less friendly to the British Empire. So there were wheels turning within wheels and not least were those in the Navy Department. When President McKinley sought Commodore Dewey's advice, Dewey said that at least the United States ought to retain a base there. "Luzon is in almost all respects the most desirable of these islands, and therefore the one to retain . . ." he wrote. The landlocked bay of Manila was ideal for a naval station. And the United States needed naval stations, he said, given the growing involvement in Pacific affairs. So McKinley was convinced and embarked on a colonial policy. The first naval base in the Philippines had already been established in Manila Bay at the end of 1898. Cavite became both a naval base and a camp for the American marines who came to the islands to help put down the insurrection. Olongapo in Subic Bay was occupied in December, 1899, by the marines. The old Spanish naval yard there became a second American naval base. But the precise manner in which the new bases would be used was so important a matter that the Navy Department created a General Board to establish policy in this new period of American development. The navy was influential in convincing the President and the Secretary of State that Germany was a potential aggressor in the Pacific. Germany's ambitions still conflicted with those of America at Samoa. America's seizure of Guam in the Spanish-American war upset the Germans. In February, 1899, German restlessness brought German traders and officials to set two Samoan chiefs to warring. Indignantly, the United States Navy sent the USS *Philadelphia* to Apia to land marines with the usual duty of "protecting American lives and property" and, incidentally, to keep the Germans from taking power. This same aggressiveness against the Germans caused the navy almost immediately to send a marine garrison to Agana and to establish the naval station in Guam. Early in 1900, the first governor of American Samoa was appointed—a naval officer, Commodore Seaton Schroeder—and as a warning to Germany, Tutuila and the nearby islands of the Samoan group were placed under Navy Department authority by President McKinley.

An uneasy solution had been found to the difficulties with Germany over

Samoa with the agreement that the Germans would rule over Savaii and Upolu islands; but it only emphasized the need for a new naval doctrine.

The creation of the General Board of the Navy was an indirect warning to Germany that America proposed to become a first rate naval power, and the appointment of Admiral Dewey, in the wake of his heroic welcome back to America, was an indication that the policy of this board was going to be aggressive. The succession of events that occurred in the spring and summer of 1900 in China, plus the continued difficulties in the Philippines that year, made certain that the board would establish a firm and expansive naval policy for America. The American navy was on the move.

8

The Boxers Really
Didn't Want to Box....

AMERICAN EXPORTS TO ASIA more than doubled in the last fifteen years of the nineteenth century, and American businessmen looked with approval on the extension of American naval influence in the Pacific. By 1900, Alfred Thayer Mahan's concept of a powerful fleet as an instrument of trade ("trade follows the flag") was generally accepted. And in the last few years of the nineteenth century American trade with China became a major factor in the development of the fleet. American exports to China had risen from $8 million in 1888 to $18 million in 1897, with most trade in cotton goods that went to North China and Manchuria. American manufacturers began to express growing interest in the Chinese market, and with the acquisition of the Philippines the steel industry advocated colonial expansion as a method of increasing the markets for American goods. But the McKinley administration was in no mood for further foreign adventures, having so much trouble in digesting the Philippines. Further, it was obvious that an American attempt to join the pack and seize a piece of China would be met with opposition, particularly from Russia, Germany, and Japan, all of which nurtured unfulfilled colonial ambitions in North China.

So the Americans contented themselves with a policy calling for an "open door," or equal trading opportunity in China for all nations. But the Europeans wanted no such competition from a country that was rapidly becoming the most powerful industrial nation in the world, and in a sense the Open Door Policy hastened the territorial acquisitions of Europeans and brought the Chinese to a point of rebellion against the incursions of foreigners in their land. The unrest produced an organization called the Boxers, which was on the surface an athletic or self-defense-teaching organization but underneath was dedicated to driving the foreigners from China. When the Boxers organized, the imperial court at Peking took a not unfriendly view of the proceedings. When the Boxers began murdering missionaries and Christian Chinese and burning missions and foreign establishments, the government intervened, although not always promptly nor with much enthusiasm. So the situation in the countryside went from bad to worse. By May, 1900, the American State Department was enough aroused that it asked for and received an American legation guard for Peking. Captain John T. Myers of the Marine Corps, twenty-eight marines, and a detachment of sailors landed from the USS *Oregon,* which had come to Taku, off Tientsin, to show the flag. Myers and his men took the train to Peking to set up the legation guard.

As Myers landed on May 24, the Boxers had already begun moving against the foreign legations in Peking. Rear Admiral Louis Kempff, the deputy commander of the Asiatic Fleet, came to Taku in the *Newark.* Other naval contingents from Britain, Germany, France, Japan, and Russia also assembled at the mouth of the Pei Ho to await developments. On May 31, a large force for that time—three hundred foreign troops—reached Peking and set up inside the wall that surrounded the legation quarter. On the other side the Boxers were encamped, demonstrating, haranguing, and whipping up enthusiasm for a direct attack on the embassies. The attack soon began, but the wall and the defenses of foreign troops kept the Chinese from overrunning the legations. By June 10, however, the situation looked so bad and the Chinese government was doing so little to help the besieged foreigners that the international military consortium in Taku harbor decided to take action. The senior officer, Britain's Vice Admiral Sir Edward Seymour, led the force. The first move was to send a train and troops down the railroad toward Peking to repair the line the Boxers had torn up and to isolate the capital from foreign influence. On June 10, 1900, Sir Edward sent a force of two thousand men on that mission. They did not march far. On June 11, the troops encountered a large force of Boxers on the railroad line a few miles from Lofa. Many of them carried guns, but others had only sticks and lances. Some of the leaders wore swords, and many wore sashes that were stitched or painted with incantations. The Boxer leaders had assured their followers that because their cause was just, the gods had granted them immunity from the foreign devils' bullets. When the column stopped it was attacked furiously by the Boxers, who seemed to show no fear at all. The foreign troops began to fire, and Boxers dropped. But others ran over the bodies and for an hour the fighting was brisk. When the Boxers had lost several hundred men, they retreated, but not far. They holed up in villages near Lofa, but these were cleared out that day and the next by the British. Then the expedition repaired the roadway and proceeded toward Peking.

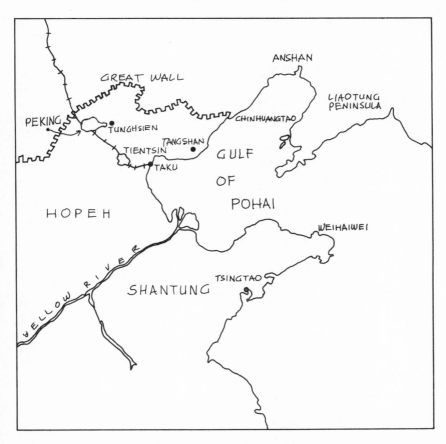

Scene of operations of the Allied Expeditionary Forces during the Boxer Rebellion

On June 13, the Boxers again cut the road near Anting. And then it was learned they had also cut the line at Santsun and several other places. The damage was so extensive and the Boxer harassment so serious that the expedition stopped at Santsun so the repairs to the train could be made. The expedition then again turned westward toward Peking and reached a point about fifty miles from Peking on June 17. At that time the international force of warships at the mouth of the Pei Ho River was undergoing harassment by Chinese government troops who threatened to cut off supply to the troops ashore. The forts began firing. One of the ships under fire was the USS *Monocacy,* now old and tired but blessed (for this operation) with a shallow draft that let her move in close to Taku. Commander F. M. Wise, although attacked by the guns of the fort at Tong Ku, did not return the fire. The other foreign ships did fire, and parts of the forts were destroyed.

Until this point, the Chinese imperial government had officially remained aloof from the conflict. But with the bombardment of the forts, the Chinese army joined the struggle against the foreigners, and the situation of the expeditionary force on the rail line became desperate. On the night of June 17, near Lang Fang, the expedition's train was attacked by more than four thousand Boxers and Chinese troops. The fight lasted all day on June 18. Next day, Sir Edward decided to move. The railroad was being cut faster than it could be repaired his scouts said. Further, the active support by the Chinese army of the Boxers meant that the railroad line behind the expedition could not be protected. They were indeed cut off and were threatened by annihilation from overwhelming force. The only thing to do was fight their way back to Tientsin and the protection of the naval force. A few hours after Sir Edward made this decision came the word that the Chinese had captured the city of Tientsin and denied access to the railroad station to the western powers.

Meanwhile the international powers at Taku had mounted another force to retake Tientsin, including a detachment of one hundred thirty United States marines who had just come in from Manila aboard the USS *Nashville*. The force set out to relieve Tientsin and was attacked just outside the city by a large number of Chinese troops.

By June 21, the foreigners were engaged in China on three fronts. The Seymour expedition was fighting its way toward the imperial arsenal at Hsi Ku, hoping to capture that bastion and deprive the Chinese of guns and ammunition. The international powers from Taku were surrounded and fighting desperately for survival just outside Tientsin. And the Boxers and Chinese military in Peking, learning of the successes against the foreigners, began a determined attack on the legation quarter.

In this crisis, the best asset of the foreigners was a result of the antiforeign attitudes at the imperial court. The dowager empress had forced the sequestration of the foreign embassies in one quarter of the city, isolated from the Chinese by a high wall. The wall that was supposed to protect the Chinese people from the foreign devils now protected the foreigners instead. For once, under common threat, the people of the various foreign powers were able to see eye to eye. Russian, British, German, Italian, Japanese, and American troops and diplomats banded together to fight the Boxers. When the German ambassador was killed, the German women and children were moved into the British embassy for security. And the siege began. Day after day the Boxers would mount ladders against the walls of the embassy quarter, and the troops would shoot them down and hurl the ladders off the walls.

On June 25, 1900, the Seymour expedition fought its way along the road to Hsi Ku. (The railroad engines and equipment and much of their personal

66

equipment were abandoned when it became impossible to keep the road open.) That day Seymour's troops captured the Hsi Ku arsenal. Two days later, the Russians and the United States marines from Taku captured another arsenal outside Tientsin. The Chinese were thus deprived of their major sources of military supply.

Sir Edward spent the next few days regrouping and preparing for a new assault to free Tientsin from Chinese military control. On July 9, a force of two thousand men, including nine hundred Americans, mounted an assault on Tientsin, which was defended by an estimated twenty-two thousand Chinese troops. The fighting lasted five days. In the end the superior fire power of the modern western weapons carried the action, and Tientsin was "freed."

By this time the Taku forts had been captured, and there was no way the Chinese could keep the foreigners from bringing in numbers of troops and quantities of supplies. The fighting around Tientsin continued, but the allied forces were successful in driving off the Chinese as troops from the Philippines, Japan, Manchuria, and Hongkong joined those in China. By August 4, the foreigners had assembled an army of eighteen thousand six hundred men, including two thousand five hundred American troops. Admiral G. C. Remey, United States commander in the Philippines, had come to supervise the naval action.

In Peking, each day the situation of the embassy people became more perilous. Food ran short. So did ammunition. But the great wall, fifty feet high and fifty feet thick, protected them. The Chinese kept launching attacks, and kept falling back with frightful losses. Finally they began the construction of a huge assault tower against one section of the wall defended by American marines. Here the fighting went on day and night, as the Chinese tried to come up and the marines forced them back down. One defender after another was killed or wounded, and the sense of attrition grew daily. But the marines continued to hold and so did the Germans, the British, and the Japanese in the other sectors.

With his reinforced military unit, Sir Edward Seymour launched a new expedition to relieve Peking, and early in August this strong force began to move west. The Boxers continued to charge at the guns, mindless of the death that faced them. The Chinese troops did not fight so wildly, but more effectively, and the allied advance was slow. But on the afternoon of August 14, 1900, the defenders on the walls of the embassy fortress heard the sound of machine guns. The Chinese had no machine guns, so the defenders knew that relief was on its way, and late that afternoon a United States Marine detachment of 482 men attacked the Chinese outside the east wall of Peking. The fighting was hard, but the troops broke through and scaled the wall. That day the Boxer rebellion ended.

This military victory first seemed to put the Americans in the international camp of powers that were determined to cut up China for their own colonial purposes. The newfound "brotherhood" of the European powers at Peking soon evaporated in various national auras, and the Japanese joined in as well, all seeking a piece of China for themselves. But the Americans held firm for free trade for all nations in China, and thus reaffirmed their standoffishness in international affairs. In the Boxer rebellion, for the first time, the Americans had allied themselves with European powers in a colonial venture and were welcomed; but they backed off, assessed the American situation, and decided enough was enough. That was the internationalist position. More insular was the attitude of most Americans who, if asked, would deny that the United States ever had any colonial aspirations and assert that the two great oceans east and west were all the protection America ever needed. That myopia, particularly in Congress, was to continue for the next forty years.

9

The Great
White Fleet

AS FAR AS AMERICANS WERE CONCERNED the major result of the Spanish-
American War and the Boxer Rebellion was a new interest in international
trade. At the turn of the twentieth century, the domestic needs of the people
of the United States were more than met by American industry, but if that
industry was to continue to profit, it must have foreign markets. The two
military excursions had pointed the way: trade abroad doubled and the country
did prosper but not, however, in the way that naval strategists of the period
hoped. For although America had inherited a shipping tradition from
England, the insularity proposed by George Washington became a reality.
Before the Civil War two-thirds of American trade was carried in American
ships. Afterwards, the figure fell steadily until in 1914 only one-tenth of
American trade was carried in United States's ships.

Americans were isolationist without doubt. Such an attitude offered serious threat to the future of the United States Navy until the emergence of
Theodore Roosevelt in the presidency changed the atmosphere. Roosevelt was
a student of naval affairs as well as an assistant secretary of the navy. (He
wrote the best history, even by today's standards, of the War of 1812.) The
navy loomed large in Roosevelt's foreign policy. In Latin America, where
Germany and other European colonial nations were casting covetous eyes, he
had no qualms about sending United States troops to protect American interests. The Panama Canal occupied Roosevelt further and in this, too, he saw an
aggressive role for his beloved navy.

The early 1900s were years in which it was popular to send ships abroad
on "goodwill" tours to show the flag and impress the world with the power

of the navy involved. It was a changing era; everyone, it seemed, was building battleships. Britain, Germany, Russia, and Japan were building them as
fast as their legislatures would allow. Even Sweden boasted of her battleships,
and Brazil, virtually bankrupt, still found the money to commission a British
shipyard to build a 27,000-ton behemoth which was touted as "The World's
Largest and Most Powerful Battleship."

President Roosevelt entered the competition in 1903, when he ordered
an admiral and four cruisers to France, Germany, and England. When the
secretary of the navy said those cruisers would not make much of a splash the
navy also dispatched the old ship *Kearsarge* and camouflaged the venerable
tub with wood and canvas panels designed to look like the newest armor
plate. In the next few years the British, French, and Germans returned the
visits to the United States but with real armored ships. American public reaction to "big ships" was so positive that Roosevelt was able to bulldoze a
reluctant Congress into voting for a fleet of battleships for the American navy.
But that was not enough for the ebullient T. R. He wanted to build respect for
American power, partly because of a serious concern over growing Japanese
strength. During the Russo-Japanese war the tsar had sent Russia's home fleet
around the world. It was destroyed at Tsushima strait, a Japanese victory that
brought the end of the war. President Roosevelt intervened to mediate the
settlement at the Treaty of Portsmouth, and the result was cession of the
northern half of Sakhalin Island to Japan, the Russian promise not to interfere
in Japanese behavior in Korea, the return to China of some territory, and the
transfer of Russia's lease on the Liaotung Peninsula to Japan. In American
eyes this was an eminently fair settlement, but in the eyes of a growingly
powerful officer class in Japan, the Americans had made victory meaningless.
There had been no reparations payments and no grand acquisition of territory.
This Japanese sense of irritation was accompanied by another: since the Japanese had come to America in increasing numbers following the exclusion of
the Chinese in the 1880s, a strong anti-Japanese sentiment had grown up on
the west coast of the United States, founded on the fear of working people
that these small, brown, vigorous strangers would steal the bread from their
mouths. As the Japanese prospered in farming and other enterprises, the
resentment grew and in 1907 was marked by anti-Japanese rioting and other
unfriendly activities in California that were quite as serious as the anti-
Chinese behavior of the 1880s. Nor had the irritations of the Hawaii annexation been forgotten in Tokyo. Roosevelt was well aware of anti-American
feeling in Japan, and recollection of the victory of the Japanese navy at Tsushima gave him something to consider.

The thought that Japan could be an American enemy in the Pacific made
Roosevelt seek the opinions of his experts about Japanese war capabilities.
They assured him it would be years before Japan could recover from the vast

70

The Great White Fleet

expenditures of the Russo-Japanese war. Roosevelt decided to send a fleet of America's most modern warships around the world, particularly to impress the Japanese of American military might. Of course, other reasons for this move have been suggested: a foreign excursion to take American minds off domestic problems, practice for the navy in navigation and naval operations, a boost for the navy's shipbuilding program. All were factors, but most important was the feeling that Japan posed a threat. On June 18, 1907, Roosevelt called a meeting of a joint board of army and navy advisors and stated his concern. The board agreed that Japanese rumblings justified sending the Atlantic Fleet into the Pacific. Indeed, anti-Japanese feeling in America at this time had the newspapers (particularly on the west coast) talking of "war." So Roosevelt gave the order to his admirals to prepare by December to send United States battleships on a long cruise.

In the months of preparation, the need for training was certainly proved. During maneuvers several ships narrowly missed collision because of faulty shiphandling and ten men were killed in the turret of the battleship *Georgia* when they disregarded safety regulations and the turret blew up. On paper the United States had twenty-eight operational battleships, but Rear Admiral Robley D. Evans, who was chosen to command the round-the-world force, said that only sixteen could possibly be made ready to sail. Even these ships were unready and undermanned. Roosevelt insisted that the navy begin to repair and recruit. (Out of this activity came the navy slogan: "Join the Navy and See the World" because the major target of recruiting was the Middle West, for the navy wanted cleancut young men who had not previously been tarnished by the sea to show off in foreign climes.)

News that the American navy was planning a display of force brought a war scare. The San Francisco newspapers were virtually calling for war with Japan. *The New York Times* and *Collier's* magazine published a series of fictional stories which predicted and described war between the United States and Japan, with fighting in the Philippines and Hawaii. These statements brought renewed explosions of the Pacific coast diatribes against the "yellow peril" and hints of the unspeakable atrocities that would be wreaked upon American womanhood by an unleashed Japan. In St. Petersburgh a drunken Japanese diplomat boasted that his country, having defeated the Russians, was about to war on the United States and capture the Philippines and Hawaii. "But do you imagine that will satisfy us?" he said.

American jingoism was equalled in Japan. Japan's *Mainichi Shimbun,* one of Tokyo's two most important newspapers, fulminated against America: "At this time we should be ready to give a blow to the U.S. Yes, we should be ready to strike the devil's head with the iron hammer for the sake of civilization." The tension grew so great that before dispatching the fleet, Roosevelt sent big, good-natured Secretary of War William Howard Taft to Tokyo

Track of the Great White Fleet (December 1907 to February 1909) to placate the Japanese. To his relief Taft returned to report the Japanese government was as worried as Roosevelt was about the possibility of war.

Still, lesser authorities continued to talk of war. Great Britain and Japan had a treaty of mutual alliance, and some British politicians and naval officers predicted that Britain and Japan together would fight the United States. This sort of talk led to worries in America that Britain would attack New York while the fleet was off touring the world, and William Randolph Hearst added his bit to the fire by reminding everyone that Britain was America's historic enemy. Germany got into the arena because Kaiser Wilhelm II saw a way to drive a wedge between the United States and England, forcing America to become his ally. He declared Germany's concern over the aggressive intentions of the British and the Japanese.

Diplomatic messages, private conversations, newspaper reports, office rumors—all these raced through the capitals of the world. Everyone, it seemed, passed judgment on the American excursion, predicting various forms of disaster, until on December 12, 1906, the sixteen battleships stood in Hampton Roads, ready to depart, and the four rear admirals (after Dewey a grumpy Congress had refused to appoint any officer to a rank higher than rear admiral) assembled for the adventure. Although the modern fashion was to paint ships naval gray to decrease visibility in time of war, the American ships were dressed in white.

Because of the saber rattling, the cruise of what came to be called "The Great White Fleet" had dominated the national consciousness for weeks. In 1907, the staging of a world cruise by so many big ships was a wonder, and Roosevelt and the navy made the most of it. The departure from Hampton Roads was celebrated with flags and ceremonies, and the cruise became like a national holiday from there to California. The president came down in his yacht *Mayflower*, the fleet gave sixteen 21-gun salutes, and the national anthem was played sixteen times. A boatload of wives and sweethearts followed the procession out to sea further than husbands and lovers would have preferred before turning back, but nothing disastrous occurred, and the fleet was off on the tour of the world.

The navy and the president had handpicked a number of friendly reporters to accompany the fleet. Even so their dispatches were censored on the entire journey because the administration wanted no negativity to mar the show. A few journalists managed to indicate some of the seamier sides of the voyage, but mostly they wrote about the workings of a warship, which pleased the navy, and the troubles of the sailors, which did not. But they wrote and wrote and wrote. As *Le Figaro* of Paris put it gently, "The Americans, who are past masters in the art of advertising, make more noise than they should concerning the voyage of their fleet."

The negative was upheld by Henry Reuterdahl, a famous illustrator, who

73

had arranged with S. S. McClure, the magazine publisher, to write a series of articles. "Muckraking," or the uncovering of real and fancied wrongdoing, was then at its zenith, and McClure, who had virtually invented the form, was riding high. Reuterdahl's first article, published four days after the fleet sailed, shocked most Americans by telling about the deficiencies of the American ships. "Battleship Fleet Fatally Defective" was the headline over a newspaper account of the Reuterdahl article. The United States Senate was so upset that it launched an investigation into the methods by which Reuterdahl had learned military secrets such as the faults of the ships' armor plate and dangers of the ammunition hoists, just when all America was talking about the "greatest fleet in all the world." In Britain, the *Pall Mall Gazette* said nastily, "Now there can be no doubt that America's greatest interest is peace."

At Trinidad, the first port of call, the Americans were snubbed by the British. It was a matter of official British policy, emanating from Whitehall, which had advised the British governor to "do only what was absolutely necessary" for the Americans, in order to dramatize to Japan where Britain's loyalties lay. The result was not quite what the British expected: their snub was heartfelt by a sensitive America and aroused a surge of anti-British sentiment in the American fleet and at home. At the end, even the governor of Trinidad tried to make amends, but the fleet sailed with most of the American sailors saying they never wanted to set foot there again.

As if to underline the British rudeness, the Brazilians welcomed the fleet to Rio de Janeiro with almost unbelievable hospitality. So friendly was the atmosphere that even when drunken American sailors picked a barroom brawl that became a vicious streetfight, it was forgiven. When the fleet left, three hundred thousand Brazilians came down to the beach to wave goodbye, and several small vessels followed the Americans out to sea.

When the display was repeated in Peru, the British became alarmed by all the goodwill the Americans were evoking. The matter was particularly important just then because Australia was suffering a spell of "yellow peril" hysteria. The Australian prime minister was more than eager that the Americans come to his country to show Caucasion alliance in the Pacific but he was frustrated because in 1907 Australian foreign policy was controlled from London, so permission had to be secured from the British government. The British government was not enthusiastic, Australia threatened to become quite ugly if the permission were denied, and so Britain yielded with as much grace as possible. Japan then asked the Americans to stop by Tokyo Bay, and Peking asked them to come to Chefoo on the Shantung Peninsula. French newspapers, so critical a few weeks earlier, now said pontifically that the success of the American tour of South America "raises the American Navy to an equality with that of Great Britain." While this was anything but true of the military potential of the American fleet, the political implications were not lost in London and elsewhere. American Ambassador Whitelaw Reid, who had been virtually a laughing stock in London, suddenly was in demand everywhere, and especially at the functions of the powerful.

After passage through the Panama Canal into the Pacific, the fleet spent nearly three months on the west coast of the United States, impressing the people of western America, who felt that the eastern power structure of the nation treated the west as a colony. The visit was marked by a certain confusion of command. Admiral Evans, who had been ill during most of the boyage, gave up his command to Admiral Charles M. Thomas. Then, Thomas died in Oakland, and Admiral Charles S. Sperry took over. Finally, in July 1908, the fleet sailed for Hawaii, and there Admiral Sperry visited Pearl Harbor, which had been really designated an American naval base just three months earlier. Congress, after years of mulling, had appropriated the money to build the base, obviously injected with this new naval spirit prompted by Roosevelt's machinations. Admiral Sperry found that workmen had just begun laying foundations for port facilities and gun emplacements.

After a few days the fleet sailed for Auckland. There were incidents. En route the *New Jersey,* captained by a man who liked to pretend his battleship was as maneuverable as a destroyer, collided with the *Nebraska.* Damage was minor, but it *was* a collision at sea, yet the American public never learned of the accident; the naval censorship saw to it. On the long Pacific voyage the ship's canteens were closed down because the admiral had learned of a racket run by officers who controlled the sale of candy and tobacco and had already defrauded the enlisted men of more than $100,000. This matter did not reach the public either.

At Auckland and again at Sydney, the Americans were greeted as conquering heroes. It was the same at Melbourne, where Admiral Sperry had to deal with seventeen different invitations for a single day. The hospitality was so inviting that three hundred men deserted at Melbourne, most of them were hidden by girl friends. A young ensign named William F. Halsey was detailed to search the city for the miscreants, but virtually none of them were found.

Japanese jingoists, who learned of these desertions, claimed that the American sailors had run away because they were afraid they might have to fight the Imperial Japanese Navy.

In spite of the ''yellow peril'' banners that flew above the streets of Australia's cities, Admiral Sperry behaved as the perfect diplomat. He reassured the Australians while saying nothing to which Tokyo could take exception. The visit probably did not allay Australia's fears of the Japanese, but it did cement American-Australian relations. The British were not so sure this was a good idea, for as American prestige in the South Pacific rose, their own seemed to decline. The British showed their displeasure by refusing to send the Prince of Wales down to be official greeter in behalf of the empire and by denying the Americans British coal. Because of this, Admiral Sperry spent much of his time on the voyage negotiating for coal. Thoughtful Americans back home suddenly realized that Britain, by denying colliers, could virtually strand the American fleet. *That* was something to think about for the future.

The Japanese chose to regard the ceremonies in Australia as studied insults. To be sure, the Australians were not very subtle in declaring their fear and dislike of Japan, but the American restraint was unnoticed in Tokyo, and the press attacked the United States unmercifully. From the Australian viewpoint, the euphoric visit was soon to produce a hangover. The Aussies loved the American display. But when the Americans announced they were going to Japan, the Australians were disillusioned and furious at having been "tricked" into spending so much money on the visit. They re-embraced the Union Jack fervently, and to assure them that all was well, the Royal Navy announced dispatch of sixteen Royal Navy warships to Australia on a goodwill visit. Out of all this excitement came the creation in 1908 of a separate Australian navy, and the release of Australia from the strictures of the Anglo-Japanese alliance.

In October, 1908, the Great White Fleet reached Manila. One would expect the Americans to stage an enormous celebration there, all things considered, but no; Manila was suffering from an outbreak of cholera, so the fleet did not go into harbor, and there were no parades and no shore leave. The Americans in Manila and the Filipinos were furious, having laid all the plans, but Admiral Sperry's order stood. The crowds, ready to cheer, gathered on the docks and booed the White Fleet from afar.

The approaching visit to Tokyo was regarded with a great deal of apprehension in America and within the fleet. The Japanese were hanging bunting in the streets, but the Imperial Japanese Navy was at sea. Which was it to be, celebration or battle?

For months, the diplomats of the United States and Japan had been working to ease the tensions between the two countries. In February, 1908, the United States and Japan had concluded a "gentleman's agreement" which was to govern the immigration of Japanese into the United States: the United States promised to refrain from passing such an ignominious law as the Chinese Exclusion Act, and the Japanese promised to limit the number of Japanese citizens who would be granted permission to immigrate. This done, in March, Washington and Tokyo could finally agree that it would be useful for the United States Fleet to visit Japan. In April, the United States and Japan signed a treaty under which they agreed to arbitrate all their differences in the future. President Roosevelt was eager to placate the Japanese, and Japan, it seemed was equally eager to end tensions with the United States. But from

76

Japan there continued to come disquieting reports that suggested the visit might end in war.

The reason for this impression was the Japanese ambition in Asia, which had already been shown in the few years since the end of the Russo-Japanese war. To reach an equal footing with the other major powers Japan must industrialize further, and to that end she needed raw materials and major markets. Manchuria and China offered both, but if Japan was to expand in this area she must secure the acquiescence, if not backing, of the other world powers. Russia had already been defeated and was not likely to interfere again. Britain had been appeased by an alliance that promised Japanese support of British objectives. The United States was an unknown factor, a rather forbidding one, with a unique approach to China that apparently could not be changed by offering concessions. So America must be bullied or appeased. The Japanese decided that bullying would work better, and the Japanese ambassador to the United States, Baron Kogon Takahira, let it be known that anything less than a full-scale appearance by the Americans in Tokyo Bay would be regarded as an unfriendly act. At that point, politicians in America were quarreling whether the greater display should be made at Tokyo or at Chefoo, and the Japanese indication that an "insult" might even mean war persuaded Roosevelt to give Japan the "full treatment." But the Japanese wanted more: it would be an insult to Japan if China, hardly an independent nation, were to be given the same treatment. As the battleships entered north Asian waters, the atmosphere was clouded.

Since spring and summer of 1908 had been most alarming times, the American Pacific Fleet had gone to Samoa to be within easy reach of Japanese waters in case trouble did develop when the Great White Fleet showed up. To be sure, the Pacific Fleet consisted only of cruisers and torpedo boats, but they were ships and they had a presence. At Apia they had new orders returning them to America. The secretary of the navy had decided their presence in the Pacific was too likely to be regarded as an unfriendly act by Japan.

The Japanese planned a show for the Americans that was not quite what Roosevelt had been led to expect. The one hundred and sixty Japanese warships of the Imperial Fleet were ordered to begin "October Maneuvers" as the Americans arrived. The intent was obviously to cow the visitors. Perhaps it was fortunate that a typhoon so occupied the two fleets that they did not meet in the waters between the Philippines and Japan. On October 18, 1907, without having seen any Japanese warships, the American fleet arrived at the entrance to Tokyo Bay.

The visit to Japan began with talk about a bomb plot. What if one or more of the American ships met the fate of the old *Maine* in Havana harbor? (In 1907, the vast majority of Americans still believed the official version that had the *Maine* sunk by unknown outside influence, apparently the Spaniards. The fact was that the *Maine* had suffered an internal explosion.) The Americans particularly feared the Black Dragon Society, an avowedly militarist organization known for its proclivity for assassination of enemies of Japanese military power. There was much talk of war by Admiral Sperry and particularly by Admiral Wainwright, who expected fighting to break out at any moment. Back in Washington, President Roosevelt was so upset by the reports these Admirals sent him that he almost decided the sailors should not even be allowed shore leave, lest there be an incident.

The Japanese overwhelmed the Americans with kindness, which made them even more nervous as to when the blow would fall. Admiral Togo, the hero of the Battle of Tsushima Strait, presided over a splendid party at the Shinjiku Imperial Gardens that had Ensign Halsey and other youngsters reminiscing for years. The four American admirals were housed in the Shiba palace, and the ship captains were given a hotel for themselves during the stay. A number of the wives of officers had decided they were not going to be left out of the festivities and had taken liners to Japan. They were housed in that same hotel. The Emperor Meiji gave a luncheon for the American senior officers—and *appeared himself*, which was almost unheard of in Japan.

Worried as they were about protocal, Admiral Sperry and his officers did not make a single mistake. The speeches were just right. No one got drunk and disgraced the flag as they had in Australia, where some of the younger officers had been seen to sway and stumble on parade. The Japanese newspapers completely reversed their view of the American fleet's arrival: "our joy is great" . . . "the fleet is a cupid". . . . "we welcome the fleet of white ships with *banzais.*" But the warning was there nonetheless, quite openly stated: "our course of empire lies to the west rather than to the east." The Japanese position was that Japan was going to try to do for China what the United States had done for Japan: open the country to foreign trade. One reason, of course, was the need for foreign markets if her industry was to expand as the industrial economies of the western powers which Japan emulated. Britain had seized an empire to feed her ambitions. So had France, Germany, and the United States. Could they expect less of a country that aspired to be at least their equal? It seemed quite natural to the Japanese that they should follow the accepted course of power.

Accepted? That was not quite the word. The treaty concluded between Japan and the United States on July 30, 1907, had promised that both nations were committed to the continuation of "the status quo" in the Pacific, particularly to support the "independence and integrity of China and the principle of equal opportunity for commerce and industry of all nations in that empire." Those two provisions were not entirely complementary. All would go well as long as Japan felt she had the same opportunity that was accorded all others in trading with China. But there would come a time when Japan felt she was being left out, even though her rationale pleaded the greater need because of the growth of her industry and the greater right because of propinquity and Asian heritage. The Root-Takahara treaty was successful because each side felt it had what it wanted: the United States had the "guarantee" of the independence of China, and Japan had the recognition of her special place, which included what she had won from Russia. Secretly, the Japanese had that same year concluded a treaty with Russia which pointed more clearly to her ambition to dominate East Asia. When the Japanese newspapers spoke of what "we are trying to do for China" the Americans might well have read the preposition as *to* instead of *for*, had they not been so grateful that the crisis of immigration had ended and cut short the threat of a war that was not wanted.

Toward the end of the visit, Admiral Togo gave a party aboard the *Mikasa*, his flagship which had been put aside and honored as a national treasure at Tsushima, as the British honored Nelson's *Victory*. Admiral Sperry was seized by the Japanese officers and tossed three times in a blanket amidst loud cheers, which was a very special Japanese naval tribute. The American officers did not recognize the importance of the action for a few minutes, until Ensign Halsey saw that Admiral Togo expected the same compliment. Then they gave it, and another diplomatic hurdle was passed safely in this strange world of diplomatic showmanship.

But in the matter of diplomacy, the Japanese won this encounter hands down. The entire reception to the visit was carefully stage-managed by the government, down to the level of street encounters with ordinary citizens. In every *chome* (district) of Tokyo and Yokohama the local policemen posted instructions to the people for their behavior when the foreigners came: "not crowd around foreigners," "sticks and stones shall not be thrown at dogs accompanying foreigners," "seats on streetcars and trains," "no staring," "no spitting," "use handkerchiefs," and "no ridicule of foreign dress." All this was done so that "Washington may be kept in the proper frame of mind." To this end even the newspaper editors were warned that if they did not show sufficient enthusiasm for the Americans they would be punished. So it was small wonder that *Mainichi Shimbun* and *Asahi Shimbun* had changed their attitude and welcomed the hitherto despised Americans.

WITH A SENSE OF RELIEF AND WELL-BEING, Admiral Sperry sailed for China. In deference to Japanese wishes, Admiral Sperry did not take the whole fleet, but only half of it. To the Chinese this was already an insult, and Yuan Shih-kai, the dowager empress' most trusted minister, suggested that American behavior indicated how little store Roosevelt set by the Open Door Policy.

Yuan's surmise was quite correct; Roosevelt had already accepted as fact the Japanese domination of the Western Pacific. The Chinese were further insulted when the fleet's destination was changed from Chefoo, which was ominously close to the Japanese sphere of influence in northeast China, to Amoy on the south coast. And then came the final insult: Admiral Sperry would not attend himself but would send Admiral Emory, his second in command, with the Third and Fourth Battleship Divisions only.

The China visit was an empty celebration, carried out less than halfheartedly by both sides. The dowager empress was furious and refused to send greetings to Admiral Emory or a cable to President Roosevelt. For the most part the Chinese press ignored the visit and only lower officials were on hand to greet the foreigners. The Americans came, spent a miserable week, and left on November 5. The unfortunate effects of the visit might have been much worse had fate not taken a hand: the Emperor of China, Kuang-hsu, died on November 14 and the dowager empress died next day. (It is still suspected that the empress knew she was dying and had the emperor, whom she had never trusted, killed so he could not undo her policies.) In the social and political confusion that followed, the dreadful fiasco of the fleet visit was forgotten. Yuan Shih-kai was soon deposed, and three years later the decayed corpse of the Manchu dynasty was buried.

Leaving China, the fleet units joined Sperry at Manila, where he was waiting once more outside since the cholera epidemic was still in progress. Although all concerned were sick of the voyage now that it had achieved its end purpose to (in one way or another) impress the Japanese, the rest of the world had to be negotiated to fulfill the "round-the-world" contract announced by President Roosevelt. But Hongkong, Saigon, Singapore, and Bangkok were all turned down. The fleet stopped at Colombo, Ceylon, because it needed coal. The British, having made so many errors in judgment about the whole voyage, now tried to recoup with a generous display of hospitality, but no one was much impressed. Perhaps the White Fleet was beyond impression by this time. But every American consul and every ambassador in the Middle East and Europe felt that the fleet ought to stop at his post and so informed Washington. The difficulty was not so much how much good the fleet would do by coming, but how much ill will would be generated if it did not come. Roosevelt accepted this view, and in the places where the most ill will might be generated to the worst effect, the fleet would stop. In the Mediterranean, it was split into divisions. Ships visited Italy, France, Tangier, Athens, Smyrna, Beirut, Tripoli, Malta, and Algiers, and they all met at Gibraltar. The parcelling-out of the fleet was a godsend of an idea, removing the onus of a grand display here and nothing at all there. By the time the four divisions of battleships reached Gibraltar, officers and men were exhausted. A number of petty incidents marred the last phases of the voyage, including the courtmartial of a senior officer who was accused of drunkenness when his crime was exhaustion.

It all ended at Gibraltar, with the Americans taking the honors tiredly from the British and then going home to arrive at Hampton Roads late in February, 1909. President Roosevelt, of course, asserted that the cruise had raised American prestige immeasurably. Perhaps but it did not seem likely. It had, however, vastly increased the capability of the American navy. In the beginning, the fleet maneuvers were carried out with more bungling than the public ever knew. In the end, the fleet functioned as a unit and showed that it would also be able to fight as a unit. That *was* progress. Of course, although it had operated in the Pacific, the fleet was still the Atlantic Fleet, and after all the shouting died down, that fact was paramount. America had decided to become a world power, and its new basic world interests were in the Pacific. But the fleet did not follow the flag in this sense. The American presence in the Pacific had been relatively slight and it continued to be so.

10

The Cunning Japanese

WHILE THE GREAT WHITE FLEET was making its grand world tour, back in Washington the Army and Navy Joint Board was hard at work on a strategic study of American defense policy. For the first time a war plan was drawn with Japan as enemy. President Roosevelt said that the Philippines represented "America's Achilles' heel," the weak point that must be defended against a Japanese attack. The immediate problem was that the United States Navy did not have enough ships to defend the islands. Out of the strategic studies came a plan: the Philippines would be sacrificed temporarily if the need arose. The base established there had to be kept small enough so that it could be given up without serious harm to the defense establishment. The basic defense of America in the Pacific would be concentrated at Pearl Harbor. During the next four years Congress willingly appropriated large sums of money for construction at Pearl Harbor. This attitude persisted even after a Democratic Congress came to Washington in 1910, largely because the Japanese had begun their exploitation of Manchuria through the cover of the South Manchurian Railway, which was controlled by the Japanese government. The South Manchurian Railway acquired the Fushun Colliery, east of Mukden, which produced three thousand tons of hard coal a day, and the Yentai coalfield northeast of Liaoyang and provided electricity for half of Manchuria. It built harbor facilities at Dairen and Port Arthur. It built hospitals and schools and even a medical college. In other words, the South Manchuria Railway became the most important force in the region and made a virtual puppet of the Chinese government there.

Theoretically, all these "rights" would expire in the 1920s, but by 1910 it became apparent that Japan would never relinquish such riches. American bankers that year tried to float a series of loans to build railways in China. The success of the plan depended on the creation of an international commission to control all the railroad lines, including the South Manchurian Railway. The Japanese said they would give up none of their power over the South Manchurian, and that was that.

The Japanese began to move again in August, 1910. They annexed Korea, whose "independence" they had guaranteed five years earlier. This action, accompanied by Japanese crowing, caused Britain to reexamine her close ties to Japan, which had damaged her relations with the United States. The American proposal to become involved in Chinese railways put an end to much of the mindless talk in the United States and in Japan about "eternal friendship." The fact was that from the moment Japan began her expansion in Manchuria her interests and those of the United States and Britain began to clash.

A new high Japanese tariff in 1910 brought another negative reaction from America, and the Japanese sensed that they had overreached themselves and had to make concessions to Britain and the United States; otherwise, they were given to understand, the western powers would retaliate in kind. Concessions were made, but the conflict was not resolved, the railway consortium of western powers failed, and Japan made it quite clear that she wanted a free hand in Southern Manchuria and China. The Russians wanted to exploit Northern Manchuria and for a time their ambitions and those of Japan seemed to go hand in hand.

In 1912, the Democratic Congress signalled the intention of making life difficult for Republican President Taft. In 1912, when the Manchu emperor abdicated and Yuan Shi-kai formed the Chinese Republic, the Japanese and Russians openly declared their imperialistic intentions on Manchuria. These so upset the United States that in the same year, after Woodrow Wilson was elected President, the country united under the Democrats to project a positive Pacific defense policy. Japanese ambition was very much responsible for the hastening of construction and increase in expenditure for the base at Pearl Harbor and for the decision of Congress that year to support a two-ocean navy.

The continuing difficulty of relations with Japan in 1914 and 1915 caused the General Board and the Joint Army Navy Board to call for naval bases in Puget Sound and San Francisco Bay that would be able to handle the needs of a large fleet. President Wilson had affirmed the traditional aims of American policy in the Far East, including the Open Door in China, much to Japan's annoyance. The people of California had again in these years raised the race issue, still antagonized by Japanese success as farmers and shopkeepers. So the navy program was given considerable impetus. The General

The Cunning Japanese

Board of the Navy wanted 48 battleships, 192 destroyers, and other vessels in such strength as to give the United States a fleet equal to any other in the world. The Navy did not get so much in 1914, although it did get more than in the past. When the war began in Europe and Asia, where Germany had several colonies, the American rush to neutrality left the navy high and dry, without even administration support for expansion. Within a year reaction set in. The result was a popular outburst in favor of preparedness, led by Theodore Roosevelt, which crossed all political and economic barriers. But the Pacific went begging; Americans were convinced that the European allies were fighting "to save democracy."

For Japan, the war was a godsend. She clothed herself in the cloak of righteousness and vowed to uphold her treaty of alliance with Britain. She declared she had no territorial ambitions—the premier, Count Okuma, said precisely that on August 18, 1914. Then Japan proceeded to attack the German colony of Kiaochao on the Shantung peninsula (with British cooperation) and seize the Chinese railroad into the interior as far as Tsinan-fu on the pretext that this was German property. She occupied Jaluit, the capital of the Marshall Islands, and suddenly her talk changed from blue sky promises to talk about property, with words as selfish as those of any imperialist. In that fall of 1914, Japan made it quite clear that she had no intention of giving up the Kwantung peninsula or the holdings in South Manchuria, and she made a new series of demands on China that meant more power to Japan.

The United States Congress and the administration awakened and protected, and the stiff United States resistance caused the Japanese government to pause in most of the demands on China, if only momentarily. But the diplomatic demarche had to be regarded as an American failure. The next American step was supposed to be the buildup of American naval power in the Pacific. The Navy Department wanted to spend $100,000,000 a year for five years to strengthen the navy, and in July, 1916, Congress passed the greatest naval construction bill in history. (Only incidentally was the European war a factor in this program.) Also, a decision was made for the first time that the Philippines would be defended as long as the United States continued to hold them. (Concurrently all concerned agreed that the Philippines were a defensive liability and should be given "freedom" as soon as possible.) Woodrow Wilson, at a cabinet meeting in February, 1917, made the remarkable statement that if he felt it was necessary to keep the white race strong to meet the Japanese threat, he would let Germany go on and on and on in her depradations. There it was, out in the open—agreement by most of America's responsible leaders about Japan as the most important enemy in the future.

The steady progress of Japanese imperialist policy was convincing. That year, 1917, Field Marshal Count Masakata Terauchi became Premier of

Japan, and he was committed to expansion in China and the Pacific. Viscount Ichiro Motono, former minister to St. Petersburgh and another expansionist, was made foreign minister. The course was clear. America was rearming her navy, not so much to enter the war in Europe as to protect American interests against what the Wilson administration perceived as the real enemy.

In 1917 and 1918, this fact was obscured by the activity of the United States in the war against Germany. The needs of the fleet for future defense in the Pacific had nothing to do with the needs for prosecution of the Germans in the Atlantic, and the latter drew all public attention. Congress got off the track. Once the war was over, the call "bring the boys back home" came loud and clear from the American countryside and the Congressmen heard. In such an atmosphere the whole burden of pressure was *against* expansion of the American navy and *for* dismemberment of the American defense establishment. For example, aircraft, built by the thousands, were junked. Ships, built by the hundreds, were put in "mothballs" or sold abroad. The conception of a strong two-ocean navy, which hit its zenith in 1916, was lost in Congressional debate. The argument against a system of Pacific naval bases insisted that America was quite well protected by its two oceans and that America must not expect more. The Republican administrations of the next twelve years turned inward to isolationism.

Japan had emerged from World War I stronger than ever, her industry profiting by the war, and her defense policy, not subject to the public whim, moving toward continued expansion. Japan held more of China than ever. She held islands dotted through the Central Pacific which provided a string of naval bases. As historians Harold and Margaret Sprout put it, writing in 1938, "these results, together with other developments, compelled American naval strategists to envisage a war fought under enormous technical difficulties, thousands of miles from home, in virtually the local waters of a militant and expanding Japan whose navy seemed at that time to be rapidly approaching unchallengeable supremacy in the Western Pacific."

Given such definition, given the attitude of the American public which overwhelmingly favored "return to normalcy" (Warren Harding's phrase) and rejected any sort of emphasis on defense, it was inevitable that the American navy would decline, and it did.

The surface activity belied the truth. The Pacific Fleet, which had virtually ceased to exist during World War I since the action was in the Atlantic, was reestablished with 8 battleships of the then modern "dreadnought" class, 6 old battleships, 54 four-stack coal-burning destroyers, 1 scout cruiser, 14 submarines, 2 tenders, 12 minesweepers, and 22 auxiliaries. In 1920, the fleet was divided into Atlantic, Pacific, and Asiatic Fleets, each with its own submarine force, air force, and surface force. That same year naval aircraft in war games sank the captured German cruiser *Frankfurt,* which had been seized to use for just such purpose, but the naval authorities (and the army) were unconvinced that aircraft could be effective in fighting against naval surface units. Aviators were able to secure the creation of a Bureau of Aeronautics of the Navy, but that did not presage a drive to naval air power.

The whole atmosphere of the 1920s precluded an ambitious approach to naval affairs. In July, 1921, Congress and the Harding administration organized a conference whose purpose was the limitation of naval armament. Thus the world saw the Washington Naval Disarmament Conference at which Japan made all sorts of representations about her peaceful intentions. The main result of the Washington Conference was to give the Americans, and to a much lesser extent the British, a false sense of security. Under the Washington Naval Treaty the United States scrapped seventeen completed capital ships and dumped eleven that were under construction. The Americans and British paid attention to the limitations set down in the treaty that came out of the conference, and these limitations affected their designs. The Japanese were already planning super-battleships and super-carriers, although they did not then build them, the moderates holding the radicals back. But the planning was all there to enable the Japanese in the 1930s to create the most modern navy in the world, more powerful than the American Pacific and Asiatic Fleets combined.

As Japan planned naval expansion, with or without international consent, the American navy went the other way. In 1922, the United States Atlantic and Pacific Fleets were combined into the United States Fleet. The principle, impeccable on paper, held that by using the Panama Canal the fleet could move to one coast or the other as need be.

In the 1920s, the United States Asiatic Fleet was preoccupied with unrest in China, where Generalissimo Chiang Kai-shek was trying to cement the Republic of China's power by bringing various warlords in the provinces under central government control. The result was almost constant warfare, punctuated by Chiang's falling out with the Communists in the Republic. The Communists made "the long march" to the northwest and began to regroup. Chiang's forces were engaged in the south and in central China, and foreign gunboats were stationed at Canton, Tientsin and other ports, and particularly along the Yangtze River from Shanghai and west to Chungking.

The American position in the Pacific, again on paper, was very strong. At Washington the Japanese had agreed to a five-five-three ratio of naval power, Japan to maintain only three-fifths of the strength of either the United States or Britain. The rationale was that the American and British navies had two oceans to police, and the Japanese only one. From the Japanese point of view, it was still five-five-three, or inferiority, and in the late 1920s that matter became subject to serious argument in Tokyo, which ultimately led to the decisions to disregard the treaty and build power as it seemed needed.

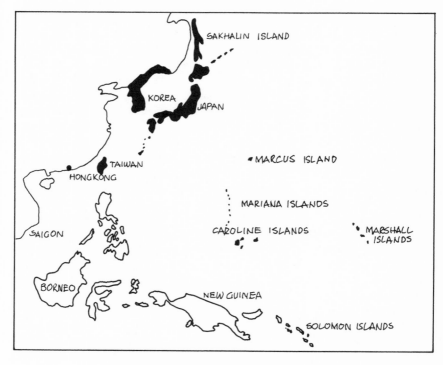

The Japanese Empire in the 1920s (in black)

After all, as Congress said, America could, at least in theory, put her whole United States Fleet into the Pacific. From the Japanese point of view the one great advantage of the treaty (other than political) was the American agreement not to fortify the Philippines, in exchange for Japanese agreement not to fortify Taiwan and the islands of the Japanese mandate in the Central Pacific (the old German colonies).

In the 1920s Japan continued her activity to dominate China. She was hardly alone. Britain had never stopped her efforts. France was also eager to gain business in China. In 1924, an International Settlement was established in Shanghai, which created an extraterritorial situation for several nations, including the United States. Each nation sent its troops to Shanghai to police its area, and the number of foreign naval craft on the rivers and at the ports was raised. In 1927, the river force was heavily engaged in fighting around Nanking, but there was no difficulty among the international powers. The occidentals regarded each other in a friendly if wary fashion—"civilized people" thrown into a foreign and not always friendly environment. The occi-

The Cunning Japanese

dentals faced the Japanese with generally courteous toleration. The Japanese responded with courtesy, until the 1930s. China, of course, was an uneasy meeting ground for Americans and Japanese.

In the 1920s, American enthusiasm for the Philippine colonial experiment had strengthened. Leonard Wood, President Harding's governor of the Philippines, said once that the United States must never give up the islands. More or less, that view represented Republican policy, and in these Republican years, the navy was ordered to plan an active defense of the Philippines. This policy made the Japanese nervous, because a fleet large enough to defend the Philippines was large enough to attack Japan. More and more the commercial interests of the United States and Japan came into conflict, particularly as the United States talked much (but did little) about promoting trade through the Open Door of China. By 1931, for example, Japan had thirty-five percent of her total foreign capital invested in China, while the United States had invested only six percent. Japan wanted markets in the Philippines, in the Dutch East Indies, and in the South Seas, and American diplomatic and consular officials reported constantly on Japanese aggressiveness in business. The United States, for emotional reasons as well as economic, was concerned with Japanese "penetration." Japanese nationalism led the Tokyo press to heights of fury every time the United States did something to affect relations. For example, 1925 had been selected as a test year for the American fleet's ability to protect United States interests in the Pacific, and United States fleet maneuvers were planned for the Hawaii area, followed by a cruise to Australia. When the plans were announced, the Japanese press erupted in anger and retold all of the negative developments of United States–Japanese relations, back to the American insistence on curtailment of Japanese immigration. The Americans did not understand the extent of the sense of injury the Japanese felt about American racist policies. To be sure, most of the immigrants to America were the poor and uneducated—hardly Japan's first citizens. This was as it had been with the Chinese. But, the greatest enemies of oriental immigration were the manual workers of America: Anglo-Saxon, Irish, and German. Also, between the governments, over the years, there were many areas of disagreement; as American policy became more China-oriented than ever, with much discussion of the Open Door and "territorial integrity," the Japanese growled in annoyance.

In 1925, the navy had fully accepted the principle that the Japanese were "the enemy." War plans were quite open about it. The Immigration Act of 1924, which laid severe restrictions on the Japanese, brought a return of the compliment. In 1927, the American War College class studied the logistics of an American-Japanese war, Orange-Blue, it was called. By then the American naval attaches in Tokyo and the rest of Asia were reporting home that Japan's plans called for "domination of Asia." This claim was taken to Congress as a reason for the building of an even greater navy, and the pebble thus thrown began to reverberate in political waters.

In Japan and the United States, without obvious official sanction, writers were discussing the probable war to come between the nations. One of the most influential was Hector C. Bywater, a correspondent for the *Baltimore Sun*, who wrote widely in American magazines, suggesting that war was just around the corner. Much of this writing was aimed to produce a greater defense establishment in the Pacific, but it was only partly successful. The American battle fleet was reassigned to San Diego. The navy wanted enlarged bases at San Francisco, Puget Sound, and Pearl Harbor, but Congress had other matters (including its pork barrel) to consider. It was remarkable (to a layman) how prophetically the naval planners of the early 1920s saw the prosecution of a war against Japan. Manila Bay must be held or retaken (assuming a Japanese occupation) and the rest of the Philippines taken too. The Japanese mandated islands of the Central and South Pacific (Marshall Islands, etc.) must also be taken. Japan must be blockaded economically and possibly bombed into submission. (Some of the more hardheaded admirals held that bombing into submission was an impossibility.)

For various reasons, in the 1920s, the United States, Britain, and the Netherlands drew closer together in their Far Eastern policies. The American navy had never managed to secure the sort of defenses in the Philippines that it wanted; there was too much difference of opinion in Washington over the ultimate disposition of the islands to make a total commitment. So when the British built the great naval base at Singapore in the early 1920s the United States looked to that base as a major defense of western power in the Pacific. The Dutch also built up their bases as much as they could, although they were constrained by a home government that was unwilling to commit the sort of money needed to build major bases. But the Dutch, perhaps more than any other westerners, were suspicious of the Japanese intentions toward their islands. They were, of course, faced with the most economic penetration, and they recognized the enormous value of the Sumatra oil fields.

While these affairs were in progress, various attempts were made to exert more political control on military building. The politicians wanted to limit naval arms further. The navies of the United States and Japan resisted. Assistant Secretary of the Navy Theodore Roosevelt, Jr., referred to the politicians as "soft-headed pacifists." A conference on arms limitation was arranged for the summer of 1927 in Geneva. It failed.

Two years later another naval conference was held in London. It became apparent to the Japanese that the Americans and British had a confidential understanding that isolated Japan. At the London Naval Conference of 1930 Japan tried to produce a ten-ten-seven naval ratio. The American navy was most upset by the suggestion; the United States building program had been sharply restricted and the admirals in charge suggested that the whole western Pacific would have to be sacrificed if it were accepted. The diplomatic isolation of Japan by the American and British private discussions was most alarming to Tokyo. It was a warning to Japan that the United States and Britain regarded their Pacific interests as joined, and therefore that Japan would have to be prepared to contend against both navies in time of war.

So the decade of the twenties ended, and that of the thirties began, with entirely new problems on the horizon, not the least of which were occasioned by the world-wide depression that had begun in 1930. The economic climate caused every nation to look to its own interests more narrowly than before. The United States went off the gold standard to the dismay of most other countries. Japan, which needed markets desperately, saw Manchuria and China as the solution to all her problems. The suspicions of the past decade had reached the point of no return, and the 1930s were marked by the hardening of attitudes in the east and west that made it almost impossible for the old methods of diplomacy to function. Self interest was the watchword of the decade. After the London conference, the Japanese naval planners threw off the old restraints and began to build their modern navy.

11

The Wicked Japanese

~~~~~~

IN THE 1920S, on an operational level the United States Navy learned a good deal about air warfare and carrier operations. After the courtmartial of Billy Mitchell, the army's foremost advocate of air power, for his revolutionary theory that air power could win wars, the "battleship" admirals basked for a time in their superiority. But on the fleet level, the first demonstration of dive bombing in the fall of 1926 showed that a force of bombers surprising a surface force could indeed sink battleships. The bombers came in from twelve thousand feet on the battleship force as it was sailing out of San Pedro and before the guns could be trained the "enemy" was on top of the fleet. Had real bombs and torpedos been employed, half the ships might have been destroyed.

Various experiments with air power were in process. Two of the cruiser hulls that might have been scrapped after the Washington Naval Conference were converted to *aircraft carriers*. On January 5, 1928, Lieutenant A. M. Pride made the first takeoff and landing on the USS *Lexington*. Three weeks later the dirigible *Los Angeles* landed aboard the USS *Saratoga*. The aviation enthusiasts were very high on lighter-than-air craft just then, and considered the dirigible to be as important as the heavier-than-air craft.

In 1929, night flying became a requirement for fleet pilots and marines, for who knew when a pilot might have to try to board his carrier after dark? But carriers still were objects of deep suspicion by the battleship admirals even after the maneuevers of January, 1929, when the carriers *Lexington* and *Saratoga* "destroyed" the Panama Canal. In spite of the distaste for aviation of the Bureau of Ships and the chief of naval operations, the Bureau of Aer-

93

onautics continued to make progress. In February, 1929, the first ship to be built from the ground up as a carrier was authorized by Congress. She would be christened the USS *Ranger*. At the end of the year, the *Lexington* gave a *tour de force* of another sort that brought welcome national publicity; she supplied electric power to the city of Tacoma for thirty days when Tacoma's power plant failed. At least, the battleship men sniffed, the carriers were good for something.

In 1930, the first monoplane carrier plane was delivered to the navy, and the 1,000-pound bomb for carrier planes became a reality. That year naval aviation moved out of the experimental stage when the chief of naval operations made aviation an official arm of the fleet.

When the 1929 crash came to Wall Street and the Depression began, it took time for the economic wave to strike the navy. But it came in 1932, and every aspect of naval life felt the impact. An economy-minded Congress resented moneys spent on war games. Consequently, although the submarine force was improving with streamlined submarines that would lead to the development of the fleet submarine, submarine operations were reduced to austerity. The fleet was not allowed to fire live torpedoes in maneuvers. Instead, the torpedoes were fixed with dummy heads which made a satisfying "thwunk" when they struck a ship but did not explode and so could be recovered and used again. After all, a torpedo cost $10,000 and in the Depression there was no room for waste. So no one really knew if the torpedoes *would* explode in action.

In 1933, the building of PBY flying boats began and the next year a squadron of flying boats made the crossing from California to Hawaii, emphasizing the importance of Pearl Harbor as the nation's first line of Pacific defense. Changes came almost monthly; and two years later the *Langley,* the first converted American ship to be made into an aircraft carrier, was deemed obsolete and converted to a seaplane tender.

During all these years, the pressure of events in the Pacific mounted. The Japanese had never forgotten the Immigration Law of 1924; although that law did not specify that it was aimed at Japan, it did say that people of countries who were ineligible for United States citizenship would not be admitted. If one wanted an argument, it could be taken back to the Japanese practice of insisting on dual citizenship for all Japanese who went anywhere. This policy was anathema to Americans, conjuring up pictures of disloyalty, and the United States did, after all, have the example of Japanese behavior during the Hawaiian Kingdom.

The Japanese did not appreciate these western sensibilities, particularly since the doors of Canada, most of Latin America, New Zealand, and Australia were already closed to the Japanese. Underneath was another problem. Japan's victory in the Russo-Japanese war was misunderstood at home. To achieve it, Japan had come close to the edge of bankruptcy. Another year or two of war might have brought quite a different outcome, and many knowledgeable Japanese said President Roosevelt stepped in just in time to mediate before the Japanese economy collapsed. Japan had walked away from the war with territory but no monetary compensation, and at home an incensed public blamed the United States for protecting the Russians. The overtones of American racism toward Japan were unmistakeable.

Another result of the war was the restoration of the Japanese military's prestige, which had been cut down greatly by Emperor Meiji in the 1880s. The army, having tasted glory, was eager for more; it did not come. Instead, a strong movement arose calling for reduction of the army, and this brought about an army campaign for self-preservation that soon extended beyond ambition. The army propagandists pulled on every emotional chord, from national pride to national fears. For example, they pointed to population: in the United States the density was 31 people per square mile of territory; in Japan it was 400 people per square mile. In offering solutions, the army indicated it was Japan's historic mission to expand in Asia and bring the results of the new westernization to others and that the major obstacle to this progress was the United States. By 1925, these seeds were sown and sprouting. A whole generation of Japanese growing up in the 1920s believed devoutly in a sense of mission. The west was painted as the enemy.

During the early 1920s, the Kwantung Army had been gaining strength in southern Manchuria. That army was like a Roman Legion, so far away from the homeland that it responded to its leadership far more readily than to the military or political leadership in Japan. In this matter, the structure of Japan's defense establishment was a primary factor. The minister of war and the minister of the navy were not in direct control of either the army or the navy. Virtually on the same level were the commanders in chief of these establishments. Thus it was common for the politicians to pursue one course while the military pursued another (or several courses) and for the former to be kept almost completely in the dark about the latter.

The manifestation of trouble began in 1928. Chiang Kai-shek, heir to Dr. Sun Yat-sen's Republic of China, had made enormous progress in subordinating the warlords of China, and it was obvious that soon he would have behind him a unified country and that there could be no further excuse of "confusion" to justify foreign encroachments. With billions at stake in southern Manchuria, and a whole economy that was based on expansion, the Japanese could hardly reverse course. From the Japanese point of view, the answer was that Chiang Kai-shek must be eliminated. The instrument the Japanese government chose to use was Marshal Chang Tso-lin, the warlord of Manchuria and North China. But when approached by the Japanese, who offered the support of the Kwantung Army, Chang Tso-lin rejected them. The

Kwantung Army's response was swift. Late in May, 1928, with Chiang Kai-shek's troops pounding at the doors of Tientsin and Peking, Marshal Chang ordered a special train to move his center of operations south to Mukden. On June 4, as the train passed under a bridge of the Japanese-controlled South Manchurian Railway, Colonel Daisaku Kawamoto of the Kwantung Army staff ordered his assassination. An army captain pushed a plunger and Chang Tso-lin's private car went up in smoke and debris, injuring him fatally. As Chang's bodyguards came charging out of the debris, soldiers of the Kwantung Army opened fire and killed most of them.

The Kwantung Army hushed up this incident; the published story said the old Marshall had been murdered by his enemies, true in the sense that Japan had become his enemy. Japan did not want the story to get out; even the imperial cabinet suppressed the scandal, and by so doing the government put itself in the hands of the military. This incident was the beginning of a long struggle between civilian and military leaders for control of Japan.

In the next two years, matters in Manchuria took a turn that the Kwantung Army deemed dangerous. Chang Hsueh-liang, the old marshal's son, made his peace with Chiang Kai-shek, and the Chinese tried to flood Manchuria with Chinese immigrants to offset Japanese influence. The Kwantung Army, its power threatened, began pressing for further Japanese expansion, and the policy struck receptive ears in Tokyo where the "overpopulation" myth had taken hold even among the most peaceful civilians. But for insurance, the army men took other actions. They established several secret societies within the military. Foremost of these was the Cherry Society, dedicated to the assassination of all who opposed the aims of the Kwantung Army, aims that in these years were accepted by the whole officer class.

On the night of September 18, 1931, the Kwantung Army struck again. This time soldiers blew up a section of the South Manchurian Railway north of Mukden, then attacked a Chinese military unit in barracks there and declared that they had been forced to "defend themselves." The enormity of the lie was such that some people believed it, and a world debate began over Japanese intentions. The Japanese cabinet, at first aghast, was maneuvered by the army into keeping quiet. But by 1932, Japan's course was clear in the rest of the world. That year Cartoonist Harold Talburt of the *Washington Daily News* won a Pulitzer prize for an editorial cartoon that showed Japan making a flaming torch of the Nine Power Treaty, the Kellogg Peace Pact, and the League of Nations. Japan was committed to aggression and all the lesser sins that course involved: espionage, outright lies, and scrapping of alliances. The Japanese navy, as well as the army, prepared for expansion. The ships that began coming off the ways were not the ships specified in the five-five-three ratio of the naval conferences. Like the Japanese army, Japan's navy was talking peace but preparing for war. Major General Hideki Tojo, then chief of the Japanese war ministry's military research bureau, an intensely political organization, warned that Japan's situation relative to the Western powers would become critical within the next few years. Tojo had studied in Europe, and was familiar with General Karl von Clausewitz's theories of politics and warfare: particularly the contention that a small power, faced with a large one, must strike quickly in difficulty before the larger power could assemble its resources. His sense of urgency was increased in the late 1920s and early 1930s by the international depression, and the creation by the United States and other Western powers of new tariff blocks to Japanese industrial export. If Japan was to have markets abroad, she must make new ones. The quickest way to secure markets was to force them, and the logical place to force them was China.

The early thirties were marked by brutal assassinations of those who stood in the way of the militarists' ambition. In November, 1930, after the Japanese government accepted the London Naval Conference decision to limit Japanese warships again to sixty percent of those of the United States and Britain, a gang of young officers shot down Premier Osachi Hamaguchi. In the spring of 1932, a gang of young officers called the "Blood Brotherhood" assassinated Junosuke Inouye, former finance minister, who had spoken out against military aggression, and Baron Dan, managing director of the Mitsui holding company, who had also gone on record against violence. On the night of May 15, a gang murdered Premier Inukai. This murder aroused public sentiment and forty defendents were tried and sent to prison. But military sentiment was unchanged. In 1935, young militarists murdered Major General Tetuzan Nagata, one of the leading army planners, in the belief that he was "soft." In February, 1936, a group of young officers tried to seize control of the central government, and took over a number of offices. Several officials were killed, and one young officer invaded the sacred Imperial Palace, before being frightened away. Thus, by the middle of the 1930s through assassination and intimidation the militarists were doing as they wished.

The anti-Western behavior of the militarists soon became impossible to ignore. Travelers were kept from military installations, which included such places as bridges. Tourists with cameras were watched. Most American visitors were suspected of espionage. In the summer of 1937, the aviator Amelia Earhart undertook a flight across the Pacific and disappeared. The United States Navy made an extensive search for her, then concluded that she was lost. But there were some who suspected she had landed in the Gilbert or Marshall Islands and had been murdered by the Japanese.

In July, 1937, Japan attacked China at the Marco Polo Bridge near Tientsin. It was another of those Kwantung Army incidents. These incidents and the string of reports from the naval attaches in Tokyo made the American navy well aware of the attitudes and patterns of the Japanese navy, but as time went on, detailed information about ships and aircraft became difficult to obtain. It was known that the Japanese had built up their armament without regard to treaty commitments. In December, 1937, came the most serious of proofs of Japanese intent: Japanese aircraft attacked and sank the United States gunboat *Panay* in the Yangtse river. The excitement that followed the unprovoked attack had a salutary effect on a United States Congress that had opposed heavy investment in self-defense. In May, 1938, the navy's expansion program passed Congress, permitting the building of the new carriers *Hornet* and *Essex* and the addition of a badly needed 3,000 aircraft for the naval force. Of course this construction could not begin immediately. *Hornet* was begun in 1939 but *Essex* not until 1941. But had they not been started when they were, the outcome of the events of the next few years would certainly have been different.

With outbreak of the European war, President Roosevelt declared a "limited" national emergency, which made it possible for the Executive Department to avoid some of the red tape of controls under the American system. Shipbuilding increased, largely to provide ships for Britain and her allies. America was neutral, but the administration was not; the president recognized the dangers of a victory by the Rome-Berlin-Tokyo axis. Aircraft production was stepped up to 50,000 a year, old four-stack destroyers were recommissioned, a new naval act called for building 167,000 more tons of ships. Attention to the Pacific Fleet varied through the years 1939–41. The initial shock of the war in Europe led the navy to turn its attention to the Atlantic. The American Neutrality patrol, operating from Maine to the Canal Zone, demanded many ships, even though it was never effective. It was 1940 before Chief of Naval Operations Admiral Harold Stark, could go to Capitol Hill and ask for a true two-ocean navy.

In 1940, it was understood on every level of the American military that Japan was the potential enemy in the Pacific. Diplomatic affairs went from bad to worse; the Japanese kept talking about peace but they were unwilling to withdraw from China where they had more than a million troops. It was a matter of "face" as much as anything else because the Japanese military policy in China had failed. No one in Tokyo could say that openly, but it was apparent. With all their study of von Clausewitz, the Japanese generals had neglected the study of Napoleon's Russian adventure and so they were repeating it.

The warning signals to America from Japan were unmistakeable. In February, 1939, Japan occupied Hainan Island off the Indo-China coast. In March she annexed the Spratly Islands halfway between Indo-China and North Borneo. In these actions Japan was the vulture, picking up pieces of the French empire when France was occupied by the Nazis. The action was reminiscent of the Japanese seizure of German colonies in 1914, but even

98

The Japanese Empire in 1940 (in black)

more indefensible because Japan had remained uninvolved in the war in
Europe.

These Japanese actions caused the government in Washington to react
sharply. Major elements of the United States Fleet were ordered back to the

99

Pacific. The Pacific Fleet was ordered to move from San Diego to Pearl Harbor, and Japan reacted to that move: General Tojo, the war minister, said he regarded the American fleet's movement as a threat against Japan. Of course it was a threat against Japanese expansion, which to Tojo and his cohorts now meant the "lifeblood" of Japan. But as Admiral Stark said, if the Japanese marched into the Dutch East Indies, it was debatable if the United States would do anything about it. There was in America still a reluctance to commitment; everyone knew that the American scrap steel and American oil shipped to Japan were vital to Japan's war against a China that America was trying to rescue. But when the question of cutting Japan off from steel and oil came up, the issue was avoided. It was July, 1940, before the Japanese army's establishment of a puppet government in China and continued aggressions aroused Congress enough to give President Roosevelt power to control the export of arms, ammunition, and military equipment in the national interest. Three days later Roosevelt invoked the new law against Japan and cut off strategic war materials. By the end of the month he also cut off scrap iron, steel, aviation gasoline, and iron. It was a harsh blow to Japan and it gave rise to a whole new set of recriminations and self-justifications for the Japanese leaders, who had already decided that war with the United States was preferable to ceasing their operations in China.

That question was clarified by a number of Japanese policy discussions beginning in June, 1940, when Foreign Minister Yosuke Matsuoka was asked by the army what he was doing to get bases in the South. To expand, Japan must move southward; it was part of a military policy of *hakko ichiu* which meant "bringing the eight corners of the world under one roof"—Japan's. Matsuoka replied that he could not act decisively until the military made the definite commitment that it was willing to go to war with the United States if necessary. On July 1, 1940, the Japanese cabinet made the fateful decision to build "A Greater East Asia Co-Prosperity Sphere" no matter who objected. The policy was confirmed at an imperial conference. Japan was determined to forge ahead. All the old self-pitying phrases were there: "self-existence and self-defense." The decision was couched in the peculiarly impersonal manner of Japanese speech: "Japan will not decline a war with England and the United States . . ." What that meant in essence was that the military was now certain it could win such a war. In September, Japan formally joined the Germans and Italians in the Tripartite Pact, which was directed at the United States. Each power, said the treaty, would assist the other if attacked "by a power at present not involved in the European war or in the Sino-Japanese conflict." Admiral Yamamoto among the military men was loud in his opposition to this treaty and to war against the United States. He told his contemporaries that he could, as chief of the combined fleet, "run wild" for six months. After that he had no confidence. Yamamoto had served in the United

States, and he had a better appreciation of the American industrial potential and the American character than most of his fellow officers of the army and the navy. But the army, which never had much use for the navy, ignored Yamamoto's advice to go slow.

Had the then commander-in-chief of the United States Fleet had his way, Japan could have had hers. Admiral J. O. Richardson, commander of the fleet, did not think the Japanese were worth worrying about. He did not want a war, and he did not want to get involved in Asian affairs. Nor did he want the fleet based at Pearl Harbor but brought back to California. Richardson's concept of defense apparently was defense of the continental United States and no more. Admiral Stark, the chief of naval operations, told Richardson in no uncertain terms that he was to base in Hawaii because of the deterrent effect the United States fleet there would have on Japan. But Admiral Richardson was not convinced, and so on February 1, 1941, he was replaced by Admiral Husband E. Kimmel and the fleet was renamed the Pacific Fleet to add a warning to Japan.

One reason the Japanese were so confident of their power (despite Yamamoto's dissent) could be seen in the relative 1941 strengths of the American and Japanese fleet elements in the Pacific.

	JAPAN	UNITED STATES
Carriers	10	3
Battleships	10	9
Heavy cruisers	18	12
Light cruisers	17	9
Destroyers	111	67
Submarines	27	64

Further, the Japanese ships for the most part were newer and more effective than the American. The Japanese counted their carriers first. The Americans counted battleships at the head of the list rather than carriers. The Japanese battleships were almost all faster than the American. Two of them, the *Musashi* and the *Yamato,* were the largest and most heavily armoured ships in the world, with 18-inch guns. The Japanese carriers, most of them built in the late 1930s, were faster than the American as well as more numerous. They carried fighter planes (Zero or Zeke) and torpedo bombers (Kate) which were faster, could fly further, and maneuver better than the American planes. The Japanese cruisers were heavier, better armed and faster than their American counterparts. The Japanese destroyers were the finest in the world. Japanese submarines were also superior; the I-boats, or long distance boats, could be equipped with seaplanes for reconnaissance. The Japanese torpedoes were far superior to the American.

Although the Japanese superiority was great it was only skin-deep, as Admiral Yamamoto knew. If these were lost, Japan did not have the industrial capability to replace them in a hurry. And that was the catch he told all who would listen; the Americans, half asleep in 1941, had the power to harness an enormous industrial plant to a war machine once they woke up. No matter, said others; whatever material superiority the Americans might bring to bear, it was no match for the spirit of *Bushido,* the will of the Japanese people to win over all odds. *Bushido,* a revival of the code of the Samurai who dominated Japanese society until the Meiji reformation of 1868, was basically the army's. *Bushido* was designed to create in a force of drafted soldiers the spirit that had been the mark of the professional warrior class in times past. It proved so successful that it became an essential part of the Japanese society of the 1930s and 1940s. All Japanese were taught that they must live and die for the emperor and the homeland. The mistake of the Japanese leaders, not apparent in 1941, was to hypnotize themselves into the belief that *Bushido* could conquer steel. Thus already in 1941, Japanese soldiers were primed for those incomprehensible Banzai charges that would begin at Guadalcanal the next year.

Given a veneer of military superiority, given the spirit of *Bushido,* and the argument that Japan must have "living room" (although only a few hundred thousand of Japan's millions ever immigrated to Manchuria, China, or the new acquisitions) the Japanese willingness to forge ahead on an aggressive policy was self-fuelling.

By the summer of 1941, as the Japanese moved, the British, Dutch, and Americans came together to discuss common defense policies, and this activity convinced the Japanese that they were being encircled. The American embargo of oil, steel, and scrap shipments to Japan brought new protest, and negotiations between the Japanese and the Americans. Privately, General Tojo, who had become premier, planned for war, although the Japanese ambassador, Admiral Nomura, negotiated sincerely, hoping that his efforts could forestall war. Even as Nomura met with the Americans, the order to prepare for battle was issued in Tokyo. At an imperial conference on November 5, 1941, Japan's leaders decided that if diplomacy failed to reach a settlement in the last hours of November 30, the preparations for war would begin. Following that conference Admiral Yamamoto issued the orders that put into effect plans for war that had been laid months before.

The Japanese war machine was in motion in the first week of November. It could still be stopped, but. . . .

12

The Nefarious Japanese

~~~~~~~

FLEET ADMIRAL TOMOSABURO KATO, who later became Japan's prime minister, was one of the principal architects of the Washington Naval Treaty that came out of the conference of 1922. As long as his influence continued, Japan abided by the letter and spirit of the treaty. Kato died in 1923, but his proteges still controlled the navy until the London Disarmament Conference of 1930. Two of Kato's aides at these conferences were Admiral Nomura, later the negotiator, and Admiral Yamamoto, later commander of the Combined Fleet. Admiral Keisuke Okada, later prime minister, and Admiral Mitsumasa Yonai, later navy minister, also believed in Kato's philosophy that for Japan a war with the United States was unthinkable. But the years took their toll. On February 26, 1936, a group of young naval officers tried to kill Prime Minister Okada, and he was saved only because an assassin mistook Okada's brother-in-law for the prime minister. The Kato influence was fading; Admiral Yamamoto was a delegate to the first round of the London discussions in 1934, but by this time he admitted to friends that his influence and that of his mentor were minimal. The "Young Turks" were gaining rapidly within the navy, and the result was an attitude so stubbornly insisting on Japanese advanced naval construction that the London talks of 1935 failed. That autumn Japan gave notice that the Washington Naval Treaty was going to be allowed to lapse, and then began building pell-mell. Actually, it was obvious that the planners had already provided for such a contingency. The blueprints for the mighty new battleship *Yamato* were all ready. A slip at the Kure Naval Yard had been waiting for a year. The building materials were all laid out.

Admiral Yonai, naval minister in 1937, and Admiral Yamamoto fought valiantly against Japanese militarism. They tried to stop Japan from signing up with Nazi Germany and Fascist Italy but were overwhelmed. Admiral Yonai was chosen premier in 1940 when the army's influence waned a little. But the army sabotaged his government and it fell within six months and General Tojo became premier. Tojo was above all a loyal army man who accepted every outrageous army breach of tradition and discipline without a qualm.

Yamamoto in a sense owed his appointment in 1939 as Combined Fleet commander to his opposition to the war policies. His views were so ardently expressed that his friends in the navy feared he would be assassinated by the extremists and sent him to sea to get him out of the way. Yamamoto might have been expected to pursue a soft policy toward America in matters of strategy. Not at all. He was a disciplined naval officer serving in a hard school. His views were known, and that was the end of it. Given the task of preparing the Combined Fleet for possible action, Yamamoto undertook it with thoroughness and dispatch. As assistant navy minister he had been responsible for a number of changes in strategy: in 1939 he extended the Japanese "empire" for naval purposes to include the Marshall Islands. The next year he extended the possible battle area of the fleet to the Hawaiian Islands, after that he began to consider what methods he must use if war came. Yamamoto took a leaf from Admiral Togo's book of the Russo-Japanese War. Togo had struck Port Arthur and severely damaged the Russian fleet while the Russian and Japanese politicians were still talking "peace" at St. Petersburgh. Yamamoto's plan of 1940 called for the Japanese fleet to strike "a decisive blow" against the Americans at Pearl Harbor, and it was inherent in the plan that the blow would come before the Americans could be prepared.

Yamamoto made the plan for a surprise attack on Hawaii. Japanese intelligence knew that the American Pacific Fleet habitually homed in Pearl Harbor with the battleships lined up in a neat row alongside Ford Island and the lesser vessels clustered about the rest of the harbor. In January, 1941, Yamamoto assigned Rear Admiral Takijiro Ohnishi the study of the attack procedure. In April, Ohnishi reported with a plan. Yamamoto detailed it to his staff, who were not enthusiastic, and Ohnishi said that the chances of success were not more than fifty-fifty. But Yamamoto knew better than any others the inherent weakness of the Japanese long-range position. If Japan was to succeed in her war effort, she must get the jump on the Americans. He decided that the chance must be taken. The secret—if one would call it that—would lie in the skill and dedication of the men who would carry out the plan. Some skills had been perfected in the China war; naval pilots had gained experience in bombing Nanking and other cities. Navy planes had bombed the American river gunboat *Panay* in 1937. Much practical skill had been gained in these years and if more was needed, Yamamoto was willing to provide it.

A special training ground was established at Kagoshima Bay in southern Kyushu, a place remarkably like Pearl Harbor. The carrier *Akagi* and several others came to the area, and the training began. Day after day the pilots of torpedo planes, level bombers, and fighters would roar in over Shiro Mountain, then dive down into Iwasaki valley and head out for the shore. Actually, Kagoshima Bay was probably even more taxing than Pearl Harbor where, after crossing the Koolau mountains of central Oahu, the fliers would have a much broader expanse of valley to follow to the home of the Pacific Fleet.

In October, 1941, the Japanese pilots were surprised when a large model of the whole Pearl Harbor set-up was put on display aboard the *Akagi*. It showed in minute detail the features of the terrain, the buildings, and the usual location of the ships at mooring. Never before had the "war games" been so real, never before had they used so many live weapons. A young commander named Minoru Genda was placed in charge of the training, which soon involved five separate areas on Kyushu. Armour-piercing bombs had to be modified to assure explosion in the sort of low level attack that the Japanese fleet would deliver. Torpedoes presented a serious problem because in the shallow waters of Pearl Harbor they would porpoise, or sink to the bottom. The aerial torpedoes had to be modified, and it took many practice drops to discover the optimum altitudes and speeds for launching. To accomplish all this the pilots and carrier crews were kept on duty endlessly but no one complained. The discipline of the Japanese armed forces was complete. Japan had been on a war footing since 1931, and what was happening now was simply an extension.

In the fall of 1941, Admiral Yamamoto hoped that new negotiations in Washington would be a success, but if he had confidence in the beginning, it was quickly eroded. The Japanese government took the position that the United States must back down from its policy of economic containment of Japan and that Japan would not end her attempts to conquer China. That was the real sticking point since the United States would not cease its support of Chinese independence. In November, it became obvious in Tokyo that war was going to come, barring a complete collapse of the American stance. Admiral Yamamoto was ready, and on November 26, the Pearl Harbor Attack Force sailed out of Tanranh Bay in the Kuriles. It was understood by Admiral Nagumo, commander of the carrier force, that a miracle might occur and they would be called back before the strike. But on December 2, Tojo's cabinet decided on war, and next day headquarters sent the message "Climb Mount Niitaka," the code telling Nagumo that the attack was on. Barring an emergency callback the fleet was to strike on the morning of December 7, Hawaii time.

Admiral Nagumo had under him the largest force of aircraft carriers ever assembled, six of Japan's ten. The *Akagi* and the *Kaga* had been built in the 1920s on hulls originally designed to be battleships. Their configuration was low, without the "island" that had come to symbolize the carrier. The *Hiryu* and the *Soryu* were more recent but smaller carriers. The prides of the fleet were the *Zuikaku* and *Shokaku,* the most modern carriers in the world. They were accompanied by two battleships, two heavy cruisers, one light cruiser, and a dozen destroyers. All these ships were fast: the battleships, for example, could make thirty knots. There were no transports. This was a sleek attack force, not an invading armada. The purpose was to make a hit-and-run strike on Pearl Harbor, and then return to Japanese waters. They were on their way. On the morning of December 3, the crews of the ships were assembled and given the official government line:

> "A gigantic fleet is concentrated at Pearl Harbor. This fleet must be destroyed at the start of hostilities. If our plan fails, our navy will be unable to regain the upper hand. Our surprise attack will be the Waterloo of the war which is about to start. For this, the Imperial Navy has concentrated the cream of its forces, in ships and aircraft, in order to assure the initial success. . . . Heaven is witness to the justice of our cause . . ."

The men of the ships were ecstatic. For months they had been primed. The United States had been painted as the ogre that was trying to strangle Japan, deprive her of the means of existence. To the young sailors the attack was "a dream come true." As for the pilots and crews of the aircraft that would carry out the attack, they were under no illusions about their chances of survival. During the preliminary training, these had been placed at under fifty percent. But the Japanese military system had taken all this into consideration. To die for the emperor was the supreme ecstasy. From the days of the Samurai Japanese warriors had compared themselves to the cherry blossoms, and now one of the pilots wrote home about his feelings, expressing his hopes that his spirit would flee to the Yasukuni temple, the shrine of Japan's heroes.

> The tender cherry blossoms
> Fall from the branches
> Without regret
> At the moment of their opening.
> Like shattered pearl
> My bones shall crumble
> In the bay of the Pearl.
> And dawn gleam bright
> In exultation find us
> At the temple of Yasukuni.

The Nefarious Japanese

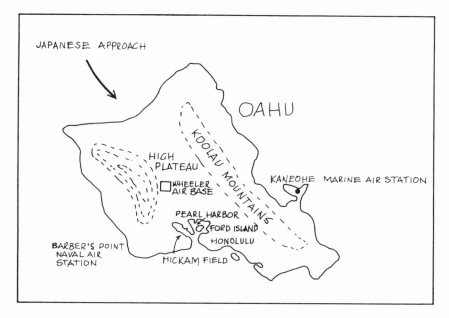

Pearl Harbor attack, December 7, 1941

As the attack force steamed on, the enthusiasm grew. Commander Mitsuo Fuchida had been designated to lead the air strike, and he bubbled over. It was too bad Admiral Yamamoto and the politicians had not decided to send a landing force, he said. If they only had the troops, they could seize Hawaii as well and be masters of the Pacific, from the China shore to California.

Admiral Nagumo did not know just where the American fleet would be found. The regular place on a weekend was Pearl Harbor, since the fleet worked a six-day week, with Saturday night in port and Sunday to sleep off the effects of the revelry. If maneuvers were in progress, the fleet might be found on the weekend at anchorage in Lahaina on the island of Maui, near the little island of Kohoolawe, which was set aside for target practice. As the hour for the attack approached, intelligence would tell Nagumo where. A dozen submarines had been dispatched to the Hawaiian area, and the consul at Honolulu was making regular reports to Tokyo. On Saturday, December 6, the force intelligence officer, Lieutenant Commander Takeji Ono, reported that eight American battleships of the fleet were in Pearl Harbor. As for the carriers, the *Enterprise* had sailed a week before and the *Lexington* had sailed on December 6. The *Saratoga* was in San Diego for repairs. The *Yorktown* and *Hornet* were at sea somewhere in the Pacific and expected. The *Wasp* was in the Atlantic Ocean.

107

The aviators were disappointed that the carriers were not in harbor and so was Admiral Yamamoto. For if they could put the battleships *and* and the carriers out of action, the United States would be totally defenseless in the Pacific. The Asiatic Fleet, operating out of Manila, consisted of a handful of cruisers and the ancient carrier *Langley,* which had been converted to a seaplane carrier; altogether a force that could be destroyed in short order. However, since the carriers were not there, and no one knew when they would be, the Japanese must concentrate on the battleships.

At 5 o'clock on the afternoon of December 6, the Japanese attack force was less than 500 miles from Pearl Harbor. Admiral Nagumo issued his orders: the attack would be launched early in the morning and the planes would fly in over the Koolau range to hit the harbor. The launch would be made from a point 275 miles out, far enough to escape detection by the carrier forces with any luck.

The two heavy cruisers out front increased their speed that night and pushed on ahead so they could launch float planes very early to reconnoiter Pearl Harbor and report on the presence and position of the ships. Before 6 in the morning, they reported back: the ships were in harbor in exactly the position that had been indicated in maps drawn back in Japan and distributed to the pilots. Everything was ready for the attack.

In the darkness of early morning the planes were launched: the torpedo bombers, high level bombers, dive bombers, and fighters. Commander Fuchida was first in the air; one by one as the others took off the crews of the carriers gathered on deck to cheer them forward.

The planes headed south. Soon the sun came up. Below them clouds concealed the water but when Fuchida estimated that they were nearing Oahu they dived down through the murk and shortly after 7:30 in the morning saw the outline of Oahu ahead, with the mountains reaching up into the clouds.

They ascended, crossed the northern cane fields that extended down to the beach and then crossed the mountains, coming out above the cane and pineapple fields of the central part of the island. They were below the cloud cover and ahead lay Pearl Harbor, the morning mist blowing gently in the trade wind. Scarcely a soul seemed to stir. The ships were silent, their boilers cold, their crews below deck. Even the barracks were quiet. Pearl Harbor was sound asleep. The Japanese could not have asked for a better target.

There was a good reason for Pearl Harbor's somnolence, if one understood the American character. The Japanese occupation of Indo-China, the blocking of shipment of war materials, the cutoff of oil, had all brought the American forces to alert beginning in 1941. For the first six months of 1940, the army and the navy *were* alert, concerned about an attack on Pearl Harbor. Admiral Harold Stark, the chief of naval operations, had warned on April 1 that all naval districts must be particularly watchful on weekends. Navy Sec-

108

retary Knox, Secretary of War Henry L. Stimson, and General George Marshall had all added their warnings to those of Admiral Husband Kimmel, commander-in-chief of the Pacific Fleet, and Major General W. C. Short, commander of army forces in the Pacific. The commander of the naval air forces in Hawaii and the commander of the army air corps had joined forces, studied the problem, and warned their commands that the most likely form of attack would be a carrier attack, that it would come on a weekend, from the northwest, and that it would come very early in the morning. On April 1, Admiral Stark had warned specifically that Hawaii must be alert *every* weekend.

The trouble was that the Americans were over-warned. For too long they had lived with the possibility of this attack—it was written into the basic navy war plan. The military forces in Hawaii had become like the villagers who live on the side of an active volcano: they know it is alive, they know it may erupt at any moment without warning, and yet they cannot remain alert forever. So each week without attack, each Japanese-American crisis that passed without war, brought the Americans to a point of insensitivity bordering on stolidity.

Besides, Thanksgiving was just past, and the Christmas season had begun, with its bustle of shopping for gifts and the round of entertainments that were even more frenzied than usual because of the constant "crisis." The Sunday newspapers' society sections reflected the tensions of the times. The weekend *Star-Bulletin* "society" section was full of military weddings and engagements. The life of mingling with the civilian population went on; Rear Admiral Raymond Spruance had just moved into a house in the fashionable Kahala district of Honolulu.

Captain Charles H. McMorris, the Pacific Fleet's war plans officer, told Admiral Kimmel and General Short in a briefing just five days before December 7 that the Japanese would never attack Pearl Harbor from the air. All autumn the fleet had heard reports of Japanese military and naval activity. The head of British intelligence in the Philippines, Major Gerald Wilkinson, learned of the Japanese buildup of troops and supplies in Indo-China, and warned both the Asiatic and Pacific Fleets of the dangers. But at Pearl Harbor all the Indo-China buildup indicated was a probable attack on some Southeast Asian point, perhaps the Philippines, but more probably the Dutch East Indies, Admiral Kimmel believed. This evidence was even more indication to the Americans that there would be no attack on Pearl Harbor, because it seemed to them impossible that the Japanese could launch more than one operation at one time which would involve a large naval force. American naval intelligence had lost track of the half dozen carriers involved here for the past three or four weeks but this had not disturbed anyone. The Japanese had become exceedingly devious in recent years and were careful to monitor

109

their own radio transmissions. In Tokyo the American naval attache's office was of the opinion that the carriers were in the Kure Naval Base, and thus silent.

Even in Washington, the air of crisis could not be maintained. In October, Admiral Stark had written Admiral Kimmel that he did not expect the Japanese to attack at all.

So Pearl Harbor slept this Sunday morning as the attack force of bombers and fighters droned on over the Koolaus. The American radar was in action and it was sweeping a radius of fifty miles from the mountains of Oahu. One radar installation picked up the blips of a large number of aircraft but the young officer in charge was as securely anchored in the somnolence of peace as any other at Pearl Harbor. The American carriers were out, and these should be Halsey's planes from the *Enterprise* or a new contingent of *B-17* bombers that was expected to arrive from the mainland. It did not occur to the radar officer that the planes might not be friendly so he ignored the blips on the screen. The Japanese strike force continued to bore in through the clear air above the harbor. As the lead plane approached, Commander Fuchida saw that he had achieved complete surprise and ordered the entire attack force to strike.

Actually, not all Pearl Harbor was as unaware as the quiet skies indicated. Four hours before the attack began, the watch officer of the minesweeper *Condor* sighted a periscope as the ship was making a routine search of the harbor entrance, a practice that had been followed for weeks as part of the "alert." The officer, Ensign R. C. McCloy, passed the word. It reached the destroyer *Ward*, which was also on night patrol. The *Ward* began to search. Nothing was sighted until around 6:30 as the light began to emerge before sunup. A navy flying boat sighted a periscope following a repair ship that was heading for the harbor (hoping to slip through the anti-submarine net behind the American vessel) and dropped smoke pots in the area. The *Ward* came to the smoke pots, saw the periscope, and opened fire with guns and depth charges. The *Ward* also sent a message to the commandant of the fourteenth Naval District, which was entrusted with defense of the harbor. But ashore the communications section of the Fourteenth Naval District was half asleep. The message was not decoded immediately and the duty officer did not get it until nearly half an hour later. The duty officer called Rear Admiral C. C. Bloch, commander of the Fourteenth Naval District, who ordered the destroyer *Monaghan* to help the *Ward*. At sea the American response was prompt and effective. No one was certain at the moment, but the *Ward* had actually sunk its submarine (one of five midgets released by the submarine attack force that had ringed Oahu to assist in the strike).

For years, the advocates of air power had been saying that air attack on a target had the enormous advantage of complete surprise, and on December 7 this adage certainly proved to be true. Admiral Bloch notified the Cincpac duty officer of the attack on the submarine. The Cincpac duty officer promptly tried to get in touch with Admiral Kimmel. But the Cincpac switchboard was busy, handling calls that involved morning golf games and other items of weekend importance, and the duty officer had to wait precious minutes before he could get through. Admiral Kimmel was brief and to the point. He would be right down, he said, and hung up the phone and hurried toward the Cincpac offices. By the time he arrived, so had Commander Fuchida and his planes. The bombs and torpedoes began to fall.

More midget submarines were moving around the entrance to the harbor. One of them managed to slip through the open submarine net, but inside the alerted *Monaghan* sank it before it could reach Ford Island where the battleships were moored in neat rows. But there was nothing to stop the bombers as they came in.

The fleet was just getting up. The wardroom waiters were busy with orders for bacon and eggs, and especially for coffee. On the decks of the battleships, seamen lounged in the morning sunshine. A few of them idly watched the first planes, a group of bombers circling at about 5,000 feet. This group was waiting for Commander Fuchida to give the order to attack, but to the Americans below, accustomed to seeing their own planes flying above Oahu, the formation was unexceptionable.

Rear Admiral W. R. Furlong, commander of the fleet mine force, was strolling on the quarterdeck of the USS *Oglala* after his breakfast and his eye was caught by a plane flying low over Ford Island. Suddenly he saw a bomb explode on the seaplane ramp at the south of the island and thought it must be a terrible mistake—one of the fleet's own planes had jettisoned a bomb. Then the plane turned up the main channel of the inner harbor and came roaring past so close to the *Oglala* that Admiral Furlong could see the bright red Rising Sun insignia on the side of the fuselage. Then he knew. The "impossible" had happened.

At Cincpac the word went out almost at that same moment: "Air raid, Pearl Harbor. This is no drill."

Had anyone doubted the effectiveness of the Japanese consulate's intelligence activities over the past few months, they were disabused just then. The line of attack of the enemy aircraft was precise against Battleship Row. Within half an hour the battleship *Arizona* was wrecked and burning, the *Oklahoma* had capsized, the *West Virginia* had sunk, and the *California* was sinking. Every battleship was sunk or badly damaged except the *Pennsylvania*, which was protected in drydock across the channel of East Loch. But that ship, the *Tennessee*, and the *Maryland* were at least able a few days later to steam to Bremerton, Washington, for repairs. The *Nevada*, which had been beached at Waipio Point when her captain feared she would sink, was refloated and went back to the mainland under her own power separately.

Most of this damage was done in the first fifteen minutes of the attack. The later waves of planes, finding that the battleships had been hard hit, sought other targets. One group attacked four ships in a line on the other side of Ford Island. The light cruiser *Raleigh* was seriously damaged. The target ship *Utah* turned turtle. The light cruiser *Detroit* escaped altogether. The *Oglala* was sunk, and the cruiser *Helena* was torpedoed, but stayed afloat.

Once the initial shock was absorbed, the Americans began to fight back, but not very effectively. They were valiant enough, however. The anti-aircraft gunners of the *Nevada* shot down two planes. The destroyers moored in East Loch began firing and knocked down some more. As for aircraft, the Japanese attack on the air installations was so effective that few planes got off the ground. At the Naval Air Station on Ford Island thirty-three planes were destroyed on the ground. A handful of United States planes appeared in the sky, having taken off from the carrier *Enterprise*, which was still hundreds of miles away. Several were shot down, and none of them managed to do damage to the enemy. At Kaneohe, the seaplane base on the north side of the island, the Japanese destroyed twenty-seven of the thirty-six PBY patrol planes. At the Marine Air Corps Station at Ewa, forty-nine planes were on the ground, most of them sitting wingtip to wingtip on the field. The Japanese fighters came down, strafing along the line, and set most of them afire. The bombers found the lines made beautiful targets. When they left, thirty-three of the forty-nine planes were destroyed.

The reason the planes were parked so close together was for protection against sabotage. For weeks a cordon of guards had been kept around the area to keep the aircraft safe from "intruders." The potential saboteurs, of course, were members of the Japanese-American community of Hawaii, who were regarded as questionable in the matter of national loyalty.

The same system had been adopted at the army's Wheeler Field, in the center of Oahu, and Hickam Field, on the edge of Pearl Harbor. At Hickam, eighteen planes and most of the vital installations were destroyed in a few minutes. At Wheeler, the *B-17* bombers and most of the *P-40* fighters were set ablaze. It was nearly 11:30 A.M. before the first plane took off from Hickam Field. By this time the Japanese planes were back on their carriers, and the carrier striking force had turned and was heading toward Japan, with a total loss to the attackers of twenty-nine aircraft.

The war had begun in disaster for the Pacific Fleet. But that disaster gave rise to changes and developments that more than repaid the Americans for all they had lost. In the months that followed there would be no more hesitancy. Changes were made, some of them brutal, but there was no time for nicety.

The Nefarious Japanese

Out of the debacle of Pearl Harbor, spurred by American indignation at the "nefarious Japanese," grew an American fighting spirit that (as in 1898) most of the world did not believe existed. Within a year the tide was to be turned, and the Pacific Fleet would begin to roll up the carpet of the Japanese empire.

13

Debacle at Wake

FOLLOWING THE ATTACK AT PEARL HARBOR, many naval men wondered why the Japanese did not come back with a second strike. "Armchair philosophers"—the naval term for military historians—have suggested that they lost a chance to wipe out the navy yard installations, and thus put the American war effort much further back, or even to capture the Hawaiian Islands. Admiral Yamamoto had conceived of the Pearl Harbor strike only to smash the American fleet, and this had been accomplished satisfactorily with the single foray. The Japanese plan had never called for an outright investment in Pearl Harbor *at this stage*. Further, the major Japanese effort was not directed this far east, but where everyone expected the attack to come, in Southeast Asia. The Pearl Harbor assault was icing on the cake, and as the Japanese strategists learned only much later, it was in its way unnecessary and a disaster for Japan. It was unnecessary because the purpose was to prevent the United States fleet from attacking the Philippines. The Japanese did not know that the American navy war plan called for abandonment of the Philippines and all the other American outposts in the western Pacific as too difficult and wasteful to defend at the beginning of hostilities. The attack on Pearl Harbor was disastrous to Japan because it unified the badly divided American nation in one stroke. So made-to-order for President Roosevelt's policy was the sneak attack that forty years later some die-hard Roosevelt haters still claimed he had forced the Japanese hand to get America into the war. Any Americans who so believed on December 8, 1941, had to keep their heads down and their mouths shut. The nation had one object in view: the successful prosecution of the war and the punishment of Japan and her German and Italian allies.

Japan's leaders sensed this American reaction, and there was much explaining to be done in Tokyo as to why Admiral Nomura's breaking off of diplomatic talks with Secretary Hull had come *after* the attack. Of course, Nomura's breakoff was not a declaration of war and in effect the Japanese attack was a greater breach of international law anyhow; but all these explanations were secondary. The primary matter at hand was that war had begun.

Admiral Yamamoto had sent the First Fleet against Hawaii. Meanwhile the Third Fleet, under Vice Admiral Takahashi, moved sixty transports filled with Japanese army troops toward Luzon, the central island of the Philippines. The force was equipped with modern landing craft and had been trained in amphibious techniques. At almost the same time the Second Fleet, under Admiral Kondo, sailed for the Pescadores Islands to cover Japanese army landing operations on the Malay Peninsula. As far as Tokyo was concerned Malaya was the primary target and the most worrisome responsibility. The British naval base at Singapore posed a serious threat to the Japanese flank as the navy moved south. And south, of course, lay the most valuable prize, the oil of the Dutch East Indies. Once Singapore fell and Malaya was taken the objectives would be Borneo, Sumatra, and Java. (The course of the battle for these areas is not within the scope of this book nor was it the responsibility of the Pacific Fleet). To protect the lines of communication, the Japanese had to conquer two more American outposts: Guam and Wake. There was no way the Americans could do anything to save Guam. It was one of the Marianas Islands, and the other major islands, Saipan and Tinian were part of the Japanese empire. It was one of the few places that attracted Japanese citizens. Thousands of Japanese had immigrated to these islands to set up a Japanese culture that overwhelmed the native Chamorros. Guam, then, had become an anomaly. The capture was entrusted to Vice Admiral Inouye and the Fourth Fleet. It was such a simple matter that Admiral Inouye did not even accompany the invasion force but sent Rear Admiral Goto up from Truk in the cruiser *Aoba*. Five thousand Japanese troops landed to assault a defending force that consisted of 30 naval officers, 6 warrant officers, 5 nurses, 230 enlisted men, 7 marine officers, 1 warrant officer, 145 marines, and 246 members of the Chamorro Insular force. They had three patrol boats and an old oiler. Within an hour the fighting was virtually over, and the Japanese had a new island base. They set to work almost immediately to build an airfield, which the Americans had often promised but never done. Guam, then, was to become an important factor in the defense of the Central Pacific in the Japanese war effort of the next three years.

But Wake Island was a different matter. Whereas Guam obviously had to fall by default, Wake had a more important potential defensive role in a war against Japan. Located a thousand miles west of Midway, it was particularly valuable as a base for long-range aircraft. Congress had agreed that

Wake would be an air and submarine base, and while no attempt was made to strengthen Guam, which also might have been a base, more hope was seen for Wake, and in the early months of 1941 engineers began building an air field. Admiral Kimmel, nine months before the outbreak of war, wrote Admiral Stark that Wake ought to be held, because it would offer the United States a chance to make a swift attack on Japanese naval forces inside their own empire. He also warned that unless the island atoll was defended stoutly it would be lost, because he expected it to be one of the major targets of early Japanese naval operations.

In the summer of 1941, the defenses of Wake were shored up—a little. About two hundred men were sent to Wake with a dozen naval and anti-aircraft guns. As part of the Pacific defenses, Wake was scheduled to become a base for flying boats. One squadron of Grumman Wildcat fighter planes was assigned to the island, and on December 4, 1941, the twelve planes arrived under the command of Major Paul Putnam of the United States Marine Corps. On December 8, the day that Pearl Harbor was attacked (western time zone), Wake's garrison consisted of 430 Marines, 68 navy men, a handful of army troops, 70 civilians from Pan American Airways, and about 1,150 civilian construction men.

The Japanese wanted Wake badly. Admiral Yamamoto also had assigned Wake to Admiral Inouye's Fourth Fleet. That admiral sent Rear Admiral Kajioka to take the island. The invasion force moved to Kwajalein atoll in the Marshall Islands on December 1, and waited. On the morning of December 8, Major James P. S. Devereux, senior officer of the American force at Wake, was finishing his breakfast when he received a message that Pearl Harbor was under attack. In seconds the bugle began to blow and men began to run. The Pan-American China Clipper, a flying boat which had come in from Hawaii the day before, had taken off at dawn for Guam but it came back to Wake. The captain of the clipper offered to fly a patrol around the island with fighter escort and the marines began fuelling his flying boat. But before the fuel was in the tanks a swarm of Japanese bombers came out of the clouds and attacked the island. The first strike came as a complete surprise; the Japanese dove down out of a rain cloud above the island. Four of the United States Wildcat fighter planes were hit directly and destroyed. Fire burned three more and damaged another (which was later repaired). The surprise was so complete that the men on the airfield did not even have time to take shelter. Twenty-three marines were killed or wounded. The bombers then worked over the land installations, destroying the hotel that had been built for the civilian passengers of Pan American Airways and most of the airfield facilities. The Clipper, riding in the lagoon, was shot up by machine-gun fire, but not seriously damaged, and that same day the captain took off for Midway, flying a planeload of civilians back to safety.

117

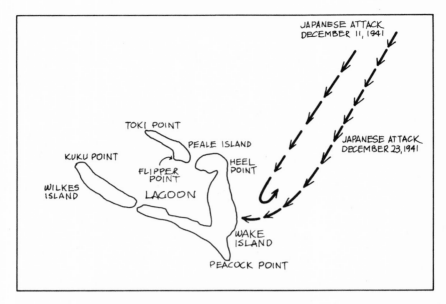

Wake Island, December 1941

The marines worked all that night to build defenses against bombs and the paratroops they expected. In the morning the three operational Wildcats took off to patrol above the island. When the Japanese came, Lieutenant D. D. Kliewer shot down one bomber, assisted by Technical Sergeant W. J. Hamilton in the second plane. The anti-aircraft guns shot down one and damaged several others.

Major Devereux began moving his gun batteries around. On the morning of December 10 the Japanese were back again, bombing, but they concentrated on the old gun emplacement sites and did not hit the guns. They did hit a construction dump with 125 tons of dynamite inside, which went up with an enormous roar and caused ammunition in the gun batteries to explode. This attack brought five more casualties to the Americans. Captain H. T. Elrod, aloft in a Wildcat, shot down two Japanese planes.

Early in the dark hours of December 11, observers on the island saw the Japanese invasion force of about a dozen ships. Rear Admiral Kajioka in the light cruiser *Yubari* led them in. The shock troops were 450 special naval landing troops, similar to the American marines. The rest of the force consisted of garrison troops who would come ashore when the shock troops had established the invasion beachhead.

The invasion began at six o'clock in the evening. The Japanese ships came along the southern shore, and as they came in range the five-inch guns of the defense opened up. Two shells caught the *Yubari* and damaged her enough so that she deserted the invasion force and headed back toward Kwajalein. Another battery began firing and put several shells into the leading destroyer, the *Hayate*, which blew up and sank. They hit another destroyer, the *Oite*, and she retreated. They hit one of the two transports, which also retreated, and a light cruiser, which steamed away trailing smoke. Four other destroyers came in: one marine battery scored a hit on the destroyer *Yayoi* and the other three turned away. These destroyers were chased by the four Wildcats left on the island, and the *Tenryu* and the *Tatsuta* were both damaged by bombs. Captain Elrod's Wildcat was so badly damaged that he crash-landed on the beach, but not before he had bombed the destroyer *Kisaragi*, which was carrying a load of depth charges. One of his light bombs hit among the depth charges, and the destroyer blew up and sank. So the Japanese first effort to take Wake had failed. They had lost two destroyers and about five hundred men, and suffered damage to seven other ships that was almost unbelievable given the size of the defense force.

Back at Pearl Harbor, Admiral Kimmel had devised a plan for the relief of Wake. Vice Admiral Wilson Brown, with the *Lexington*, was to make a diversionary raid on Jaluit in the Marshalls. Vice Admiral William F. Halsey was to take the *Enterprise* west of Johnston Island and be ready to support Rear Admiral Aubrey W. Fitch, who would take an improvised task force and the carrier *Saratoga* (which was then on her way from San Diego carrying Marine Corps Fighter Squadron 221 and eighteen planes to reinforce Wake). But instead of giving command of this force to Fitch, an experienced naval aviator, Kimmel gave it to Rear Admiral Frank Jack Fletcher, who knew much less about carrier war because he was the senior officer present. From the beginning the relief force ran into trouble. The *Lexington* encountered such rough weather that she could not fuel at sea. Admiral Brown, scheduled to attack Jaluit, was nervous because that island was supposed to be an enemy stronghold. (Actually it was not.) He secured permission from Admiral Kimmel to retire if he felt threatened. All that Brown heard from the intelligence officers worried him more: that the Japanese had occupied the Gilbert Islands with an enormous force; that Jaluit was a major submarine base; that Makin Island had been made into a huge air base. None of these reports was true; they were a part of the frantic thrashing of an American intelligence system which had been caught by surprise.

More important even than the intelligence was an order from the "Commander-in-Chief of the Pacific" on December 20, just when Admiral Brown was worrying. The order came from Vice Admiral W. S. Pye, not from Kimmel, for Kimmel and General Short had been relieved of command in the immediate search of the Washington authorities to find scape-goats for the extent of the surprise of the attack that had destroyed the effectiveness of the battle fleet. The plan for Wake's relief had been Kimmel's, and at this point it appeared that anything Kimmel had approved was likely to bring trouble. Pye had been the battle force commander until his battleship fleet had been shot out from under him. Now he was waiting for the new commander of the Pacific Fleet to appear, and in naval life there can be no vacuum, so he had been given temporary command. It was not a very comfortable position for Admiral Pye, nor one calculated to bring about positive action. Should he take the responsibility for ordering Admiral Brown into what Brown believed was a Japanese trap, and thus possibly sacrifice the *Lexington* for no good cause? Pye determined to be more conservative. He ordered Brown to turn north and give support to Admiral Fletcher's force that was heading toward Wake. That order put Brown safely out of trouble—and action.

Admiral Fletcher's force was slowed by the oiler *Neches*, which could only make twelve knots. So Fletcher ambled along across the Pacific while the Japanese regrouped and launched their assault on Wake again. Fletcher was a cautious commander to say the least. Naval doctrine held that the commander should always try to fight with full fuel tanks, and so he stopped to fuel on December 22 although his ships were in no immediate need. Meanwhile the Japanese were attacking Wake and Fletcher was still six hundred miles away. If he had gone on he could have caught the Japanese but instead he wasted a whole day. Admiral Kajioka had returned to Kwajalein and secured more ships and more troops for the assault on Wake. To make sure there would be no slipups this time, Admiral Inouye also sent along Rear Admiral Goto with four heavy cruisers and a number of destroyers, and from the Pearl Harbor striking force Admiral Nagumo detached the carriers *Soryu* and *Hiryu* for the Wake operation.

On December 21, 1941, as the Americans on Wake were attacked by the first wave of bombers—land-based planes from Kwajalein—from Pearl Harbor came a succession of foolish dispatches, regarding such matters as dredging the channel between the islands of the Wake atoll. Obviously officialdom at Pearl Harbor was taking a long time in converting from a peacetime to a wartime manner of thought. The bombing continued on December 22. On December 23, as Fletcher continued to fuel six hundred miles away, the Japanese attacked the island with a landing force of one thousand men. Within a few hours they had established a firm beachhead, and the end was in sight. There was no way the handful of marines could win unless they were reinforced. As far as reinforcement was concerned, with the departure of Admiral Kimmel from command the chances grew dimmer every moment. Pye was certainly not encouraged to vigorous action by Admiral Stark's comment from Washington that Wake Island was a "liability" which perhaps ought to be evacuated rather than defended. Pye, Stark, and Fletcher could all agree that

120

the Pacific Fleet was essential for the defense of Hawaii, and about all that was left of the fleet's major units was the carrier force. So there was a general reluctance to risk the carriers.

At 7:30 on the morning of December 22, 1941, (which was December 23 at Wake) a dispatch came to Cincpac from the island stating that the enemy was landing and the issue was in doubt. Admiral Pye, not at all sure what to do, called his chief of staff, Rear Admiral Milo F. Draemel, who until recently had been the fleet commander of destroyers. They conferred with Captain McMorris, the officer who had said the Japanese would never make an air attack on Pearl Harbor, and together the three decided that it was too late to do anything about Wake. Given Admiral Fletcher's desultory performance, this was certainly true, but it was not too late to steam to Wake and assault the enemy. The *Lexington* and *Saratoga* could both be employed. Admiral Halsey's *Enterprise* could not, because Halsey had been constrained to stay home and protect Hawaii. The three-man committee hemmed and hawed, and finally decided that fighting was not a good idea, so they called the two task forces near Wake to come home. Gladly, Fletcher and Brown turned away from battle. Only Halsey was unhappy. His force might have gone on to help the others and create a badly-needed American victory had Admiral Pye been willing to risk a fight. Could one blame Pye, Draemel, McMorris, Fletcher, and Brown for their timidity? Certainly the political leaders in Washington had not helped any; the immediate relief of Admiral Kimmel after the attack at Pearl Harbor showed all of them what could happen to a naval man's career if he fell afoul of the politicians. Kimmel's recall was made by President Roosevelt on the advice of Secretary Knox.

But what was apparent in Washington among the political leaders was the need for change of command. Admiral Stark's actions showed that he was not the aggressive man Roosevelt wanted, nor were the officers now in charge at Pearl Harbor. It was ironic that the one officer who had moved to engage the enemy immediately—Admiral Kimmel—was in disgrace for reasons over which he had virtually no control. There was no going back in the face of public opinion—America had to have someone to blame for the Pearl Harbor disaster, and Roosevelt was certainly not going to let it be himself. So a whole new naval leadership was necessary, the President decided. On December 20, 1941, Admiral Ernest J. King, former commander of the Atlantic Fleet, was appointed commander-in-chief of the United States Fleet, a new post, superior to that of chief of naval operations. King was one of the most aggressive men in the navy, a firm disciplinarian who demanded and usually obtained the utmost effort from his subordinates. In the Pacific, King's principal assistant would be Chester W. Nimitz, the fifty-nine-year-old chief of the Bureau of Navigation, a more genial and less abrasive officer than King, but equally aggressive in his attitude. Nimitz was jumped two ranks, from rear admiral to full admiral, to take the job as commander-in-chief of the Pacific Fleet. A whole new command and a whole new attitude were about to emerge at Pearl Harbor. Admiral King had drawn a line from Midway Island down to Samoa, Fiji, and Brisbane, Australia. Beyond this point, said King, the Japanese must not pass. They must be held at the line until the United States could gather the resources to begin the drive to retake Wake, Guam, the Philippines, and any other territories that had to be sacrificed now, and then to move onward to defeat Japan.

This attitude was just what Admiral Yamamoto, the chief of Japan's Combined Fleet, had been worrying about. He felt even more strongly that he must swiftly secure a victory large enough to negotiate a peace that would allow Japan to pursue her territorial and trade objectives in Asia. The rapid string of victories in the Philippines, in Malaya, among the Pacific islands, were still being digested in the last days of December, but Yamamoto was not happy. Since the signing of the Tripartite Pact with Germany and Italy he had been concerned about war with America, and his stubborn belief that it could never end in victory for Japan. Yamamoto was growing irritable as he contemplated the difficulties ahead. In the first flush of victory no one in Tokyo was willing to discuss the steps that must be taken to end the war. Almost alone among the officers of the Imperial Japanese Navy, Yamamoto was conscious of the true manner in which the Russo-Japanese war had been brought to an end just in time to prevent Japan's downfall because her economy was overextended. The first stage of the war, Yamamoto said in December, was obviously going very well for Japan; but the real outcome would be decided by the second stage, and in this politics and strategy would be far more important than any tactical development. Late in December, without knowing just who was going to be managing the American war effort, Yamamoto sensed that the effort had begun. The future that concerned Yamamoto as much as it did Admiral King.

14

Confusion
in the Coral Sea

~~~~~~

ADMIRAL NIMITZ arrived at Pearl Harbor on Christmas morning and was immediately taken to the house of the commander-in-chief of the Pacific Fleet. It was empty. Admiral Kimmel, reduced to his permanent rank of rear admiral, had moved across Makalapa Drive to the house of Admiral Pye, where he would remain until recalled to Washington to face Congressional inquisitors and answer impossible questions about the failures of army and navy to protect Hawaii from the surprise Japanese attack. Just before Nimitz arrived Admiral Pye made an estimate of the situation faced by the Pacific Fleet. It called for purely defensive action. When Nimitz learned this, he was silent. He knew that President Roosevelt and Admiral King would never accept a "defensive" approach, but he also did not want to say so just then. He needed some time to assess the situation of the fleet for himself, and particularly the capability of the commanders with whom he would have to work. All these senior officers had been leading figures in the peacetime navy, but whether or not they would do as well in war was another matter, one that had suddenly become enormously important. One of Nimitz's first moves was to call his staff together and say with an apparent air of finality that he intended to make no changes in staff. If that statement lulled the fears of the Cincpac staff it would be useful; even as Nimitz said the words he knew very well that the changes would be coming soon and in wholesale lots. He was the new broom and there was much sweeping to be done to create a powerful fighting spirit. From the moment that he arrived, then discovered the sad truth that the Wake Island relief expedition had been abandoned, and why, it was apparent that major changes in the staff would have to be made. Further, he learned how damaging had been the negative policy of the politicians between the wars. To save money too many corners had been cut. There were shortages of ammunition, shortages of aircraft beyond the damage caused by the Japanese, shortage of trained officers because too many had been transferred to fight the Germans. The torpedo pilot shortage, for example, was nearly desperate and could not possibly be rectified before the spring of 1942. One deficiency even Nimitz knew nothing about was the ineffectiveness of American torpedoes. No one in command knew that the firing pins of the fleet's torpedoes were defective and that often they would not explode the warheads on impact. No one had ever learned of this basic problem because in peacetime the navy was not allowed to fire and sacrifice real torpedoes. Even as Nimitz arrived in Hawaii, the pilots and submariners of the Asiatic Fleet were learning the sad truth in abortive attacks on Japanese warships of the Philippines.

Now that the Japanese had captured Wake, there was no way in the world that the Americans could retake the island, no matter what force Nimitz might be ready to commit. The Pacific Fleet did not have a single amphibious command or any amphibious watercraft. In other words, there was no way the fleet could launch an invasion of anyplace. Although the United States Navy had a war plan, it had not been developed to the point of planning for a real war. The peacetime philosophy was that pervasive.

So the Japanese retained the initiative, and for Admiral Yamamoto, the victories kept piling up. Yamamoto was not fooled. While others rejoiced, he was depressed. They had been lucky, he wrote a friend two weeks after the Pearl Harbor attack; he had no illusion about the future. The war might go on for years. The one chance Japan had of emerging from the war with honor was to run up the string of victories and then hold. For that reason by early January Yamamoto was depressed because Nagumo had not found those three carriers at Pearl Harbor; for it was apparent in the news broadcasts and from the reports of naval intelligence that "America in particular is determined before long to embark on fullscale operations against Japan." If Yamamoto had nightmares, there was the cause; he had no faith in the abilities of the military leaders who had taken ascendance in Japan, and particularly those of the navy. He was particularly distressed as he saw and listened to the news reports from Tokyo which puffed up the victories. "Once you start lying, the war's as good as lost," he said. Imperial Headquarters had already started lying on the excuse that it was essential for the national morale.

In the first week of January, almost before Admiral Nimitz had unpacked his bags at Pearl Harbor, back in Washington Admiral King began agitating for action against Japan. He was responding to President Roosevelt who knew that action was essential to the rebuilding of American morale. But Japanese air raids and submarine activity in the South Pacific indicated the Japanese thrust had not ended yet. The best Nimitz could do at the moment was send carriers to escort four transports filled with marines who were going to bolster the defenses of Samoa before it was too late.

As the Australians knew much better than Washington, the key to control of the South Seas lay in what the Australians called "the Northeast Territories" whose "metropolis" was Rabaul on the northern tip of New Britain Island in the Bismarck Archipelago. The Japanese landed a new invasion force at Rabaul without opposition except from a tiny Australian garrison. Soon they had expanded along the coast of New Britain and to New Ireland. Next they took the northern coast of Papua, New Guinea, and the northern Solomon Islands. They began building Rabaul as a major Japanese air and naval base. The next step would be capture of Port Moresby and that would end effective Australian military opposition in the area.

In January, King ordered the United States carrier fleet to begin raiding Japanese bases, but in Washington few realized how slender was the strength of that fleet. For example, Admiral Wilson Brown was to hit Wake with the *Lexington*'s task force, but when the oiler *Neches* was torpedoed by a Japanese submarine and sunk, Brown had no way of fueling his ships, so he had to return to Pearl Harbor. Then, when the carrier *Saratoga* was torpedoed on January 11, 1942, she barely made it back to Bremerton, Washington, for repairs. The carrier force was again reduced to three. Admiral Fletcher's attempted raid on the southern Marshalls and Gilberts was a failure and cost the *Yorktown* half a dozen planes. About all the fleet got out of that effort was practice. Admiral Halsey's *Enterprise* did successfully raid the Marshalls.

One by one, the bastions fell. Hongkong had gone in December. Malaya was taken, Singapore was captured, and it was apparent that there was no way the Americans could hold out for long in the Philippines. The Australians were concerned about an attack on their country, and when the Japanese aircraft raided Darwin on February 27, 1942, the fear grew.

Very early in 1942, the Imperial General Staff and the Combined Fleet were considering the next step, or second phase of the war. Four plans had been advanced: to strike the Soviet Union from the west, adding immeasurably to Hitler's war launched against the USSR half a year earlier. It was rejected as too confining, without bringing any immediate result to Japan. The second suggestion was that Australia be invaded. Members of the Naval General Staff had seen that the American effort to fight back would be launched from Australia. (They were less than half right.) They expected the Americans to begin offensive operations in 1943. Before that they proposed the seizure of the Solomons and all the islands around Australia, including Samoa. The idea was to cut America off from Australia. This plan was the favorite of the Naval General Staff and the reason for the build-up of Rabaul. The ambitious young men of the planning section were even beginning to lay out invasion plans for Australia.

The third plan, which was advanced by Admiral Yamamoto and his staff, called for an attack in the Indian Ocean: assault Ceylon with an army invasion force, lure and destroy the British Far Eastern Fleet, use Ceylon as a base to launch a major invasion of India, and then link up with the Germans in the Caucasus, sequestering the Middle-East's oil for Germany and Japan. This plan would have resolved one of the navy's perennial problems, the assurance of a fuel supply. But the army did not approve.

With opposition in various quarters to all the other plans, the Combined Fleet then suggested that the perimeter of Japanese power be advanced in the Pacific to the east. The key was Midway Island, from which attacks on Hawaii could be conducted and perhaps even an invasion of Hawaii staged. At the same time, a small military force would invade the Aleutian Islands, expanding Japan's power to the edge of North America and creating a diversionary effect. Yamamoto expected the Midway invasion to bring out the remainder of the American Pacific Fleet, which he hoped to destroy. Then Japan would indeed have prepared the way for peace talks that could not help but be favorable, given the United States's inability to protect even its own shores. The Naval General Staff was to have the final say. Within the staff there was violent opposition to the plan as pushing Japan too far and straining the navy's resources. But Yamamoto was obdurate; they had to keep moving and hope that the politicians would act at the right time. He said that every month the war lasted meant another month for America to gain military strength. And barring the move west to the Persian Gulf, without a swiftly negotiated peace, he expected Japan to lose all in the end. Thus the Midway gamble was completely in character for Yamamoto. If he could destroy the American fleet, he would buy Japan time.

The Yamamoto plan might have gone begging except for one development: in the spring of 1942 the unthinkable happened. The military had been promising that no foreign soldier would ever set foot in Japan, nor would any foreign aircraft ever bomb her cities. But on April 18, 1942, thirteen B-25 medium bombers struck Tokyo and three others hit Nagoya, Osaka, and Kobe in a raid led by Lieutenant Colonel James H. Doolittle of the Army Air Corps. The raid was planned for morale purposes more than anything else, and it succeeded in raising American morale remarkably. The reaction of the Imperial General Staff was immediate: the Midway operation was approved. On May 5 the orders were issued.

As the plans for the Midway assault were being laid the buildup of Rabaul brought thousands of men to that base. Lae and Salamaua in New Guinea were occupied, and the stage was set for the capture of Port Moresby, which housed a big Australian seaplane base, and Tulagi in the Solomon Islands, where a Japanese seaplane base would be built. An air base was also planned for Guadalcanal Island. Once these bases were complete, the Japanese navy could assume control of the air over northern Australia and cut off communication with the United States. All was ready early in April, except that Japan's carriers were off on other missions. Admiral Nagumo had sailed into the Indian Ocean with the striking force; he had sunk the carrier *Hermes* and neutralized British power there. At the end of April the carriers were home in Japanese waters, and although most of them were scheduled for the Midway operation, the two biggest carriers, *Shokaku* and *Zuikaku,* were assigned to cover the Port Moresby invasion. It was indicative of the importance of the mission that Admiral Inouye, commander of the Fourth Fleet, moved his headquarters from Truk to Rabaul.

The latest intelligence report on allied activity indicated that the allies had only 200 effective fighter planes in northern Australia. One American task force was somewhere in the area, but that meant only one big carrier against Japan's two. The British were said to have a battleship in these waters and two or three cruisers and some destroyers, and the Americans had sent some submarines down from the Philippines, but since Japan had lost no ship larger than a destroyer so far, the allied naval presence was not regarded as a serious threat. Admiral Inouye, then, had no qualms about ordering the Port Moresby operation to proceed on the night of April 30.

A hundred and fifty land-based aircraft would cover the Port Moresby landings from Rabaul. The two-carrier striking force was led by Vice Admiral Takeo Takagi. The invasion force was led by Rear Admiral Aritomo Goto and was split: one transport and covering ships would assault Tulagi and eleven transports would land troops at Port Moresby. Admiral Goto's protective force for Port Moresby consisted of two light cruisers, a seaplane carrier, and the light carrier *Shoho* which could launch twelve fighters and nine torpedo bombers.

The Tulagi force landed on May 3 without opposition. There did not seem to be an Australian on the island. The *Shoho* sat offshore ready to launch planes, but no planes were needed. It was even easher than the Japanese had expected.

On May 3, the ships moved into position for the assault on Port Moresby. The carriers *Shokaku* and *Zuikaku* had been ferrying planes down from Truk to Rabaul all week, but they were freed of this task and sent to sea ready to fight with their own aircraft: forty-two fighters, forty-one dive bombers, and forty-two torpedo bombers. A fight for Port Moresby was expected, but the Japanese also were supremely confident. The events of the past five months indicated that the allies were no match for the Japanese navy.

But in Washington, Admiral King had drawn his line down the Pacific. Thousands of troops had been sent to New Caledonia and so had several squadrons of Army Air Force planes. Samoa had been reinforced. Efate in the New Hebrides was an allied base now, and Tonga was to become one.

Battle of the Coral Sea, May 1942

Confusion in the Coral Sea

Admiral King was determined that the Japanese would not come closer to Australia and would not cut off communications between that continent and the United States.

The sorting out of commanders had already begun. Admiral Wilson Brown, on his return from the abortive mission to the South Pacific, aroused the wrath of Admiral King, and very shortly afterward he was shipped off to San Diego to head a new amphibious force there. Nimitz also had concluded that Brown did not have the qualities necessary for a fighting command. Brown's great experience had brought him to the top of the peacetime navy, but the navy in war was quite a different service, as Brown's performance indicated. The qualities that made a man successful in peace—conservatism and adherence to the rules—did not serve so well in war.

Nimitz planned a more aggressive role for Admiral Pye, former commander of the battle force. He was to go to the South Pacific to coordinate the activities of commands in New Zealand, Fiji, and New Caledonia, which were within the Pacific Fleet's area. With the escape of General MacArthur from the Philippines to Australia, the Pacific had been divided. MacArthur was given the Southwest Pacific and Nimitz was given the Central Pacific, but they overlapped just where the action was about to begin.

Nimitz kept Admiral Draemel as his chief of staff, but it was obvious to the well-informed that Draemel's days in that post were numbered. He was another of the old school; when King had announced the Doolittle Tokyo raid and assigned it to Halsey to perform, Draemel had declared that it was a dreadful waste of America's slender air resources. Everyone knew that the B-25s involved would never make it back to the Pacific command; Doolittle had hoped to land the planes in China although in fact all of them were lost. So Draemel was right, but being right was no excuse. King needed morale boosters and at this time of the war they were far more important than any material considerations. Halsey was exuberant about the chance to hit the enemy; Draemel worried about the consequences. That was the difference between them and it was to shape their careers. Naval history rings with the name of Halsey, while that of Admiral Draemel is almost forgotten.

Early in 1942, Admiral King adopted the practice of meeting with Nimitz every month or so, usually in San Francisco, so King could keep his hand on the pulse of the Pacific War. He expressed himself at the March meeting as less than satisfied with Admiral Fletcher's performance. Nimitz saved Fletcher's command for the moment. Let them see how Fletcher did in the next operation, he pleaded, and King grouchily agreed. But he did not agree about Pye. He overruled Nimitz and so instead of Pye, Vice Admiral Robert Ghormley was sent down to the South Pacific cammand. There was going to be fighting down there, King said, and he wanted an aggressive commander. Ghormley would be assisted by an untried aviator, Rear Admiral J. S. McCain.

Admiral Fletcher's task force had been operating in the South Pacific since March without accomplishing much. As King saw it Fletcher spent most of his time fuelling or reprovisioning instead of fighting. King and Nimitz expected Fletcher to move in on Rabaul and attack the enemy's buildup there, but Fletcher hemmed and hawed. He wanted to wait for the Japanese fleet, he said, and not waste his ammunition on lesser game. Still, Fletcher was the senior officer present, and under naval rules, that meant he was in charge of operations. When word came in the first hours of May 1, 1942, that the Japanese were on the move, Fletcher met with Admiral Aubrey Fitch, who commanded the *Lexington's* task force, and Admiral J. G. Crace, commander of the Australian forces in the area, which included several cruisers and destroyers. On May 3 came the word that the Japanese had landed at Tulagi. Fletcher moved then, and the next day his planes attacked Tulagi, sank a pair of destroyers and several other ships and crippled the Japanese force there. The Japanese radioed for help, and Admiral Takagi with his big carriers *Shokaku* and *Zuikaku*, came up to search for the Americans.

The Japanese attacked first. Admiral Takagi's search planes found the destroyer *Sims* and the oiler *Neosho*. They sank the *Sims* and turned the *Neosho* into a floating hulk whose survivors would sit and wait for days for rescue.

Admiral Fitch's planes from *Lexington* then sank the light carrier *Shoho*, which was covering the attempt to land at Port Moresby. So far the trade was better than even for the Americans. On May 8, planes from *Yorktown* attacked the *Shokaku* and *Zuikaku*. The torpedo plane attacks failed. The Americans still had not learned that their torpedoes were fatally defective, but the bombers put two bombs into *Shokaku* and damaged that ship enough so that she could not launch planes and had to retire from the fight. Japanese planes bombed and torpedoed the American carriers. *Yorktown* took one 800-pound bomb that did considerable damage and killed or wounded sixty-six men, but did not destroy the carrier's ability to fight. *Lexington* was torpedoed twice by those effective torpedo bombers of the Japanese and at the end of the battle she was severely damaged, with a heavy list.

Still, Admiral Fitch was a fighter and he was determined to save the carrier. He tried valiantly. The fires were put out, the list was righted by flooding, and *Lexington* was again able to launch planes. But one of those enemy torpedoes, which seemed only to have damaged the fresh water tanks, had actually done much more. A concentration of aviation gas fumes built up in a compartment next to the ship's generator room, and suddenly the gas exploded. The explosion blew flames and vapor throughout the vent pipes of the ship, and fires started simultaneously in half a dozen areas. The explosions cut the ship's fire mains, and the men of the *Lexington* found that they had no way to fight the fires. Late in the afternoon the ship was abandoned and sunk by an American torpedo.

Confusion in the Coral Sea

So the score was changed, the Japanese had sunk an American fleet carrier and damaged another. The result was even worse than it seemed, for the ratio of Japanese carriers to United States carriers in the Pacific was three to one just then, and Nimitz could ill afford to lose one of his major weapons. The loss of *Shoho* to the Japanese hardly compensated. Actually the score might have been worse for the Americans, except that Admiral Takagi showed the same conservative characteristics that Admiral Fletcher had shown and retired. Admiral Inouye, shaken by the events of the day, cancelled the Port Moresby invasion. Admiral Yamamoto was furious with both commanders, but there was nothing he could do at the moment. He could and did order Takagi to take *Zuikaku* and find and destroy the American force. But Takagi was not eager to do so, and he never regained contact. So the battle of the Coral Sea ended. Back in Tokyo, the spokesman for Imperial Headquarters announced that it had been an enormous Japanese victory, further proof that the Americans could not stand up to the superior fighting ability of the Japanese, who were obviously aided by Divine Providence. Secretary Knox and the American navy had a certain amount of egg on their faces: an American naval spokesman had announced on May 7 the attack on Tulagi and the destruction of *Shoho* and a number of lesser vessels. The tone was triumphant. But after the loss of the *Lexington* the tone changed, and the Japanese propagandists leaped upon this as further evidence of America's growing weakness.

Aboard the battleship *Yamato*, Admiral Yamamoto was annoyed and distressed by the Imperial Headquarters propaganda. To him the outcome of events meant defeat. Port Moresby had *not* been invaded. Tulagi had been so hard hit that there was no hope for creation of an effective base there. The move toward Australia had suffered an enormous setback, and he had lost one carrier and was going to have to do without *Shokaku*'s services for several weeks. All the more reason that the Midway Operation must proceed satisfactorily and on schedule. The Americans were showing a new aggressiveness and Yamamoto knew that it would not be long before this was matched by a new power as more ships began to come into the Pacific area. If Japan was to have the time and the opportunity to negotiate a successful peace, the American fleet must be crippled immediately. Midway was Yamamoto's chance.

131

15

Turning Point at Midway?

~~~~~

WHERE THE TURNING POINT of the Pacific War came is a matter still for conjecture and American and Japanese naval historians disagree. But the Americans said it was Midway, and from their point of view it was, even if the Japanese saw the war's basic change in emphasis as coming much later. The Japanese still held the initiative in May, 1942. Despite the setback at Port Moresby, which Yamamoto blamed largely on the timidity of Admirals Inouye and Takagi, Yamamoto laid plans to retain that initiative. He would take Midway in May and establish a base in the Aleutian Islands. In July, the Combined Fleet would put the army ashore at New Caledonia and Fiji, then stage a series of carrier raids on Australia to cripple the allied defense buildup. In August, the Combined Fleet would strike Johnston Island and the Hawaiian Islands. There were some in Tokyo who advocated more than a strike. Once Midway was established as a Japanese base, then why not occupy Hawaii? In Tokyo, the occupation plans were complete, but Yamamoto did not allow himself the luxury of planning that far ahead. One step had to be taken at a time. But it was apparent that if Yamamoto's plan succeeded, and the American fleet was lured out and destroyed at Midway as he intended, then there was nothing to stop the Japanese forces until they reached the shores of California.

For the Midway operation, Yamamoto hoped to have the use of *Zuikaku* and *Shokaku*, although the two big carriers had already been committed to the Port Moresby operation, when the Midway orders came down from Imperial Headquarters on May 5. A few days later *Shokaku* was damaged in the Coral Sea and sent home to Japan for repairs. *Zuikaku* suffered the loss of a number

133

of planes and pilots, her stores had to be replenished, and there was not time to make all the changes and still use her in the coming operation. However, Admiral Yamamoto still had four fleet carriers available, the *Akagi*, the *Kaga*, the *Soryu*, and the *Hiryu*. The best intelligence estimates showed only the United States carriers *Enterprise* and *Hornet* operational in the Pacific. Considering the damage to the *Yorktown*, which was roughly the same as that to the *Shokaku*, Yamamoto would have an edge of two to one.

The Japanese intelligence was correct. The *Saratoga*, damaged by a torpedo, was at San Diego but would not be ready for sea until June 5. The *Wasp*, which was scheduled to come to the Pacific, was still on the other side of the Panama Canal.

Admiral Nimitz and his staff tried to anticipate Admiral Yamamoto's plans. They could estimate that he knew America's industrial power would soon produce enough ships and planes to change the balance of forces in the Pacific. It was only logical that Yamamoto should try to move quickly to take advantage of his greater strength. More important was another sort of information, secured by Lieutenant Commander Joseph J. Rochefort, head of the Pacific Fleet Communications Intelligence Unit, a small group, most of them fluent in Japanese, whose job it was to monitor Japanese radio broadcasts and ascertain Japanese intentions and actions.

The intelligence men had managed to break part of the code used by the Japanese navy. Based on these partial code breaks, the volume of Japanese radio traffic, and movement of Japanese planes and ships in April, Lieutenant Commander Rochefort predicted that the Port Moresby operation would be quickly followed by one much larger aimed at the Central Pacific. Early in March, the Japanese had sent a flying boat around Midway. The Communications Intelligence Unit intercepted the plane's transmissions and warned the marines. The flying boat was shot down. Early in May, radio traffic from Yamamoto's headquarters indicated a Japanese buildup of forces in the Marshalls Islands, centered at Kwajalein. Suddenly, in May, a new two-letter word appeared in the coded radio traffic. Time and again the messages mentioned *AF*, which was obviously a place name. But where? Rochefort's men had already deduced that *AFG* meant French Frigate Shoals, north of Hawaii. They assumed then, that *AF* should be a point somewhere in the Hawaiian chain of islands. One message referred to an "occupation force" for *AF*, and the intelligence unit aroused Admiral Nimitz's command with the suggestion that Hawaii might be next on the invasion list.

But as the traffic continued, Rochefort got a better picture, and it did not seem to indicate an assault on Hawaii. He convinced Nimitz's fleet intelligence officer, Lieutenant Commander Edwin T. Layton, that a big operation was coming and that Midway was the target. At that time the carriers *Hornet* and *Enterprise* had gone to the South Pacific to join the *Yorktown* and *Lexing-*

ton but had arrived too late to become involved in the Battle of the Coral Sea. They remained in the south until May 16, when Nimitz was convinced of the enemy buildup for a Central Pacific operation and recalled them. Meanwhile, *Yorktown* limped home to Pearl Harbor. Admiral Fitch estimated that under normal dockyard conditions the damage probably would take three months to repair. So Halsey's two carriers seemed to represent the only fighting force Admiral Nimitz had.

Was *AF* really Midway? That was the question that Rochefort was unable to answer. With the breakdowns it had made, the radio intelligence unit was able to read about a third of any message. But since *AF* was an arbitrary geographical designation, there was no way that confirmation or denial could be made by analysis. *AF* could be Oahu, and Admiral King thought it was, but Nimitz was sure it was Midway. He flew there and sent additional fighters and patrol planes to Midway. He reinforced the marine garrison. Every available submarine was detailed to the Midway area. Nimitz persuaded General Delos C. Emmons, commanding general of the army forces in Hawaii, to send eighteen of his precious *B-17* bombers to Midway, thus reducing the Oahu defense force.

That was the dilemma. United States naval doctrine held that a defending force must prepare for the enemy's action by considering the utmost of the enemy's capability—and that could mean an attack on Oahu, which Yamamoto certainly *could* launch; that was King's inclination. But Nimitz was told by his radio intelligence men that they were absolutely certain the target was Midway, and he risked everything on that hunch. If he was wrong, and the Japanese did attack Oahu when the defenses were at Midway, then there would be hell to pay. King continued to believe the target was Oahu and ordered the old battleships to leave Oahu and head for the west coast instead of adding their strength to the Midway defenses. If Nimitz was wrong, California would become the first line of defense.

The key to Midway had to be Halsey's carrier force, with the *Enterprise* and *Hornet*—unless somehow the *Yorktown* could be repaired in time for the battle. It seemed hardly likely; she was scheduled to arrive in Pearl Harbor on May 28, and Nimitz expected the attack in the first week of June.

In the interim the radio intelligence unit came up with an idea: Commander W. J. Holmes knew that Midway had a new fresh water distilling plant. What if the plant broke down? It would be a serious problem and one the Japanese would understand because they held a number of similar atolls. Rochefort took the idea to Nimitz, and together with Admiral Bloch they conspired to send a secret message to the commander of Wake, asking him to send a message in the clear saying that Midway's fresh water distillery had broken down. He did, and Bloch then sent back an answer, also in the clear, that a barge load of water would be sent immediately.

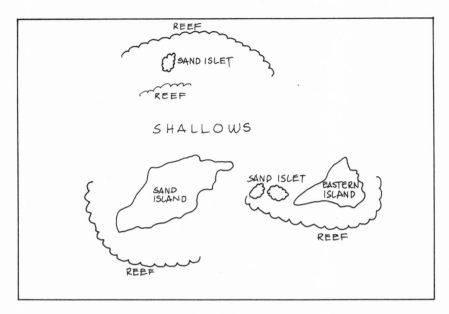

Midway, May 1942

This exchange produced the desired results: in a matter of hours, the Wake island radio station advised Admiral Yamamoto that *AF* was short of water. So the hunch was confirmed.

On May 26, 1942, the radio intelligence team brought word that the Japanese force heading for *AF* had sailed from Saipan where it had been assembling for several days. That same day Admiral Halsey pulled into port with his two-carrier fighting force and made his duty call on Admiral Nimitz. One look at Halsey told Nimitz his best fighting commander could never participate in battle in a week or so. Halsey's nerves were shot. He was a sick man who needed a rest. Nimitz hustled him off to the hospital and then had to find a new commander to carry the vital battle that was coming up.

He chose Rear Admiral Raymond Spruance for several reasons. One was that he had decided to make Spruance his chief of staff. Draemel had not worked out in that position. If Nimitz had needed a brake, Draemel would have been the man for the job; but what Nimitz needed was support and ideas, and Draemel was much too conservative. He was shipped off to California to take Wilson Brown's place as amphibious commander, for Brown had made the mistake of saying he thought he needed a rest, and King exiled him to the First Naval District command.

There was another reason for choosing Spruance. Once this operation was out of the way, and Halsey had recovered from his indisposition, Nimitz wanted Halsey back in action. If he gave a commander the Halsey task force and then took it away there was bound to be ill feeling, but not if the temporary commander was going back to be chief-of-staff to the commander-in-chief of the Pacific. By choosing Spruance, Nimitz made sure there would be no post-operational complications; it was the sort of organizational maneuver at which Nimitz excelled.

Vice Admiral Fletcher showed up in Pearl Harbor the next day, and after a discussion with Nimitz, retired to his cabin to write up an explanation of his ineffectiveness in the South Pacific. King was very critical, and Nimitz needed some answers. Meanwhile, Nimitz launched the repair of the *Yorktown* on an emergency basis. She was put in drydock, and one thousand four hundred men with torches and tools went aboard to repair the damage done by that Japanese bomb. The three months' repair job was completed in two days and two nights, and the *Yorktown* was ready to sail. That was a great relief to Nimitz; the odds were shortened; the Americans would have three carriers. He did not know how many carriers the Japanese would bring, but he was sure there would be more than he had.

Fletcher's explanation satisfied Nimitz, at least enough so that after indicating King's past displeasure, he left Fletcher in command of the task force. Moreover, he left him in command of the whole defensive operation, because when he got right down to it, he did not have anyone else to put in. Spruance was not an airman and was untried as a task force commander. Nimitz was certain that Spruance would do a good job, but with the defense of the entire eastern Pacific riding on the outcome of this battle, as was obviously the case, Nimitz could not risk an untried man. If Fletcher would perform as he now promised, everything should work out all right. So Nimitz drafted the orders. "You will be governed by the principle of calculated risk. . . ." he wrote. Fletcher could not but know what that meant. This time his performance must satisfy King, or else. . . .

Oddly enough, although Admiral Yamamoto was determined on the Midway-Aleutians operation, many of his commanders were negative about it. They regarded Midway as a wasted effort because they believed that after Midway was taken, supply and maintenance would exert an enormous drain on Japan's resources. That was as far as they thought. They were, of course, dead wrong in their estimates, as the Americans knew well. A victory at Midway, and the destruction of the American carriers would set back the United States war effort for years. All Nimitz's efforts were turned to eliminating that danger.

So the Japanese came on, contemptuous of the enemy they had already defeated so many times. One Japanese air squadron sent a message back to the fleet post office in Tokyo requesting that mail be forwarded to Midway from June on. Admiral Nagumo, the hero of Pearl Harbor and Trincomalee, suggested that the Americans would come out to fight, as Yamamoto hoped, but his opinion of American "fighting spirit" was so low that he anticipated an easy victory.

The force they brought was impressive. The light cruiser *Nagara* was in the lead, followed by twelve destroyers. Behind them were the heavy cruisers *Tone* and *Chikuma* and the battleships *Haruna* and *Kirishima*. Behind them came the four proud carriers, *Akagi*, *Kaga*, *Hiryu*, and *Soryu*, with 260 aircraft to be launched against Midway and the American fleet. At sea the force formed into the famous Japanese fighting circle, with the carriers in the middle for protection. Sailing separately came twelve transports loaded with invasion troops, escorted by the light cruiser *Jintsu* and eleven destroyers. To offer further protection, from Guam came the cruisers *Suzuya*, *Kumano*, *Mogami*, and *Mikuma* with another eleven destroyers. They were followed by the cruisers *Nachi*, *Atago*, *Chokai*, *Myoko*, and *Haguro*, the battleships *Hiei* and *Kongo*, the light crusier *Yura*, and seven more destroyers. Last, up came Admiral Yamamoto in the flagship *Yamato* with the *Nagato* and *Mutsu* (all battleships), with the light cruiser *Sendai*, and eight destroyers. Finally, in this covering force were the four battleships *Ise*, *Hyuga*, *Fuso*, and *Yamashiro*, the light cruisers *Kitakami* and *Oi*, and the carrier *Hosho* with thirteen escorting destroyers.

Once Midway was secured, part of this covering fleet would steam on to offer support to the Aleutians invasion, which was to be guarded by the carriers *Ryujo* and *Hayataka*, the heavy cruisers *Takao* and *Maya*, and three destroyers.

Without knowing the exact composition of the Japanese fleet, Admiral Nimitz knew that this was the biggest operation yet launched, much larger than the Pearl Harbor strike. The future depended on that thin line of ships he could put into the waters around Midway and particularly on those three carriers. Against the ninety-six warships sent by the Japanese, Nimitz dispatched what he had: Admiral Spruance's task force, consisting of the *Enterprise*, the *Hornet*, six cruisers, and nine destroyers; and Fletcher's task force, consisting of the *Yorktown*, two cruisers, and six destroyers. Odds of four to one against the Americans.

Both sides had their submarines out for scouting. The Japanese submarines arrived late. Not knowing that the Americans were prewarned, there was no reason for them to expect that the United States forces would have sailed before the threat to Midway was announced by Yamamoto's bombing and bombardment. So the submarines set up picket lines about halfway between Midway and Pearl Harbor, but the Americans had already passed that point. Yamamoto had been careful; he had provided for seaplane observation of Pearl Harbor, or thought he had. But when the flying boats arrived at French Frigate Shoals, where they were scheduled to meet two submarines that would refuel them for the flight to Hawaii, the flying boats found two American seaplane tenders and two American flying boats there. Nimitz had taken no chances; from his point of view it was imperative that the Japanese *not* be forewarned that the United States forces had already sailed. So the Japanese flying boats turned around and went back west, and Yamamoto's force steamed on, comfortable in the belief that the American fleet was safely tied up at Pearl Harbor and could be drawn out and annihilated once the Midway operation began.

The Japanese invasion of Midway was right on schedule. On June 3, 1942, the minesweepers headed in to make sure the water would be safe for the troop transports. But just after nine o'clock in the morning an American search plane from Midway spotted the Japanese ships and the word was passed. That afternoon *B-17s* from Midway came out to bomb the Japanese minesweepers and the transports behind them. But these were army bombers, trained in high altitude bombing against stationary land targets. The Japanese ships twisted and turned as the bombs came down, so the *B-17* bombs did no damage at all.

At dawn on June 4 the Japanese carriers launched the first air strike against Midway, seventy-two bombers protected by thirty-six fighters. Everything from Midway that could fly was put in the air: twenty-seven fighters circled the islands of the atoll; *B-17s*, half a dozen *B-26* medium bombers, and marine dive-bombers went for the Japanese carriers. The *B-17s* again bombed from 20,000 feet and hit nothing. The *B-26s* came in at 2,000 feet, hit nothing, and five of the six were shot down. The marine dive-bombers, all inexperienced pilots, hit nothing, and a dozen of them were shot down. The American performance did not increase Admiral Nagumo's respect for American fighting power. There were obviously more American planes at Midway, and he decided to eliminate them in the next go-around, so that they would not interfere when finally the American fleet was drawn out to face its annihilation. The bombers of the carriers *Akagi* and *Kaga* had been loaded with torpedoes for an assault on the American ships. But since Nagumo had no reports of American ships in the area—and he did not expect any yet—it seemed only sensible to take this opportunity to neutralize Midway. He ordered the bombers to switch from torpedoes to bombs and then to knock out the island air installations.

Nagumo did not know that the Americans had found his carrier force that morning. Admiral Fletcher told Admiral Spruance, who was closest to the Japanese, to attack as soon as possible. Spruance, who was a cautious man, wanted to wait until he reached a point about 100 miles from the enemy, because the *TBD* bombers had a range of only 175 miles, but Captain Miles Browning, who was really Halsey's chief of staff and was now lent to Spru-

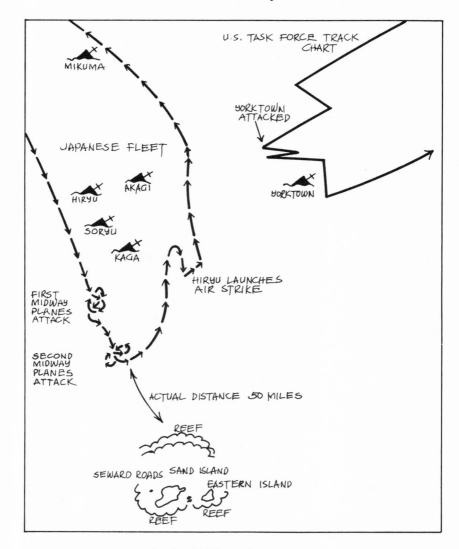

Battle of Midway, June 4, 1942

ance, advised otherwise. Browning was an experienced airman. He knew that the Japanese planes had struck Midway already. That meant they were on their way back to their carriers. If the American planes could hit the carriers just as the enemy aircraft were landing, the decks would be crowded with planes, and the Japanese would be caught unready for defense. Spruance

140

agreed. The planes of the *Enterprise* and the *Hornet* began launching just after seven o'clock in the morning when the Japanese were about 150 miles away.

As the American planes headed toward the area where the Japanese carriers had been reported, a Japanese search plane discovered the American carriers. Admiral Nagumo was surprised; the Americans should not have been so close. As a normal precaution, he changed course, and so by the time the American planes arrived at the expected rendezvous with the Japanese carriers, the carriers were nowhere to be seen. Then began the tedious search.

The planes of the *Hornet*'s Torpedo Squadron 8 were the first to find the Japanese carriers. They had lost touch with their own fighter escort and had to go in alone if at all. If at all was a good question. The delay in finding the fleet had used up the fuel margin; Lieutenant Commander John C. Waldron, leader of Torpedo 8, looked down at the Japanese carriers and at his fuel gauge and asked for permission to withdraw and refuel before attacking. The answer was negative. "Attack at once" was the order from Admiral Spruance. The TBDs these pilots were flying were old, slow planes, and without fighter protection, heading into the Japanese defense circle was going to be suicide. Back on the *Enterprise*, Admiral Spruance and Captain Browning knew that just as well as Lieutenant Commander Waldron did. But the bombers were expendable. In their attack, everything was at stake.

Waldron's planes attacked, and as they did, those fast, maneuverable Zero fighters bored in on them from above. They flew rings around the slow American bombers and shot them down, one by one. Most of the torpedo bombers managed to launch their torpedoes, but not one struck home, and every one of the TBDs was lost. Only one pilot survived, Ensign G. H. Gay, who crashed in the sea but managed to escape the sinking plane and inflate his "Mae West" life preserver. Gay watched, then, as the torpedo bombers from the *Enterprise* repeated the performance. Their record was slightly better; they did not score any explosive hits on the carriers, but four of the fourteen TBDs managed to get back to the *Enterprise*. No one will ever know whether or not the torpedo bombers hit the Japanese ships because American torpedo performance was so poor at the time. In a sense, the poor performance of the torpedo bombers turned the tide *for* the Americans. The Japanese fighter pilots grew excited in the chase, and their director made the fatal error of pulling down all the Combat Air Patrol from the heights to pursue the torpedo bombers. Scarcely had this occurred than the dive-bombers from the *Enterprise* discovered the *Kaga*, *Akagi* and *Soryu*. They formed up and came screaming down in sections of two on the three carriers.

The *Kaga* and the *Akagi* were preparing to launch planes for the second strike, and as Captain Browning had hoped, their decks were full. The SBDs screamed down, and Ensign Gay swore that the pilots did not even use their dive flaps, but came all the way at full speed, and then pulled out just above the water and sped away, their bombs striking home.

Bombs exploded on the planes that were ready to take off and below, on the hangar deck. Admiral Nagumo's flagship, *Akagi*, began to blaze. Commander Genda, the air officer of Nagumo's staff, had been pleading for the admiral to rearm the planes with torpedoes. These too began to go up in blast. One bomb hit amidst planes being serviced on the hangar deck and started an enormous fire. Another struck aft on the flight deck, in the middle of torpedo-laden planes, and a second huge fire began. The *Akagi* turned into the wind, to push smoke and flames aft, but the heat was so intense that the damage control parties could not get near the fires. The captain of the *Akagi* told Admiral Nagumo he ought to leave the ship. The *Akagi*'s radio was going out. But Nagumo would not leave. Soon the fires became so bad that the captain ordered the ship abandoned, but the admiral furiously refused to leave his bridge. Reason prevailed when the captain said he could no longer even send a talk-between-ships message. The flagship was entirely out of touch with the fleet. Then, had the crewmen of the *Akagi* been of ironic turn of mind, they would have wondered at the sight of the hero of Pearl Harbor scrambling down a hawser to board a destroyer, followed by an officer bearing the carefully wrapped portrait of the emperor.

At almost the same time that *Akagi* was hit, other sections of dive-bombers went after the *Kaga*. The first bomb blew up the bridge, killing the captain of the ship and every other man there; the second went through the flight deck and exploded on the hangar deck, and in a moment the deck was alive with flames. Bombs and torpedoes began popping like giant firecrackers. More bombs struck, but they were not needed; that second bomb had done its work. The emperor's portrait and a thousand men were taken off; the rest stayed to fight the fire.

The *Soryu* was almost ready to launch planes, when three waves of American came out of the sky. One bomb struck near the forward elevator, one near the aft elevator, one went straight into the hangar deck. The story was the same as with the other two carriers. In minutes the fires were out of control, and after twenty minutes the captain gave the "abandon ship" order.

Only the *Hiryu* remained. At noon, Admiral Nagumo had moved to the cruiser *Nagara*, where he had a message from the captain of the *Hiryu* that his planes were attacking an enemy carrier. It was the *Yorktown*, and the Japanese bombers repaid her for what had happened to their three carriers. One bomb exploded in the funnel and put several boilers out of action. Her speed fell from twenty knots to six, and then the *Yorktown* went dead in the water. Other bombs continued to fall on her. One hit a storeroom near some gasoline storage tanks on the hangar deck and exploded in the ship's supply of oakum, tree bark used to stuff the cracks on the flight deck. This highly flammable material began to burn fiercely, but the fire fighters managed to control it and the other fires. In an hour the boilers were repaired and the *Yorktown* was making twenty knots. In the meantime, Admiral Fletcher had transferred his flag to the cruiser *Astoria* and given tactical command of the battle to Admiral Spruance. Japanese planes attacked again and started more fires, and *Yorktown* was abandoned.

The *Hiryu* continued to operate until five o'clock in the afternoon, when the planes of *Enterprise* came back for a second strike. Not all these planes were actually those of the *Enterprise*'s squadrons. After the *Yorktown* was hit, its planes landed on the *Enterprise* and the *Hornet*. So several strikes were launched, and one of these found the last remaining Japanese carrier. Soon the *Hiryu* was a mass of flame, then she was abandoned. Rear Admiral Yamaguchi, commander of Carrier Division Two, decided that since his *Soryu* and *Hiryu* were both destroyed, he would go down with the latter ship. All the officers and men were sent off to rescuing destroyers, and Yamaguchi and the captain of the *Hiryu* waited on the bridge for the end. "We will watch the moon together," said the admiral.

As the moon came up and the carriers went down, Admiral Spruance was struggling with the biggest decision of his career. Should he give chase to the enemy fleet, now that four carriers were destroyed? He knew that out to the west was a large enemy fleet, just how large he did not know, but he had to assume that it contained several battleships. He had none. Nor were the Americans well-skilled at night fighting, while the Japanese were expert. Another consideration was the possibility of attack from one or more enemy carriers. No one knew the whereabouts of those other carriers, but the Americans did know that Japan had more than were apparently committed at Midway. Balancing danger and opportunity, Spruance decided to head east, away from the enemy.

Spruance's decision probably saved his fleet. Admiral Yamamoto wanted a surface engagement that night. After he learned of the fate of his carriers, Admiral Nagumo transferred control of the battle to Admiral Abe, aboard the cruiser *Tone*. Admiral Abe ordered the attack force to withdraw. Admiral Yamamoto intervened and ordered Admiral Kondo to take the striking force to Midway for a night bombardment, hoping to draw the Americans into a surface action. Spruance's decision thwarted Yamamoto's hope.

In the morning, the Japanese defeat was underlined by the collision in mid-ocean of the cruisers *Mikuma* and *Mogami*, which headed immediately for Truk for repairs. As dawn came, the Americans turned west and launched planes again. All day long they searched, but they did not find the main striking force. Spruance now supposed that the major elements of the fleet had turned back, and he still hoped to catch up with the last crippled carrier (*Hiryu*), which he believed to be still afloat. So he headed west that night.

The next morning search planes found the damaged *Mogami* and *Mikuma*. Dive-bombers sank the *Mikuma*. The *Mogami* was so badly damaged in this attack that when she reached Truk, she was in the repair yard for a full year.

So the Japanese failed to take Midway Island and lure the American fleet to destruction. Their one shred of satisfaction was in the sinking of the *Yorktown*, hit by bombers first and finally torpedoed by a Japanese submarine. But for the first time in the war the losses to Japan had been enormous. More than five hundred of her most highly trained airmen went down with their planes or the carriers, a loss that was to dog Japan through the rest of the Pacific war. The loss of the four carriers put an end to the "striking force" as a major element of the fleet.

As for the Americans, the Midway battle proved the incompetence of the American torpedo squadrons; not that the pilots were less than brave or less than efficient, but their aircraft were built for the previous war, not this one, and although they still did not know it, the torpedoes they carried were more likely to malfunction than to sink ships. As constituted, the aerial torpedo squadron of the United States Navy was little more than a suicide squad, and one with little chance of success. The loss of *every plane* of the "Torpedo Eight" in the first strike against the carriers was a warning. Nimitz heeded it. He called the *TBD*s "fatally inadequate" and moved swiftly to get them out of the fleet. Happily, the navy was already producing the new *TBF*, a much faster and better protected plane than the old bomber. But torpedo experts were not yet paying attention to the reports of malfunction of both aerial and submarine torpedoes.

The battle of the Coral Sea had been a new experience, the first sea battle in which two opposing naval forces fought without ever laying eyes on one another. The British attack on the Italian fleet at Taranto and the Japanese attacks at Pearl Harbor and Trincomalee had established the aircraft carrier as the prime naval weapon of this war. (The sinking of the *Bismarck* had helped too). The Battle of Midway showed beyond doubt how important the carrier had become. The battle had been fought by the men of the carriers and the men of the submarines, and those elements of the fleets had decided everything. After the Battle of Midway, Admiral Nimitz said he believed it was the greatest sea battle since Jutland and that it would end Japanese expansion in the Pacific.

He was not quite right. When Admiral Yamamoto went limping home to Tokyo, tight-lipped and self-confined to his cabin for several days, he kept his thoughts to himself. Admiral Nagumo came aboard the *Yamato* before the fleet docked, weary and bedraggled, and announced to his aides that he would commit suicide. He was dissuaded from this course, but his career was wrecked. He was sent ashore and ended the war, and his life, as a garrison commander in the battle for Saipan.

Turning Point at Midway?

Admiral Yamamoto had never liked Nagumo, but he did not openly blame his underling for the defeat. Indeed, readers of Japanese newspapers did not know there had been a defeat. On June 10, 1942, Imperial Headquarters announced that two United States carriers had been sunk, one Japanese carrier had been lost, and that Midway was a resounding victory for Japan. To make sure the country continued to believe that story, the surviving officers and men of the striking force were immediately confined to base in Kyushu so they could not tell the true story, then transferred swiftly to other posts. The enlisted men were moved immediately to the South Pacific, and never saw their families until the end of the war—if they were lucky enough to survive.

Japan had suffered a blow, but she had not yet changed policy. The Imperial General Staff had not decided to curtail expansion, and the buildup along the line from the Bismarck Islands to New Guinea continued. It seemed apparent that the Japanese would soon move to cut Australia off from the United States.

Yamamoto had worried that the Tojo policy of building national morale by bragging would lay the country low in the end. For the first time, after Midway, the government embarked on a program of outright lies to the people, concealing losses, a policy that would continue until the end of the war.

That was when Admiral Yamamoto knew that all was lost.

16

Carlson's "Foolish" Foray

~~~~~~~

THE AMERICAN VICTORY AT MIDWAY had saved the war, but it did not mean the war was anywhere near over. The basic problem facing Admiral Nimitz, with which he had lived since December, 1941, was the American commitment to the war in Europe, which demanded first priority. To Nimitz the Pacific was everything but to King it was just then less than half the problem. Beginning shortly after Pearl Harbor the Nazis had launched a U-boat attack along the east coast of the United States which had cost the allies far more than the disaster at Pearl Harbor. In a few days in January, Commander Hardegan's *U-123* alone had sunk fifty-three thousand tons of American and British ships off the United States coast, damage equivalent to that accomplished by thirty thousand bombing missions. In the spring of 1942, the Petroleum Industry War Council assessed the damage done by the U-boats in the first three months of the year and announced that at the then current rate of sinkings half the tankers that served the east coast of the United States would be sunk by the end of the year, and there would not be enough fuel to continue the war effort. One major problem was the shortage of anti-submarine craft. The American navy had totally ignored anti-submarine warfare in the period between the wars. The destroyer was the smallest vessel built by the navy but what was needed were the smaller corvettes or destroyer escorts, which were cheaper and easy to build. That spring the situation grew so desperate on the United States's eastern seaboard that Britain lent the United States a dozen converted trawlers and taught the Americans how to use them. Much of King's effort was directed at resolving this ship problem, which was far more menacing than any other. For several months longer, Nimitz would simply

147

have to get along and fight the war in the Pacific with what he had. King did send the carrier *Wasp*, the new battleship *North Carolina*, the cruiser *Quincy*, and seven destroyers to augment the slender Pacific Fleet. He spared these vessels because he and Nimitz were already planning an offensive action in the South Pacific as soon as they could manage it. Just when that would be no one was quite certain. The landing of the Japanese in the Aleutians, which had been the one part of the Japanese Midway plan that succeeded, was a worrisome development that must be watched. The Japanese foothold was no more than troublesome at the moment; the danger would come if there was a Japanese buildup in the Aleutians. The main impetus had to be on the South Pacific for the Japanese could not be allowed to cut the lines to Australia. No matter what it cost Nimitz he would have to prevent that development.

One of the serious problems of the Pacific Fleet just then was the lack of intelligence about the Japanese forces. What little information was available came largely from the United States submarines for there were not enough long-range planes available yet to do what the Japanese did so well: scout the enemy at long range from the air. Admiral Nimitz still went to San Francisco to meet Admiral King every month, and in May they discussed the need for an aggressive operation. The Port Moresby effort of May was certainly going to be followed by the Japanese with something else. But what would it be and where would it come from?

Down in Australia the Australians gave General MacArthur a better appraisal of Japanese power in the South Pacific than the navy had. He suggested that if the navy would give him a battleship or two, and a carrier or two, he would set out and capture Rabaul. He knew (which the navy did not seem to appreciate) that Rabaul was the major Japanese base in the area. King and Nimitz were forever talking about Truk, the big naval base. But Rabaul was the key and it would continue to be. King opposed the Rabaul operation, probably because it would put MacArthur in the driver's seat in the Pacific, and so the idea died. But something had to be done.

One deficiency, which had to be remedied before the navy could ever undertake its traditional campaign to defeat Japan by crossing the Central Pacific, was to secure intelligence about the area. In the absence of long-range aircraft, the Gilbert and the Marshall Islands were unknown quantities. The Japanese had been in control there since the First World War and in the 1930s had begun fortification. What had happened since then no one knew, for at that same time the Japanese had stopped visitors from coming to those islands. The hydrographic details were kept secret and the only charts released to the world were inaccurate, probably purposefully so. What was needed then was intelligence, and somehow Nimitz had to get it.

The opportunity seemed to present itself that spring when the Second

Raider Battalion appeared at Pearl Harbor. This unit was led by Lieutenant Colonel Evans Carlson, a veteran of World War I who had spent several years observing the Chinese communist armies in action. For many years, Carlson had advocated the development of shock troops who would use new guerilla war tactics. The United States Marine high command had been impressed by the performance of British and Canadian commando troops in quick raids against the Germans so they agreed to the concept of Marine Raider units. The Raiders were to be shock troops among shock troops—for that is what the marines were anyhow. They were trained into magnificent physical condition, they knew every trick of killing, and they were on Oahu island in the summer of 1942, itching for something to do. Admiral Nimitz decided they might bring him some valuable information about the Pacific islands, and it was worth the gamble of launching a probe.

Admiral Nimitz was intrigued by his "private army" as he called the Raiders. He talked to Carlson several times about places and plans. They even discussed a raid on Hokkaido in the heart of the Japanese homeland. That would certainly give the Japanese something to think about. But that plan was rejected as too suicidal. They considered a raid on Wake, but really the Americans knew much about Wake since it had been an American base for years before the war.

Part of the Raider Battalion had been sent to bolster the defenses of Midway. But half remained on Oahu, training every day. Nimitz put two of his submarines at their disposal for training, and the men practiced landing in rubber boats, in the dark, through booming surf. One night, they staged a show for the brass: they came in by submarine off the coast, got into their rubber boats, and moved to within fifty feet of Nimitz and his staff officers before announcing themselves. If this had been a Japanese command post, it would have been all over before a shot was fired.

Everyone on the staff was impressed by that performance, not the least Admiral Spruance, who had returned to his job as Nimitz's chief of staff when Halsey got out of the hospital. Spruance also knew that Nimitz planned to make him commander of a new force to be used in the Central Pacific drive. So Spruance suggested that the Raiders could be very useful if they would secure some information about the Japanese buildup in the Gilbert Islands. Nimitz agreed, and in July it was decided. There was another reason than simply the intelligence-gathering: the plans were already made for an American strike against the Japanese buildup in the South Pacific. Carlson's raid on the Gilberts, far to the north, should confuse the Japanese and ought to cause them to divert some of their defense forces from the Solomon Islands where the major effort was to be made. Japanese aerial and submarine observers, even if they sighted the invasion fleet in mid-Pacific, might be confused into believing it was heading to support the Raiders on Makin Island, the point of the Gilberts atoll that Nimitz had selected since it was the largest and apparently most important.

The plan did not quite work out. There were delays at Pearl Harbor and there could be no delays in the Solomons campaign because on July 5 Admiral Nimitz learned that the Japanese were beginning to build an airfield on Guadalcanal Island. King had been agitating for action to stop the Japanese buildup since the Coral Sea days, and now he demanded immediate action. Nimitz said he did not have adequate forces, but King was not to be denied. The Japanese had established a perfect communications line that ran from Tokyo down to Rabaul. Planes could be flown all the way, island hopping. Supplies could be moved swiftly and relatively safely by ship. Guadalcanal and Tulagi and Santa Cruz Islands were all potentially dangerous bases for attacks against Australia, and they must be captured. "Operation Watchtower," Admiral King called it. "Operation Shoestring," Nimitz called it privately. But he did not argue. One of his great attributes was his ability to quarrel with an idea, but to accept it wholeheartedly once superior authority had made a decision.

On August 7, 1942, the marines landed on Guadalcanal. The Carlson mission could not fool the Japanese in the way it had been intended, but it still could be valuable, Nimitz decided.

Also he still needed that information, for after Guadalcanal, the next United States move would be into the Central Pacific, maybe indeed the Gilberts.

So on the submarine dock at Pearl Harbor the men of two companies of the battalion boarded the submarines *Nautilus* and *Argonaut*, singing to the tune of "Abdul the Bulbul Amir":

> They will sing of the sailor and
> soldier, I know,
> And tell of the deeds that were done.
> But Carlson's Raiders will sing for
> themselves,
> And know that the battle was won.

Morale could not have been higher as these 221 officers and men headed for Makin atoll, a thousand miles north of Guadalcanal, to carry out a mission that was now termed "diversionary."

The submarines arrived early on the morning of August 16 but waited until the darkness of night to move in toward shore and land the troops just off the beach of Butaritari Island. The weather was bad, the swells were running high, and on deck the Raiders could hardly hear orders as they assembled to go into the rubber boats. As they did so the boats took on water and the outboard motors refused to start. Carlson had predicted this when Cincpac Supply had given him this particular brand of motor. He had asked for

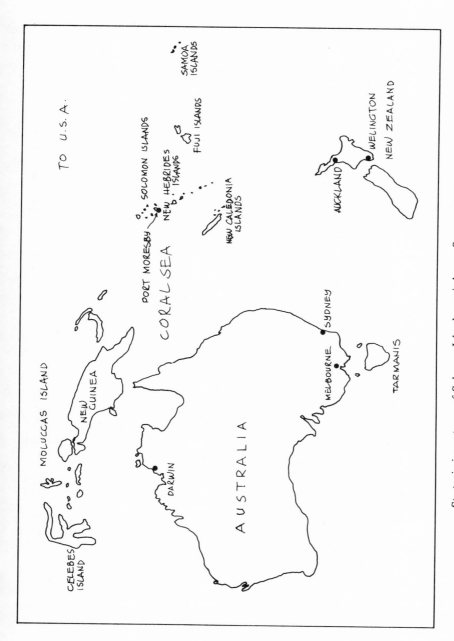

Strategic importance of Solomon Islands as air bases, Summer 1942

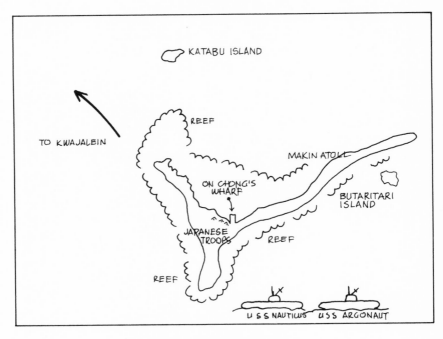

Carlson's Raid, August 1942

replacements, but outboard motors seemed a small thing to Cincpac Supply with a global war on, and he had not gotten them. So they rowed, eighteen boatloads of men heading against the wind into the beach. One boat got separated from the others and landed on the wrong beach, which put Japanese soldiers between the elements. But there were not many Japanese soldiers in between, for there were only forty-three Japanese soldiers on the whole island. They were dug in on the lagoon side, where they might expect the enemy to land. Instead the Raiders had come in from the ocean side.

On landing, one marine accidentally discharged his rifle, arousing the Japanese garrison. As the marines came up the road toward Kukianggong Point, the Japanese dug in and began firing rifles and machine guns. Some Japanese snipers tied themselves to palm trees, and they began firing too. The Japanese had half-expected some sort of attack in these islands and had alerted the defenders, but they had not had time to reinforce the garrison. The word was now out, and two Japanese freighters on the edge of the harbor, which had been coming in to On Chong's Wharf, turned about and headed for the open sea. They carried reinforcements for the garrison, but the troops never arrived that day. The *Nautilus* began firing at the ships with her deck gun and damaged one ship so badly she went dead in the water. The other escaped.

Carlson moved up the island taking notes about the defenses. His radio-men said the Japanese radio station was still working, calling Jaluit and Mille for reinforcement. In the afternoon two flying boats, two smaller seaplanes, and four two-engine Betty bombers appeared to bomb and strafe the Raiders. Four Zero fighters escorting them made strafing runs of their own. The flying boats landed in the lagoon and reinforcements for the garrison went ashore. The Raiders fired on the flying boats and damaged them so they could not take off.

By late afternoon the Raiders' position was most unpleasant. The defenders had machine guns, mortars, and field pieces, and they harassed the Americans constantly. More enemy bombers came over and bombed. Proba-bly more reinforcements could be expected that night, Carlson decided. It was time to withdraw in spite of the fact that Carlson had not accomplished his whole mission. He had intended to cover the island, destroy the radio and the port facilities, and pick up all the printed information he could, including code books and material about troop dispositions in the Gilberts. But the Japanese had responded too swiftly and were obviously going to respond even more vigorously the following day. So it was time to get out.

The marines got into their boats and tried to make it through the surf, but without those outboard motors on which they had been depending in the days ashore when the plans were made, they could not force the rubber boats through the surf. Less than half the men made it to the two submarines, and some of those swam part of the way. More than a hundred men were stranded on the beach, including Lieutenant Colonel Carlson, who had stayed until the last boat. They formed a defensive perimeter there and waited. The Japanese harried them that night. Next morning Carlson sent a patrol out for food and ammunition. The Japanese had decided all the Americans had escaped and had withdrawn to their garrison at the end of the island. But Carlson and Major James Roosevelt, his second in command, got four boats through to the waiting submarines. Five Raiders volunteered to go back to shore with food and ammunition and help get the others off. They got into a boat and made it halfway across the distance. Then a flight of seaplanes appeared over head, coming in to bomb the submarines and the beach. The subma-rines crash-dived and the boat was left alone in the water. The seaplanes came in low, strafing, and turned and came in again. They made several passes at the rubber boat, and when they moved away the boat was sinking and all five marines in it were dead.

Seventy marines were left on the beach. They stayed all day, suffering several more air raids. Finally, that night most of them got off. Eighteen marines were left dead on the island. At the very last, friendly islanders prom-ised Carlson they would bury the American dead (and they did). A dozen men were missing, somehow strayed from the perimeter. Later they were captured, taken to Kwajalein, and executed by the Japanese as "spies," a deed for which Admiral Abe, commander of the Marshalls, was finally hanged as a war criminal after the Japanese surrender.

So the men of Carlson's Raiders returned to Pearl Harbor, where they were greeted with a brass band and public relations officers made sure on Nimitz's orders that the story of the raid was given the widest publicity. In America the Raiders became folk heroes overnight. The raid was announced as an enormously successful blow against the Japanese and the intelligence aspects were not even mentioned. Carlson had secured some materials which were of use to Fleet Intelligence, but in reality, although the raid did divert some Japanese aircraft and a few Japanese troops who probably would never have been sent to Guadalcanal anyhow, it did not accomplish what Nimitz and his staff had hoped. Quite to the contrary, the raid indicated to the Japanese that the Americans were planning to invade the Gilbert Islands, and the Japanese high command in Tokyo took warning. That summer orders were given to increase the fortifications of the Gilberts and the Marshalls and to strengthen the garrisons. Instead of a handful of troops in these islands, there would be thousands. It was not Evans Carlson's fault that the American high command's planning had gone astray, but in the end, the Makin raid was to cost the Americans far more than it gained.

17

Gauntlet
at Guadalcanal

WHATEVER ADMIRAL YAMAMOTO SAID to the Imperial General Staff about the defeat at Midway, he gave no sign of distress to his subordinates, and from all outward appearances it would have seemed that he was completely assured that the next move, the assault on Australia, would be successful. Reinforcements and a steady supply of construction materials moved southward to Truk and Rabaul. The Japanese navy built up its air bases at Buka, Bougainville, and Shortlands. A seaplane base was constructed at Tulagi, and in the Lunga district of Guadalcanal Island an air base was nearly completed in July. Admiral Yamamoto's plan was to use that Guadalcanal airfield to stage day and night raids on Australia, shuttling down from Rabaul, stopping at Guadalcanal for fuel, bombing Australia and the waters around that continent, returning to Guadalcanal for refueling.

Months before, Admiral King had begun planning for an American invasion. Rear Admiral Richmond Kelly Turner, who was then King's chief plans officer, tried to persuade the army that action in the South Pacific was essential to stop the Japanese drive against Australia. The chief opponent of this view was General Dwight D. Eisenhower, who wanted every bit of American war production for the European theater. Turner had watched as the Japanese moved south. He saw that the Tulagi takeover of May 3, 1942, which resulted in the Battle of the Coral Sea, had put Japanese air power almost in position to cut off communication between Australia and the United States. One more step was all that was needed.

Admiral King had been saying just this for months at Joint Chiefs of Staff Meetings with the army turning a deaf ear. For Eisenhower was pressing—and General Marshall agreed—for an invasion of the Cherbourg peninsula in the fall of 1942. The Russians were urging the western allies to establish a second front against the Germans, and every time the Pacific was mentioned, nearly everyone but the United States Navy squelched the talk. But Australia was concerned about the growing Japanese threat and was able to arouse Winston Churchill to the danger. General MacArthur transmitted this worry to the Joint Chiefs of Staff. At the end of June, entirely on his own authority, Admiral King ordered Admiral Turner to leave his planning post and prepare for an offensive against Tulagi and the Santa Cruz Islands and to strengthen American forces in New Caledonia. Turner did not know where his offensive would be or exactly when it would start. Early in July, Turner was planning the occupation of Ndeni Island, the most western of the Santa Cruz group, the capture of Tulagi, and the capture of little Guadalcanal where he thought they ought to build an air field. He did not know that the Japanese were already building one. Then, on July 5 came the word to Nimitz's headquarters: the Japanese field was nearly finished.

It had taken a long time for the word of the Japanese advance to reach Admiral King. On May 22, an army plane saw a Japanese photo reconnaissance plane working over Guadalcanal, and Army Intelligence suggested that the Japanese were planning an airfield, which was the only logical reason for the activity. The news filtered through channels and did not get to King or Nimitz. On June 25, Army Intelligence reported that the grass on the central plain of the island had been burned off and that a wharf was under construction at Lunga.

Admiral King did learn of this and told Nimitz to find out what was going on. Nimitz ordered an aerial reconnaissance, but the air observers did not see anything. On July 1, Australian coastwatchers on Guadalcanal reported that building of the Japanese airfield was only awaiting the arrival of two Japanese construction units, and they were expected within the week. That dispatch aroused Admiral Nimitz. Then, Fleet Intelligence brought him a confirming Japanese naval radio message which named the 11th and 13th Pioneer forces as the two Japanese units and announced July 4 as the date of their arrival.

At that moment, Admiral Turner was at Pearl Harbor on his way to the South Pacific with vague orders to prepare for an amphibious landing. It was immediately apparent that the landing had to be at Guadalcanal. But when? The trouble was, as Turner saw it, that "neither the troops, ships nor aircraft assigned to the project are adequately trained in amphibious warfare." He had to remedy that deficiency in a matter of three weeks. He did have the First Marine Raider Battalion, counterpart to Carlson's Raiders, trained for just this sort of action. The First Raiders were moved from Samoa to Noumea,

New Caledonia, much closer to the Solomons. Ships and men began to assemble, to stage an invasion rehearsal in Fiji.

Admiral Ghormley, who had been made Admiral Nimitz's commander in the South Pacific, had no taste for the coming operation. When Ghormley went down to Melbourne to confer with General MacArthur, he discovered that the general did not believe it could be successful. Their common concern was that the Japanese had so many airfields and so many planes in the region that the enemy would have indisputable control of the air. The two commanders recommended that the operation be deferred indefinitely.

Admiral King was adamant. The Japanese *must* be stopped and they must be stopped at the Solomons. The request to defer was denied and preparations were speeded by the navy. In the Joint Chiefs of Staff meetings King also made much of the MacArthur-Ghormley plea that the South and Southwest Pacific did not have enough aircraft. That was true, he said, because the United States was more concerned with meeting lend-lease commitments to Britain and the USSR and building up a plane reserve for the invasion of North Africa. The army had to reverse policy, he said, and it did: the first *B-17* bombers began to move toward the South Pacific.

Still, there was so little concern among the other armed services in Washington and even in MacArthur's command, that no one paid much attention to what was going on at Guadalcanal. The Japanese construction gangs were building quickly, yet on July 10 the only note of it in the Joint Intelligence Committee report in Washington was a casual comment that "there are indications of construction of an airfield" on Guadalcanal. Ten days later there was another casual note: "runway completed." When the intelligence men did become aware of the airfield, they located it on the wrong side of the island. In fact, before the end of the month the entire airfield was ready for operations, Admiral Yamamoto had scheduled the first island-hopping mission against the allies for August 14, and the fighter planes that would use Guadalcanal had already been selected and the orders issued.

The United States invasion of Guadalcanal was to be carried out by ten thousand marines and seventy-six ships. The ships met on July 25 south of Suva in the Fiji Islands. The warships had come from the United States west coast, from Australia, from Pearl Harbor, and the troops ships had come from San Diego, Noumea, and Samoa. On July 26, Admiral Fletcher called the senior officers to a conference aboard the *Saratoga*, which was the expedition's flagship. The final decisions were made here. Admiral Turner was extremely unhappy about one of them: the American carrier force that would protect the landing would stay near Guadalcanal for only two days. That decision represented the concern of Admirals Ghormley and Fletcher that the carriers might be lost to the superior Japanese land-based air force. Like so

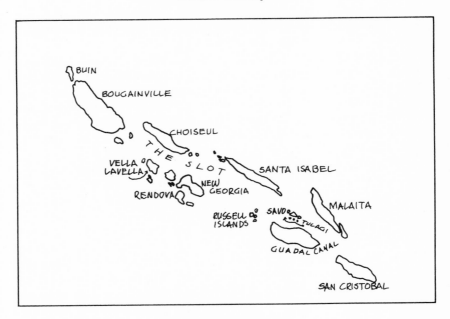

Solomon Islands

many of the admirals, these two talked of fighting the war in the way they had learned about it, and not the way the war had developed. The operation was too hurried, too badly planned, and could never succeed, said Fletcher. There was no point in that sort of argument, said Turner. The decision had been made and it was their job to carry it out. Admiral Ghormley was not even in attendance, although he had been ordered to take personal strategic command of the operation. By the end of the meeting, it was apparent that if anything went wrong, without the carriers, the landing force would be in a very tight spot. But Fletcher was not going to risk his carriers just because there was a war on. *Saratoga*, *Wasp*, and *Enterprise* must be protected.

The rehearsal for the invasion was held from July 28 to 31. It was most unsatisfactory. The foul-ups began with communications and unreadable messages. Only a third of the troops actually landed on Koro island, the "invasion point." General Alexander Vandegrift of the marines regarded the rehearsal as "a complete bust." But it was the best the Americans could do. There was no more time; the Guadalcanal invasion must go on if the Japanese expansion was to be stopped.

The run from the Fijis to Guadalcanal took six days. At noon on August 5, the United States force neared the Russell Islands, which lie northeast of

158

the Solomons. On the next afternoon, the twenty-six ships of the carrier groups broke off and disappeared to the south. (Fletcher would have his planes over Guadalcanal, but he was taking the carriers as far from harm as possible.) Fortunately for the Americans, the weather on August 6 was cloudy and rainy, and Japanese air reconnaissance flights from Rabaul and other air bases were called off, so the enemy did not see the approaching invasion force. By midnight on August 6, 1942, the United States fleet approached the shore of Guadalcanal but no Japanese activity was noted. The Japanese were completely unaware of the American approach. That somnolence continued until after dawn on August 7 when two Japanese seaplanes took off from their anchorage near Lunga point on Guadalcanal just after six in the morning on routine patrol, and there below they saw an American invasion fleet. The American ships saw the seaplanes too, and knowing they were discovered the American ships began firing on the shore.

The Japanese commander of the air base at Tulagi sent a message to Rabaul, and that is how Admiral Nimitz had his first word that the action had begun, through his radio intelligence unit at Pearl Harbor. Then, at 7:15, Nimitz had another message, courtesy of the Japanese: "the enemy has landed."

In all, nineteen thousand and five hundred Unites States marines were committed to this action. Ten thousand of the marines were to land on Guadalcanal but four thousand would take Tulagi, Gavutu, and Florida Islands, and the rest would be held in reserve. At 6:15 A.M. the landing craft had been started, and just after seven o'clock the first troops were ashore. The First Raider Battalinn and the Second Battalion of the Fifth Marine Regiment landed on Tulagi, which was regarded as a major Japanese strongpnint. The ten thousand marines landed on Guadalcanal, and others moved into Gavutu, Tanambogo, and Florida Island. After some fierce fighting, Tulagi was de clared secure at the end of August 8. It had not been a stronghold after all.

The initial landings on Guadalcanal were deceptively easy. One transport was lost and eleven fighter planes and a dive-bomber were destroyed, but that was much less damage than had been expected. Japanese submarines, which had worried Admiral Turner, were nowhere to be seen. On that first day, fourteen United States transports lay off the narrow beaches and unloaded as quickly as the beachmasters could force the pace. By the end of the second day, the marines had fought their way to the airstrip. What were needed immediately, Admiral Turner said, were airplanes, for Admiral Fletcher insisted on moving his carriers out of the area. No one of less rank than Nimitz could have persuaded him to do otherwise, for Fletcher was determined to take no risks, and Nimitz at this stage did not know what Fletcher was doing. Fletcher had lost the *Lexington* at the Coral Sea and the *Yorktown* at Midway, and he could not bear to lose more carriers. So, as the Japanese prepared to counterattack, the American forces ashore were virtually defenseless against air attack.

For the first few hours after the American landings, Admiral Yamamoto believed this invasion was a raid, like that of Carlson on Makin. But at the end of the first day the word came from Guadalcanal that this was not just a raid; there were too many American troops ashore and too many United States transport ships along the beaches. Yamamoto dispatched Vice Admiral Gunichi Mikawa with five cruisers, two light cruisers, and one destroyer to challenge the American force. Trusting in their superiority as night fighters, they intended to come down on the American ships at night.

Late on the afternoon of August 8, 1942, the Americans learned of the Japanese ship movement. Shortly after Admiral Turner was warned, he also had word from Admiral Fletcher that instead of attacking the enemy again, he was withdrawing his carriers completely from the area. Turner had been warned at the outset, but he did not expect this when Fletcher knew there was a Japanese force steaming down on him. Turner knew he was in trouble, but he did not know the full extent. The Japanese force had been sighted quite early in the day, but the pilot had failed to make a report for almost eight hours, and then it was understated. Two destroyers, three cruisers, and two gunboats were coming down, the narrow slot between islands, said the pilot. But details as to where they were heading and when they would arrive were vague. Deprived of air support, Turner decided he had to stop the unloading and move the transports away from the beaches. He warned General Vandegrift that the transports would leave the area at six o'clock the next morning.

As Fletcher retired, the Japanese came on steadily. They headed around New Ireland and then north of Bougainville and into the long channel that runs from Shortland Island to Guadalcanal, past Choiseul, New Georgia, on the one side and Santa Isabel on the other, and then past the Russell Islands.

Admiral Turner's defensive force was scattered. The sound between Tulagi and Guadalcanal was divided into three sectors. Admiral V. A. C. Crutchley of the Royal Australian Navy was in charge of the southern force of cruisers and destroyers. He had no ship-to-ship radio aboard his vessel and the Australians were not familiar with American naval procedures; there had been no time for training. Captain Frederick Riefkohl was in charge of the northern force of cruisers and destroyers. Rear Admiral Norman Scott had a force of cruisers to the eastern side and two destroyers on the west.

Admiral Mikawa came in through the destroyers, luckily (for him) finding the weakest point. Neither destroyer even saw the Japanese ships—an apt commentary on the state of American night fighting. Float planes had been put in the air above the Japanese force, and as the ships came down at three o'clock in the morning, the planes flew over the American ships and dropped flares, which lighted them brightly for the Japanese gunners. They opened

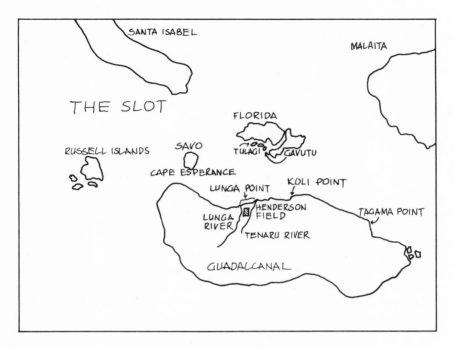

Guadalcanal, October 1942

fire with deadly accuracy. The *Canberra* was the first ship sunk. The destroyer *Patterson* was then hit and damaged. The cruiser *Chicago* was torpedoed, her bow blown off. The Japanese then turned north and struck Captain Riefkohl's ships. They sank the *Astoria*, then the *Quincy*, and then the *Vincennes*. The destroyer *Ralph Talbot* was badly damaged.

The Japanese paid no attention to the transports on the beaches, which they could have destroyed, because dawn was coming, and they fully expected American carriers to begin launching planes. Admiral Mikawa turned and sped at high speed northward to avoid the carriers.

But it was totally unnecessary; the timid Fletcher had moved far south. Captain Forrest Sherman, the commander of the *Wasp*, asked Admiral Leigh Noyes, his immediate chief, for permission to move forward and attack that morning. Noyes, who knew how Fletcher felt about risking even one carrier, did not transmit the message to Fletcher at all. So the Japanese steamed home, totally unhurt. The one effective American action was taken later that day by the American submarine *S-44*, which tracked and sank the cruiser *Kako*, far from the scene of the night's activity.

The naval battle was a stunning defeat for the Americans and showed an ineptness that was really surprising. The Americans called the battle "Savo," after the island off the shore of Guadalcanal where the *Astoria*, *Quincy* and *Vincennes* were sunk, and a junior officer aptly named the area "Iron Botton Sound." To the Japanese, who had very little respect for American fighting abilities, the thirty-five-minute battle had come out just about as expected. They were not given to romanticizing such affairs, and later called it the "First Battle of the Solomons."

Admirals King and Nimitz were more than a little upset; when the facts came out, it was discovered that Admiral Ghormley had never known what was going on that night although he was in overall command. Admiral Fletcher had left the scene hurriedly to avoid a fight and never tried to get back in. Many of the junior commanders had acted less than brilliantly. In all, it was a sad performance, and the only officers who came out of it creditably were Admirals Turner and Crutchley, who were in fact conferring aboard Turner's flagship just as the Japanese moved in.

On the morning after the battle, the transports moved out to safety, leaving eleven thousand marines stranded on the beach at Guadalcanal with only a small part of their supplies unloaded. As far as the land action was concerned, the marines were in no immediate trouble. There were only about 2,000 Japanese on the island, most of them laborers, and they had all retreated to the other side of the airfield, which the Americans now named "Henderson Field" in honor of an officer killed at Midway. But Japanese planes from Rabaul immediately began attacking the beaches and the airfield, and they came down every day like swarms of deadly bees.

Air reconnaissance told Admiral Yamamoto that the American assault was a major action which needed immediate attention, so he decided to move his headquarters from the Tokyo area to the the South Pacific. The *Yamato* headed for Truk after ordering that Guadalcanal was to be reinforced.

On August 23, Fletcher was fueling his ships far from any scene where action might occur. Meanwhile the Japanese were coming to Guadalcanal with two fleet carriers, a light carrier, an escort carrier, a seaplane carrier, and several battleships, cruisers, and destroyers, escorting several transports loaded with Japanese troops.

Fletcher was forced into a fight, with the *Enterprise* and the *Saratoga*. This "Second Battle of Guadalcanal," as the Japanese termed it, ended in an American victory. The carrier *Ryujo* was sunk and the *Shokaku* was damaged, and the army troops destined for Guadalcanal never made it there. The *Enterprise* was damaged by bombs, but not seriously.

Admiral Yamamoto arrived at Truk on August 26 to learn of the Japanese defeat. Again he ordered relief for Guadalcanal, this time by destroyers. In the next few weeks, many ships were sunk on both sides. The Japanese lost the destroyer *Mutsuki*; the Americans, the fast transport *Calhoun*. The

Saratoga took another torpedo and had to go home again for repairs. Most important, the Japanese *were* landing reinforcements, thousands of them. The land battle for Guadalcanal began then. General Kiyotake Kawaguchi had orders to retake the airfield, then the whole island and drive the Americans into the sea.

The battle of the Tenaru River was the first vicious struggle. The Americans won, but the fighting continued, and General Vandegrift's marines began to feel the shortage of supplies. The Japanese had even more serious supply problems. The two navies and air forces were fighting a battle of attrition. It was infuriating, said Admiral Ugaki, chief of staff to Admiral Yamamoto; the Japanese sent ships and planes, and they shot the Americans out of the sky and sank them into the sea, "we shoot them down and we shoot them down, but they only send in more." In Washington, where the politicians were restless after the disaster at Savo Island, Admiral King seemed almost nonchalant. The losses had been heavy, he said, but not seriously so in view of the fact that the United States was switching from the defensive to the offensive. Some more losses must be expected.

Early in September, a small man with a face like a bulldog appeared in the South Pacific dressed in khaki but with no insignia. One naval officer who saw him at Pearl Harbor thought he was the typewriter repairman from Honolulu. He was actually James V. Forrestal, undersecretary of the Navy, and a man with a shrewd eye. He returned to Washington after a few days, with strong recommendations for a shake-up in the South Pacific command.

Forrestal's talk with Admiral King simply buttressed all King's own views. At the next San Francisco meeting, he brought up the matter with Nimitz, who, if he had a fault, was that of kindliness and loyalty to his fellow officers. But King had no such tender heartstrings, and he said bluntly that he did not think Ghormley and Fletcher and Noyes were doing the jobs they should be doing. And what about Admiral McCain? His planes had let the Japanese slip through the so-called net on the day before the battle of Savo Island. Was he not to be held responsible for that error? He probably should be, said Nimitz, but Turner had said that McCain should not be blamed. Admiral King cocked a cold blue eye at his favorite commander. Well, he would see, he said. Let McCain come on back to Washington for a while and he would look him over. Also Fletcher.

In the end, Fletcher was taken out of the fighting for good, and Admiral Noyes was relieved. McCain went back to Washington and seemed aggressive enough to King so that he soon had a fighting command. It could as easily have gone the other way. There was no time for tender treatment and no consideration for personalities was permitted. Certain jobs were to be done, and the officers intrusted with them were held responsible. They had one chance. If they failed it, they were out.

The big question remaining was *command*. Who was finally responsible for the disaster at Savo and what was to be done about it? Nimitz soon learned that the Japanese were succeeding in reinforcing their troops on Guadalcanal. What had looked like an easy victory in the first days of invasion was now turning into a major struggle, with the odds favoring the Japanese. Their lines of communication were much shorter than those of the Americans. The Japanese base system allowed the Gilbert, Marshall, and Bismarck Islands to serve as stationary carriers, while the Americans had only Henderson Field and that was under constant and heavy attack. The Japanese began a major effort to retake the island. In September, 1942, General Kawaguchi's soldiers began hacking their way through the jungle from Taivu on the eastern side of the island, toward Henderson Field.

General Vandegrift had gone on the defensive after the transports left his men high and dry and short of everything that counted. Supplies began to trickle in, but he needed more troops and brought the First Raider Battalion and the First Parachute Battalion over from Tulagi, where all was quiet. On Guadalcanal the fighting intensified. The marines fought by day and the Japanese "Tokyo Express" came down on them at night. That term was the marines' colorful way of describing the train of destroyers and cruisers the Japanese sent through the slot each night to shell the western beaches and Henderson Field and to keep the marines preoccupied, while on the eastern side of the island, the Japanese landed reinforcements and supplies. The third week of September was critical. The Japanese were attacking fiercely all around Henderson Field. In a week the 750-man Raider contingent dropped to 526, and the parachute troops who had come with them from Tulagi suffered almost fifty percent casualties. It was the same with the rest of the marine units on Guadalcanal. The Japanese attacked and attacked again; by day the Japanese planes hit the American positions, and by night the Japanese navy did the same. At the end of the third week of September there were no reserves left. If the marines were to hold Guadalcanal, it would be held by those marines on the island just then. They did hold, and September began to draw to a close.

On September 28, Admiral Nimitz came to Guadalcanal to see for himself what could be done to carry out Admiral King's orders that the island must be held and the Solomons cleared of Japanese at any cost.

At a meeting aboard the American flagship, Admiral Ghormley outlined the position for Nimitz. Guadalcanal was not being held by the Americans; they only had a foothold and possession of Henderson Field. The Japanese were all around them and increasing in number. The whole area was under constant observation and harassment. The navy could send in only one supply ship at a time and that ran the danger of bombing or enemy destroyer attack.

General Vandegrift had only one division of troops and one regiment. No one could even make an estimate of the number of Japanese troops on the island, because reinforcements came in every night. What Ghormley did not know was that Imperial Headquarters in Tokyo had made the recapture of Guadalcanal a prime mission for the Seventeenth Army. For the past three weeks General Kawaguchi had tried the storming tactics that had worked so well in the past against westerners, but against the marines they did not work at all. Japanese casualties were enormous. So Lieutenant General Haruyoshi Hayakutaki, commander of the Seventeenth Army, ordered a change in tactics. Just now it was relatively quiet on Guadalcanal, but only because the Japanese were bringing in reinforcements for the major offensive. General Hayakutaki was coming to Guadalcanal himself to lead it.

Admiral Nimitz conducted a brisk series of meetings with the commanders of the navy, army, and airforces. He could not fault General Vandegrift or his marines, who were holding on. He could not fault Admiral Turner, who against all odds, was managing somehow to keep Henderson Field supplied with gasoline and the marines supplied with badly-needed guns and food. As the conversations continued Nimitz saw that the fault lay at the top. Admiral Ghormley, who had opposed the operation in the beginning, still did not like it and did not seem to understand what was required of him. "If the Japs make a maximum effort there, we can't stop them," he said at one stage. Nimitz also recalled Admiral King's stern face as he announced that the Japanese *must* be stopped at Guadalcanal.

The matter of command became paramount in the second week of October. The Seventeenth Army reinforcements arrived at Guadalcanal, their transports guarded by a number of warships. So far, the Imperial Japanese Navy had controlled the seas and Iron Bottom Sound was virtually paved with the hulks of American warships. But Rear Admiral Norman Scott, the commander of the American cruiser force in the South Pacific, had been listening when Admiral Nimitz told his commanders that they must be more aggressive and take any calculated risks that seemed indicated. Scott came across the Japanese off Cape Esperance on the northern tip of Guadalcanal, just as the enemy transports were getting ready to move in and land troops and supplies. Scott engaged, and when the firing stopped, the Japanese had lost the heavy cruiser *Furutaka*, the destroyer *Fubuki*, and two other destroyers were damaged (and sunk the next day). The cruiser *Aoba* was seriously damaged, and Admiral Goto, the commander of the Japanese force, was mortally wounded. The Americans lost only the destroyer *Duncan*, and the cruisers *Boise* and *Salt Lake City* were damaged. It was, then, the first American naval victory in the Guadalcanal campaign after a series of reverses that included the loss of the carrier *Wasp* to a Japanese submarine. But the naval victory was overshadowed by what would be more important: the Japanese had managed to land General Hayakutaki's troops and supplies. The situation of the marines could become critical at any moment.

In spite of this development and Nimitz's constant urgings, Admiral Ghormley was acting like a sleepwalker. He did not even visit Guadalcanal to see for himself what was going on. He and General MacArthur still opposed the campaign, and Ghormley did not seem to recognize that Mac-Arthur's opposition was largely because it was an invasion of an area he considered to be his command.

In view of Ghormley's behavior and the worsening Japanese threat, Admiral Nimitz could see nothing but defeat facing the Americans unless something drastic was done immediately. Admiral Halsey had bounced back from his illness, grinning and vowing that he was ready to "eat Japs for breakfast." Nimitz decided to give him a chance to try. Halsey had been assigned the Fletcher air command in the South Pacific, but by the time he reached Noumea to join the force, Admiral Nimitz had changed his mind. Orders were waiting for Halsey. He was to take over the whole Guadalcanal operation.

"Jesus Christ and General Jackson," said Halsey as he was handed the message. Then he sat down to figure out how to win the war.

18

The Solomons
Slog-Along

~~~~~

Kill Japs,
Kill Japs,
Kill More Japs.

THAT SIGN HUNG above the fleet landing at Tulagi and was painted on the buildings at the Halsey headquarters in Noumea and Admiral Halsey closed every letter with the slogan. He made it very clear at the outset of his command of the South Pacific that every officer who *fought*—and never mind the consequences—was going to get along just fine. Any officer who did *not* fight was going to be relieved so fast he would not know what hit him.

On October 20, Halsey held a meeting with his commanders. Marine General Vandegrift and Army Air General Harmon told of the enormous difficulties of supply and fighting on Guadalcanal. The Japanese had brought in thousands of troops. They had air superiority. They had control of the seas. "Well," said Halsey. "Are we going to evacuate or hold?" "Hold," said Vandegrift. "If you can get us the help."

So Halsey sent his generals back to their posts with the promise that they would have everything he could secure for them. At the moment it was not much, that "everything." Admiral King had taken a calculated risk in ordering the invasion of Guadalcanal for there were no reserves available outside the South Pacific. But Halsey could make changes, and he did.

The help was little enough. General Vandegrift's marines were sick and tired after fighting for two and a half months. More than seven hundred cases of malaria were reported every week, and the rest of the twenty-two thousand men that Vandegrift had managed to bring in were nearly exhausted. The First Marine Raider Battalion was "shot," as he put it, and needed evacuation.

Admiral Turner convinced Admiral Halsey that a new airfield should be built on Guadalcanal at Aola Bay, fifty miles east of Lunga Point. The Second Raider Battalion was to land, secure the area, and then turn it over to the army infantry and the Seabees, the navy's construction battalions. But as the marines prepared for the assignment, their orders were changed. They were to march across the island toward Lunga Point and attack a new Japanese infantry regiment that had been landed by destroyers near Henderson Field. They did so, and came just in time to meet ten thousand new troops which the Japanese managed to bring in to follow Admiral Yamamoto's orders and recapture Henderson Field. Most of these troops were part of the Japanese Thirty-Eighth Division, which had been committed to Guadalcanal. But while the troops appeared, their supplies did not. American planes found the transports—eleven of them—and sank every one. So the offensive against Henderson Field was cut off on the beaches. The Raiders marched through, linked up with the marines on the Lunga Point side, and put the Japanese back on the defensive.

At sea, the battle went back and forth. Late in October, Admiral Yamamoto sent a strong force to deal with the American fleet. Relatively speaking the odds were not much better for Halsey than they had been for the Americans at Midway. The Japanese had four carriers, five battleships, and many supporting ships. The Americans had two carriers and two battleships, with support in scale. But on October 26, carrier planes of both sides found their enemies and attacked while the fleets were far apart. At the end of the action, the Japanese carrier *Zuiho* was badly damaged, the carrier *Shokaku* was hit so hard she had to go into drydock for nine months, and the cruiser *Chikuma* was also forced to go back to Truk for major repairs. On the other side, the Americans lost the carrier *Hornet*, and the carrier *Enterprise* was damaged, but not so seriously that she could not be repaired in the South Pacific.

Once again, as at Coral Sea, this battle was a tactical victory for the Japanese, but the American sacrifice prevented the Japanese from clearing the Solomons. Since General Hayakutaki had failed, Lieutenant General Hitoshi Imamura was given command of the Seventeenth *and* Eighteenth Armies and ordered to capture the Solomons and then secure strategic points on New Guinea for subsequent operations to continue the Japanese plan of cutting off Australia. In November, after three months of fighting, the Japanese aims were still unchanged.

At first, the Japanese had been totally contemptuous of the American infantrymen. Japanese army legend had it that the moment Americans were attacked on the beaches, they would flee, bawling at the tops of their voices. The Japanese army knew so little about the United States Marines that when one Japanese high naval officer came to Rabaul before Yamamoto got there he was asked what sort of unit this "Marine Corps" was. When he replied that these were shock troops, the army lost a bit of its contempt. "Ah," said the army officer, "something like the troops of the naval special attack force?" "Something like that," said the naval officer.

Reports reaching Rabaul from Guadalcanal showed that the Japanese army of this island had encountered something new in the way of resistance. Major Masanobu Tsuji had been sent down to Guadalcanal from Imperial Headquarters as liaison officer between the army and the navy. In October, Tsuji reported that the army forces on Guadalcanal were actually starving because the navy could not get supplies through to them. During November, Japanese transport ships were sunk in increasing numbers. Each unit on the island had been forced to decrease the daily food ration until at the end of October it was a sixth of the normal. When Admiral Yamamoto heard this news, no transports were available so he sent eight Japanese destroyers. They made the run successfully to the Japanese side of the island and landed supplies. The idea of deploying destroyers as supply ships was abhorrent, but Admiral Yamamoto could not sit by and see soldiers starve to death. So what the Americans called the "Tokyo Express" was born. The destroyers came night after night. Sometimes they ran down the slot. Sometimes they were sidetracked, fought PT boats and American warships of greater size; some were sunk, others had to turn back. The Japanese sailors began to call it "the rat run."

In the beginning in the air the Japanese had it all their own way. Marines of "Fighting Five," the original air squadron assigned to Guadalcanal, hung on by their toenails for weeks. The Japanese Zeros were faster, their rate of climb and their range were better. Thus, chasing *F4F* pilots saw many Japanese bombers get away because they had to turn back or never make it home.

By November, however, supplies were getting through to the Americans in impressive amounts. New 155-millimeter artillery pieces arrived. More planes came. Army troops began to arrive.

On the sea, the Japanese still scored impressive victories. The night of November 12 went down as the "night of the long lances," after a Japanese force led by Admiral Hiroaki Abe met a United States force under Admiral Daniel Callaghan off Guadalcanal. The decisive factor in this night battle of destroyers, cruisers, and battleships was the superiority of Japanese night-fighting plus the effectiveness of the Japanese torpedoes and the ineffectiveness of the American torpedoes. Admiral Callaghan was killed by gunfire on the bridge of the cruiser *San Francisco*. The cruisers *Portland*, *Juneau*, and

169

Atlanta were hit by torpedoes. The destroyer *Laffey* was sunk by a torpedo, the destroyer *Sterett* was hit. The American destroyers fired torpedoes at the Japanese ships, and hit—but the torpedoes failed to explode, and still no one knew why.

So once again, the Americans lost tactically but again the Japanese failed in their mission, which had been to destroy Henderson Field. When the shooting was over, and Iron Bottom Sound was repaved with American ships, Henderson Field was still in American hands. The next day, American bombing planes punished the Japanese and sank several of the vessels that had participated in the night's raid. Those ships had a secondary mission, which was protection of a new force of Japanese transports to resupply Guadalcanal. The naval battle continued that day, American capital ships against Japanese, again off Savo Island. Seven of eleven Japanese transports were sunk. The Americans lost the use of, at least temporarily, almost all United States destroyers, and *Walke* and *Preston* sank. At the end of the running action, the Japanese had sunk three American light cruisers and seven destroyers, and the Americans had sunk two Japanese battleships, one heavy cruiser and three destroyers; but the United States Navy had established once and for all its ability to resupply the Americans ashore and to keep the Japanese from effectively supplying their own troops. The increase in American air power was the key. In the naval battles, the Japanese had out-performed the Americans, as in this last one, except for the battleships of Admiral "Ching" Lee, which had sunk one Japanese battleship—the *Kirishima*. The fact was that the serious damage to Japanese ships was accomplished by American planes, not American surface vessels. On November 15, a sight witnessed by General Vandegrift underlined that newfound power. He sat on a hill and watched American planes attack the four Japanese transports that had managed to beach on the island shore and land men and supplies. The American bombers set all four transports afire.

So by November 15, the tide had turned. The Americans had the offensive. At this point Halsey would have liked to strike directly at Rabaul, the major Japanese base, with the idea of letting all areas south wither on the vine. But as Halsey soon learned, the Japanese, even if they had lost the initiative, were far from finished. On November 29, a Japanese relief force headed for Guadalcanal, and Halsey sent five cruisers and six destroyers down to intercept. The Japanese unit consisted of eight destroyers of the "rat force," loaded high with provisions. The next day the two forces met. The American destroyers made a torpedo attack. But once again the American torpedoes were completely ineffectual and the only Japanese destroyer sunk was the *Takanami*, sunk by naval gunfire. The Japanese struck back with a torpedo attack of their own. They damaged the cruisers *Pensacola* and *New Orleans* and sank the *Northampton*. They blew the bow off the *Minneapolis*.

170

So here was another Japanese naval victory. Even so, Admiral Yamamoto saw he could win naval victory after victory, and yet lose the war. The weight of his predictions was beginning to bear; no matter what the Japanese sent, the Americans sent more, and the Americans were willing to fight and die. Even the Japanese army had learned they were not at all as the Japanese propaganda machine had painted them.

Early in December, as the enemy admirals assessed their situation in the South Pacific, Admiral Yamamoto decided withdrawal from Guadalcanal was the only sensible solution. He could not supply the troops, and he could not let the troops there starve. Admiral Nimitz looked with considerable satisfaction on the past month and with optimism toward the future. The American air forces now held superiority. The land forces were better armed and superior in number to the Japanese.

In Tokyo, Imperial General Headquarters was assessing the Japanese situation too, but not very realistically. The Army High Command wanted more ships and more planes sent to the south to retake Guadalcanal. But here General Tojo interfered. He was war minister as well as prime minister, and he saw the picture of the war in relation to the navy and the home front as well as the war. Japan needed those transports to bring materials from the new empire to the homeland. They could not be sacrificed on the altar of the army's blasted ambitions in the south. Guadalcanal, he told the army, must be evacuated.

The Army High Command exploded in fury, as it had done so often before. But while uniformly successful in its tantrums of the past, this time with navy backing, General Tojo resisted. The Army *demanded* three hundred thousand tons of shipping—perhaps thirty transports—for Guadalcanal resupply. Tojo said no. General Shinichi Tanaka, chief of army operations, quarreled openly one day with General Tojo. Next day he and his chief assistant were transferred to the provinces. That was Tojo's final answer.

On December 31, 1942, the Japanese Imperial General Headquarters held a conference at the Imperial Palace with the chief aide to the emperor. On January 4, 1943, Imperial Headquarters ordered Guadalcanal evacuated and a new defense line laid in the northern Solomons. In February, the Japanese evacuated some eleven hundred army and navy personnel from the island, by destroyer and submarine. To Tojo and his aides, and particularly to Admiral Yamamoto, the evacuation meant a major change in the war. Admiral Yamamoto decided he must make an inspection tour of the front, to prepare for some difficult decisions.

Halsey pressed for the invasion of Rabaul that winter, but Nimitz, assessing the numbers of men, ships, and airplanes that would be needed, said the pipeline from the United States was not yet flowing rapidly enough to stage such an operation. They would have to move more slowly. The next move would have to appease the American army, and that meant General MacArthur, who was chewing up the stems of his corncob pipes in irritation at the navy's command of operations. MacArthur would move against New Guinea, while Admiral Halsey continued to advance with his marines in the Solomons and to New Georgia. The preparations began. In the air the battle was fought fiercely, with the Americans beginning to overwhelm the Japanese. On the sea, American destroyers and other ships raided and controlled the waters around Guadalcanal. In the north, Admiral Yamamoto consolidated his bases and brought up reinforcements from Japan, expecting a new American attack.

But before the attack could come, there was another development. One day that spring, Admiral Nimitz was presented with a half-deciphered Japanese message announcing a visit by Admiral Yamamoto to Rabaul, giving a precise itinerary. The intelligence officers suggested that Yamamoto be intercepted. Yamamoto, as the Americans knew, was the most effective commander in the Japanese navy, and his death would be worth whatever it might cost. Nimitz ordered an interception. Admiral Yamamoto went to Rabaul early in April. While he was there, the Japanese staged Operation I, an all-out aerial attack on Guadalcanal that Yamamoto hoped would stop the Americans. For four days, waves of Japanese planes attacked—two hundred bombers and nearly five hundred fighters. Most of them were shot down. The American air superiority was total. One of the most effective fighter planes, just introduced into the South Pacific, was the *P-38*, with two engines, heavy armament, and tremendous speed. A *P-38* could overtake a Zero, outdive it, outclimb it, and outgun it, and the results were usually fatal to the Japanese plane. By sheer exhaustion of pilots Operation I did slow down the American advance, and Yamamoto regarded it as "more or less of a success" although the losses were enormous. On April 18, he took off for Shortlands, the advanced Japanese base, so close to Guadalcanal. It was there that the American *P-38*s intercepted the admiral's flight of two bombers and escorting fighters. Both bombers were shot down and Admiral Yamamoto died in the crash.

If to the Americans Midway had been the turning point in the war, back in Japan those who were informed enough and thoughtful enough to know what had happened in the South Pacific could now see the change. Admiral Yamamoto had hoped desperately to be able to win one more victory that would enable Japan to go to the peace table and secure her new empire. That chance was now irrevocably lost. The roles were reversed. After Guadalcanal the Americans were on the offensive and Japan was on the defensive.

19

The Carlson
Comeuppance

WHILE THE BATTLE OF ATTRITION continued in the South Pacific, the Central
Pacific Command was occupied with its own plans. Once the southern Solomons were secured that area did not need Admiral Nimitz's close attention.
Nimitz was busy in the spring of 1943 planning the recapture of the Aleutians.
On March 26, a force under Rear Admiral "Soc" McMorris engaged a Jap-
anese task force off the Komandorski Islands, and although the Japanese force
outnumbered the American ships by two to one, Admiral McMorris attacked.
The American cruiser *Salt Lake City* was damaged seriously, but the Japanese
turned away and withdrew in the face of an American destroyer attack. The
American invasion of Attu followed, with some brisk fighting which ended in
the deaths of the entire Japanese garrison of about twenty-six hundred men.
Five hundred of the defenders committed suicide rather than surrender. It was
a performance that the Americans would see repeated time and again as they
moved across the Pacific toward Japan.

The Aleutians operation was important as a training exercise for the
future. When it was over, Major General Holland M. Smith, the marine
amphibious expert, delivered a critique which emphasized the need for more
aggressive action on the part of the assault forces.

If there was any doubt of that after the Aleutians, the next American
move in the Pacific erased it, for the invasion of the Gilbert Islands, at
Tarawa, was a bloody slaughter. Before, and after, some strategists claimed
that the invasion of the Gilberts was a waste of time and American (as well as
Japanese) lives. The Americans had two rationales for the Gilberts invasion.
The strategic rationale was to link the South Pacific forces and the Central

173

Pacific forces and tidy up the lines of communication by coming up from the south toward the Marshalls and the Marianas. The practical reason, on which Admiral Spruance insisted, was that the Guadalcanal invasion had proved how much the Americans had to learn about warfare, and the Gilberts, regarded as a relatively easy target, would provide a training exercise with relatively low losses.

The trouble was, as far as this concept went, that the excursion by Carlson's Raiders to Makin in the summer of 1942 had warned the Imperial General Staff to expect an assault along the Central Pacific island line. After the disaster in the Solomons, probably the Japanese would have improved their defenses all along the outer perimeter of empire anyhow, but they might not have done so quite so soon, nor quite so effectively as they had in the Gilberts by the summer of 1943.

After the plans were made, Admiral Nimitz selected Admiral Spruance to lead the expeditions of the Central Pacific and brought General Holland Smith in to command the troops. By this time, the relative strengths of the American and Japanese naval forces in the Pacific were almost reversed. The Japanese had no more than four effective carriers in operation, and to man these they did not have enough trained men. The disasters on the Coral Sea and at Midway had cost carriers and many hundreds of pilots. Many hundreds of pilots had been lost in trying to stem the American advance in the South Pacific. Japan had begun the war with thousands of highly trained naval pilots, since the navy was given the air defense responsibility for islands of the outer empire. There were more naval pilots by far than were needed to man carriers, since under the Japanese system naval pilots were stationed among the various islands as part of "air fleets" that had no ships. But in Yamamoto's series of raids just before his death many planes had been shot down, and since that time the Americans had blasted Rabaul and gained full control of the air. There were literally thousands of planes of the United States Army Air Forces, the Navy, and the Marine Corps. United States Air Force fliers came to the Pacific to serve the Americans in the same way that the air fleets served Japan. At first, there was much friction between navy and army because the air force pilots did not know how to attack shipping; but they learned rapidly, and by the summer of 1943 the Japanese contempt at Midway for the big American *B-17*s which had flown over at twenty thousand feet and bombed ineffectually had been turned to respect for *B-24* bombers that came in low and hit hard.

As for carriers, the Americans in 1943 had an awesome force, with still more ships on the way and in the outfitting yards. For the Gilberts operation, Nimitz was able to assign six fleet carriers, five light carriers, and a dozen escort, or "jeep" carriers.

The Americans assigned the Second Marine Division the task of taking

174

the Gilberts. Even more troops were needed so Spruance was given part of the army's Twenty-Seventh Infantry Division. The marines would go to Tarawa, which was known to be the most stoutly defended of the two island atolls. The army troops would take the easier objective of Makin. The Japanese had only a few hundred troops on Makin, many of them service troops. Against them would move sixty-five hundred American assault troops. On Tarawa, the defenses had been strengthened more than the Americans expected. The Japanese had brought to Betio, the principal island, two small contingents of their "special naval attack forces" which were the equivalent in training and morale of the United States Marines. But nineteen thousand marines were regarded as a sufficient number to take the islands.

For two weeks before the landings, army and navy bombers hit the islands. They dropped almost as many tons of bombs on Makin as they did on the more stoutly defended Betio. In seven days of November, 1943, 27 tons of bombs fell on Makin, and 34 tons of bombs on Tarawa. The pilots came back to report exultantly on their accuracy, but in fact, the defenses were virtually intact when the attack transports moved in to land the troops on November 20. Then, in the pre-invasion bombardment by surface ships, the American naval forces fired 2,000 eight-inch shells against Betio. The 19 carriers mounted 900 planes that dropped 185 tons of bombs on Tarawa atoll in the two days before the invasion. All this might was aimed against two eight-inch coastal guns and dozens of smaller guns. One would think that this tremendous plastering with explosives would wipe out all life, but the fact was that it did very little damage. The Japanese had been well warned by the Carlson raid, and they had many months to dig in. There were only 5,000 troops on Betio when the assault began. When the barrage let up and the American troops began coming ashore, there were still nearly five thousand troops there to meet them. And although the bombardment had promised to "soften up" the defenses, it had not. The Japanese had built thirteen anti-tank trenches across the narrow width of the two-mile-long island, at various angles to cover the approaches to the airfield, which was the focal point of defense. Mines and water obstacles had been emplaced offshore. Barbed wire was strung on the beaches around mine fields. The pill boxes and command posts were built of reinforced concrete, and some of the concrete was twelve feet thick. The concrete was covered with coconut logs, sand bags, and coral sand. When demolition bombs struck the sand they exploded without disturbing the concrete beneath. When the battle was all over and the experts took the field they estimated that Betio's defenses were as perfect as anyone could make them. The fighting certainly showed that, for as the marines came in they were hit by very effective fire, and the casualties were much higher than expected.

One reason for the high number of casualties was an error in American

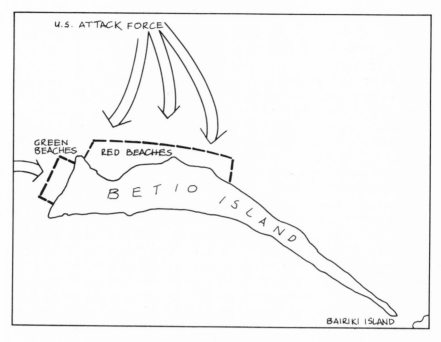

Tarawa, November 1943

calculation. The Gilbert Islands had been a British possession before World War II and well prior to the invasion Australia had been combed for former colonial officials who had served in the Gilberts. Several of them had come to Pearl Harbor to participate in the planning, since they knew the land and the ocean around it. Nonetheless, when the decision was made to land on Betio, the northern beaches were chosen. This choice meant the Americans had to come in across the lagoon instead of from the open sea, where the Japanese were expecting them. The justification for the choice was the better chance of getting a foothold on these beaches which had not been built up with defenses as heavily as those of the west and south. Since the approach to the lagoon meant crossing the reef, and the reef was often nearly exposed at low tide, the Japanese had expected the Americans to come the other way. But the Americans had believed even at low tide they could manage to cross safely in their shallow-draft landing craft. On the day of the landing, luck was against them; they were cursed with an especially low tide which no one had expected. The landing craft stranded hundreds of yards offshore and the marines had to wade in to the beach, rifles held above their heads, while the Japanese fired steadily at them. Only the amphibious tractors, and there were

176

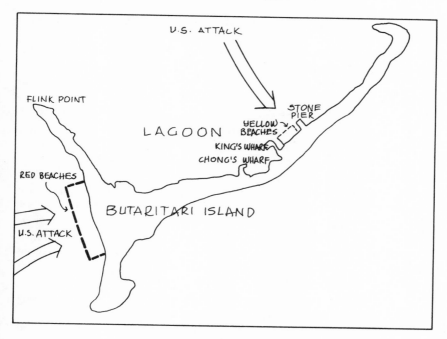

Makin Atoll, November 1943

too few of those, could make the beaches. The casualties were very high in the first assault wave and in the second. By the end of the first day, 5,000 marines had gone ashore, but a third of them had been killed or wounded. On the second day, the reserves were committed to the action, and the outcome was very much in doubt in spite of the enormous preponderance of American strength. When Tarawa was finally secured, the casualties were counted at nearly 2,900, whereas on Makin, the army lost 64 men killed and 150 wounded.

To be sure, Makin atoll was a much simpler operation than Tarawa, but there was also a vast difference in the method of approach of the army, the navy, and marines to amphibious assault or any sort of advance. The army wanted every bit of its strength to be in play at all times. First the artillery blasted the objective. Then tanks and infantry moved forward cautiously. If they encountered resistance, they stopped and called for artillery support, then moved ahead cautiously once again. Fighting on a broad land front, this tactic was entirely sensible. Any unit that charged on ahead of those to right and left was quite likely to be outflanked, perhaps surrounded, and wiped out. But in island fighting, where the whole island is a battlefield of a few thousand square yards, the shock approach of the marines was much more effective. The army went ashore at Makin using army tactics, and Major General Holland Smith became so annoyed that he came ashore and castigated Major General Ralph Smith, the army commander. The result was mutual annoyance and a deep source of irritation that was to affect the conduct of the Pacific war more seriously later on.

In the final analysis, the Gilberts invasion probably was unnecessary, as its opponents said. But at least the navy and the marines learned from their mistakes. Major General Holland Smith made a careful tour of the Tarawa battle area when the fighting ended and saw how little effect the bombing, strafing, and naval bombardment had on the defenses. Next time he promised himself, it would be different. All the effort the navy could exert would have to be put forth to soften up the defenses. Nor would there be any more excursions into adventure with the tides. Furthermore, although Admiral Turner, commander of the amphibious landing force, had scoffed at General Smith's demands for more amphibious tractors, the slaughter at Tarawa had convinced everyone that he was right. The amphibious tractors began to come into Pearl Harbor by the dozens.

Months before, Admirals King and Nimitz had begun the initial planning for the invasion of the Marshall Islands in the spring of 1944. Now, at their regular meetings in San Francisco, they were talking about attacking the Kuril Islands north of Japan, invading the China coast, and seizing Hokkaido Island of Japan proper for use as a huge air base and staging platform for the invasion of Honshu and Kyushu, the most heavily populated islands. Even as the results of the Gilberts operation were being assessed at Pearl Harbor, events were moving with the force of a juggernaut.

20

Torpedo Junction

~~~~~~~~~

DURING THE FIRST YEAR AND A HALF of the Pacific War America's most serious military deficiency in the Pacific was its lack of effective torpedoes. Two hundred and thirty-two torpedoes were lost almost immediately in the bombing of Manila at the outbreak of war. Many of the remainder turned out to be duds. The first indication came two days after war broke out when the submarine *Swordfish* sighted a Japanese convoy coming to land troops in the Philippines and fired a torpedo at a transport. The men aboard heard an explosion. After a suitable interval, the submarine surfaced and the captain saw the transport still afloat and apparently unhurt. He fired another torpedo, dived again, heard an explosion, and wrote in his log book: "sunk," but the Japanese ship was not sunk, nor were most of the others attacked by American submarines in these early days. There were some successes; *Seawolf* torpedoed the Japanese cargo ship *Atsutasan Maru* and she was run aground for everyone to see. But there were more failures. One captain, Commander Tyrell Dwight Jacobs, blamed the magnetic exploders on his torpedoes. Those devices were designed to draw the torpedo to the steel hull of a ship and explode on contact. But Jacobs saw several of his torpedoes run true and explode prematurely, and he concluded that the Japanese had discovered some method of dealing with magnetic exploders. He was right for the wrong reason; the Japanese did not have to deal with the exploders. The Americans had produced a faulty weapon from the beginning.

But the men who had devised the torpedoes and the men who supervised the manufacture of torpedoes were certain that they could not be wrong so they resisted every complaint by the submarine captains. Rear Admiral R. W.

Christie was one of the leading figures in development of this *Mark 14* torpedo. Early in the war he went to Fremantle, Australia, to take over command of the submarines of the Southwest Pacific. In spite of the constant reports from his captains that the torpedoes malfunctioned he refused to investigate. He did not believe there could be anything wrong with his handiwork. Instead, he complained whenever any higher command suggested that the captains' reports might be right, and he contended that the submariners were at fault. They were either badly trained or incompetent, he implied. But not every submarine captain could be incompetent, and nearly every submarine that went out had its share of malfunctions. So early in 1943, in spite of the foot-dragging of the conservatives, Vice Admiral Charles A. Lockwood, the commander of submarines in the Pacific Fleet, undertook a campaign to get at the facts. He sent a barrage of complaints to the Bureau of Ordnance. The bureau stuffed them away in the files and nothing happened. He complained again and still the attitude in Washington was much more that of Admiral Christie than that of the submarine officers at sea. For a year and a half the American submariner had been fighting with one hand tied behind his back. It was remarkable that the submarines achieved as much as they did in this period. For example, three submarines were sent into the Sea of Japan through La Perouse Strait in the spring of 1943. *Plunger*, *Permit*, and *Lapon* left Pearl Harbor, stopped at Midway Island for refuelling, and then went into Japanese waters. They had torpedo trouble and sank only a few small vessels. But the most telling story was that *Tinosa*, which occurred during the midsummer of 1943. In July, Lieutenant Commander Lawrence R. Daspit took this submarine on patrol in the Caroline Islands. On July 24, the *Tinosa* encountered a Japanese tanker full of oil, bound for Truk. Lieutenant Commander Daspit fired four torpedoes. He saw two of them hit and send spray as high as the foremast. The tanker did not even slow down. He fired two more torpedoes and saw both of them strike. Neither exploded. Daspit would not give up. He tracked the tanker again and fired another torpedo. It hit and did not explode. Lieutenant Commander Daspit then decided he would expend the rest of his torpedoes against this one target, just to show Admiral Lockwood how bad the torpedoes were. One after the other, he fired eight more torpedoes against that tanker. In all, the tanker was hit fifteen times. The expenditure, at $10,000 a torpedo, was $150,000. The tanker remained unscathed. Lieutenant Commander Daspit saved his last torpedo to take back to Pearl Harbor for evidence and headed home.

When he arrived at Pearl Harbor he went to see Admiral Lockwood and presented the evidence. It was just what Lockwood had been looking for. Lockwood ordered that the torpedo be disassembled. The "experts" said nothing was wrong. But Daspit and his crew had absolute evidence: fifteen torpedoes against one ship and not one explosion? Something must be wrong.

Torpedo Junction

So Admiral Lockwood did the unthinkable: he began investigation on his own, using live torpedoes. He sent submarines out to Kahoolawe, the little island off Maui that the navy used for target practice. The submarines fired torpedoes against a solid cliff—and they did *not* explode. It was like shooting an elephant gun against the side of a barn door and then finding that there was no sign of the bullet. He fired against cliffs on Oahu. The results were the same. If a torpedo would not explode against solid rock, it would not explode against anything. And Admiral Lockwood so reported to Admiral Nimitz, to King, and to the Bureau of Ordnance. The Mark 14 torpedo was a dud.

Further investigation proved that the major offender was the firing pin, but even when all the information was in hand, the Washington naval bureaucrats were slow to move, and finally Lockwood had to call on Admiral Nimitz for high-level influence. Nimitz wrote a stiff letter to the Bureau of Ordnance, not bothering to argue the facts, but demanding information as to when he could expect some improvement. King became concerned and action on the torpedoes was hastened, particularly after Admiral Lockwood reported that he had deactivated the magnetic feature of the Mark 14 torpedoes used by the fleet and that the results were much better.

The Bureau of Ordnance finally reported that work was progressing on a new electric torpedo, and it would not be long before they would be ready for use. In the interim, in 1943, the torpedomen at Pearl Harbor rebuilt the Mark 14 torpedoes with new firing pins, and the submariners began to go to sea with weapons they could trust. The course of the war changed more rapidly as the American submarines began to cut the lifeline of the Japanese to the Asiatic continent and to the Dutch East Indies on which Japan depended for her oil.

181

21

The Marshalls Campaign

BY THE END OF 1943, the American offensive force in the Central Pacific was planning to move again. The next target of invasion would be the Marshalls Islands, north of the Gilberts on the road to Tokyo. A chastened and highly embarrassed Pacific Fleet promised the marines that this time there would be a naval barrage to which "Howling Mad" Smith could take no exception. But the troubles at the Gilberts could not all be blamed on the naval bombardment or on any other single source. The Gilberts invasion was Admiral Spruance's first, and it suffered from the inexperience of most officers and a general failure to coordinate all the forces. Air power, for example, had not been exploited in the proper manner in softening up Tarawa. One reason, of course, was the failure of intelligence to give accurate information about the enemy strength on Betio Island. But that again came back to aerial surveillance failures.

Air power was a very large part of the growing American strength. The army air forces were supplying planes and squadrons for the Southwest Pacific and would soon bring planes to the Central Pacific. Admiral Nimitz insisted on retaining control of all aircraft, which were placed under Admiral John Hoover. The liaison between army and navy commands was not effective, notable more for friction than for cooperation. The island and anti-shipping campaigns of the Pacific demanded different techniques from those used in the Atlantic War, and there was no way to learn these except by experience. Midway, and now the Gilberts, had shown the ineffectiveness of heavy bombers like the *B-17* if they were not properly employed.

The key to the sort of aerial warfare to be carried out in the Pacific had

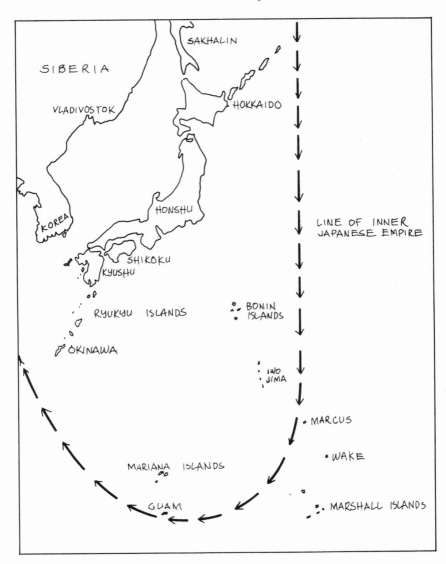

Pacific Theater of Operations, Summer 1944

to be the aircraft carrier. The Japanese still held a string of islands that extended from Honshu down to Truk in the Bismarcks. The capture of the Gilberts put a large dent in the chain but did not break the chain. The Americans had bases in the Southwest Pacific and on the edge of the Central Pacific

184

in the Gilberts, but further north they had nothing, and so the carriers must be the islands. Fortunately the carrier building-program that had begun before Pearl Harbor was now showing results. A dozen new carriers had either joined the fleet or were preparing to join. And with that increase came a basic change in the whole attitude of the fleet toward carrier warfare.

Late in August, before the Gilberts operation, Admiral Charles Pownall, as senior officer in the area, had taken the *Yorktown*, *Independence*, and *Essex* on a carrier raid against the Marcus atoll. In this operation Pownall had come to the unfavorable attention of his captains, who charged he was too cautious. After the carrier planes delivered five attacks on the targets, Pownall nervously turned away while his young captains felt there was still time and there were still enemy targets to be hit to good advantage.

Before and after the Gilberts operation, the officers of the Pacific Fleet staff had been split in their attitude toward carriers. Spruance, a "battleship admiral," regarded the carriers as just another part of the fleet, one that should stick close to the battleships for protection. But Admiral Towers and the other aviators of the new school felt that the carriers should not be held down by any ships slower than themselves. If they could make thirty knots, then only thirty-knot battleships should accompany them. The carriers could move fast, and their best protection was their own aircraft and their speed. This new idea took some getting used to with the battleship officers, and there were many brisk discussions. As of the time of the Gilberts operation the battleship admirals were having their way: the carriers were ordered to stay with the fleet.

Admiral Pownall agreed with Spruance as to the proper function of carriers, and in so doing he aligned himself against Admiral Towers and most of the other airmen. By the winter of 1943–44, most of the carrier captains at the outset of war had been made admirals. These included Rear Admirals Frederick C. Sherman, A. E. Montgomery, and Arthur Radford, all airmen of the new school who wanted to exploit the capability of the carrier and were not afraid to risk ships and planes in the process.

On December 9, 1943, Admiral Pownall led six carriers on a raid against the Marshall Islands. Everyone knew that the Japanese had many planes in the Marshalls. After Pownall arrived on the scene he became nervous. The thought of Japanese capability and his enormous responsibility for the safety of the six carriers overwhelmed him. The American planes raided the Japanese all day long, but at the end of the day, when his captains wanted more, Admiral Pownall insisted on heading home. Captain J. J. Clark in particular argued for a strike against the island of Roi, which was scheduled for invasion in the Marshalls operation. The Japanese had many aircraft there and these could be destroyed and the aviation facilities badly damaged. But Pownall was not in a mood to brook argument and the task force went back to Pearl

Marshall Islands

Harbor. There Admiral Nimitz was shown pictures of undestroyed bombers and a new airstrip on Kwajalein Island. Captain Clark, who had brought the pictures in, thought the Cincpac staff would be indignant at the sight of undestroyed aircraft on the ground. But Nimitz had been worrying about which Marshall Islands to attack first, and the picture of the airstrip settled the matter. Still, there was concern over the recent methods of employment of the growing carrier force. Admiral Towers agreed that Admiral Pownall was not aggressive enough. Spruance disagreed; Pownall was just the sort of carrier commander he wanted, for Pownall agreed with Spruance that the main task of the carrier force in an amphibious attack was to stand by and guard the landings and the ships. Even during this argument the situation had changed with the coming of a new sort of carrier, the escort. Escort carriers were originally conceived for convoy duty in the Atlantic, to bridge the gap where the German U-boats had previously enjoyed complete freedom from air attack because planes could not fly to mid-Atlantic and return. Early in the war several tankers and other transports had been converted to escort carrier duty, and then several classes of escort carriers were built from the keel up. The Kaiser Engineering Company had gone into shipbuilding, starting first with

Liberty cargo ships, and then began to build carriers. By 1943, they were coming off the ways almost daily. The airmen who ran the big carriers maintained that a handful of these small escort carriers could create a perfectly adequate air cover for an invasion force. Thus they said, the fast carriers should be allowed to range far around the perimeter of the attack and intercept any air reinforcement or naval force that the enemy tried to send. This was new doctrine, and Admiral Pownall was slow to accept it. Admiral Towers considered the complaints made privately (and some not so privately) by the "Young Turks" of the carrier force, and on December 23 he went to see Admiral Nimitz to discuss the matter. He recommended that Admiral Pownall be replaced as commander of the carriers by Rear Admiral Marc Mitscher. Mitscher had been the captain of the *Hornet* less than two years earlier when Admiral Halsey took that carrier and the *Enterprise* into the deep Pacific to launch the Doolittle raid on Japan. At the end of 1943, Mitscher was the most highly acclaimed carrier commander, and the airmen said Halsey was a fleet commander, but Mitscher was the man to run the carriers. He had an entirely different attitude toward the employment of carriers than Admiral Fletcher had shown before, or Admiral Pownall showed at this point. Fletcher and Pownall represented the thinking of the prewar days when carriers were so valuable and so scarce that each single carrier became the nucleus of a task force of battleships and cruisers.

At the meeting between Towers and Nimitz, Rear Admiral Forrest Sherman backed Towers, as might be expected, since Sherman was Towers's chief of staff. But more than that, Sherman was a young officer whom Nimitz liked and admired, and he trusted the Sherman judgment more than that of his air chief. Sherman was of the vintage of Radford and Montgomery, and he had some strong ideas about what should be done with carriers. Nimitz listened carefully as his two senior staff air officers spoke.

For the first time, a task force could be put to sea which consisted of several groups, each as large as the whole Midway defense fleet had been in 1942. The old concept of the task force built around a single carrier was completely outmoded. The Japanese had shown the way in the employment of carriers, and the Americans had learned. When Towers and Sherman laid out the new philosophy, calling for the use of the carriers as a major striking force, Nimitz listened and agreed. Since Pownall did not agree with that doctrine, Nimitz recommended to Admiral King, who retained control of the appointments of all flag officers, that Pownall be replaced by Admiral Mitscher.

There was one difficulty. Admiral Spruance wanted Pownall and did not want Mitscher. The reason for his feeling about Mitscher went back to prewar days. One day during fleet maneuvers off San Diego, Mitscher was flying in command of his Patrol Wing 2 on a scouting mission for the destroyer force when the big flying boats ran into a bad storm. Admiral A. E. Watson, commander of the destroyer force, was sitting in San Diego harbor where the sky was clear and blue, and when Mitscher asked permission to return to base because of heavy weather, the admiral snorted and denied the request. Mitscher flew on but after another ten minutes the weather grew worse and he renewed the plea. The request was again denied. Mitscher flew on, the flying boats bucking in the up and down drafts, the rain pelting so hard the windshield wipers could not keep the glass clear. The buffeting became so severe that Mitscher feared the planes would shake apart and so after another ten minutes of worsening weather he called San Diego once more. "Am returning to base unless specifically ordered otherwise," he said. And then he pulled the plug on his radio receiver.

Two hours later the flying boats landed and taxied into the Naval Air Station, and Mitscher was hailed before the furious destroyer commander for an explanation. He was sorry, he said. It must have been faulty radio equipment in his flying boat, probably knocked out by the dreadful storm they had been flying through. Since no one but Mitscher's radio man could have gainsaid him, and the radioman would have his tongue torn out first, that was the end of the incident. But Admiral Watson had unkind feelings for Mitscher ever after, and these were shared by Admiral Spruance, who at that time was Watson's chief of staff. In 1943, years after the incident, Spruance still distrusted Mitscher. He was the sort of aviator who might very well take the command of a fleet into his own hands.

Admiral Nimitz had an effective way of dealing with such matters. He called a meeting. Spruance came with Pownall. Sherman came with Towers. Nimitz and his new chief of staff, Admiral McMorris, were the arbiters. They discussed the complaints of the younger airmen against Pownall, and Spruance and Pownall made the case for the conservative use of carriers. The discussion was so heated, perhaps, that the participants did not pay enough attention to Nimitz's reactions. He had been disappointed in that last raid on the Marshalls, he said, and he referred to the many planes left undamaged on Roi Island. Then Nimitz indulged in a little gentle philosophy. Ships were always at risk when brought against the enemy, he reminded Spruance and Pownall. Carriers were no different than others, and with their new speed and anti-aircraft armament, perhaps no more vulnerable (although carrier doctrine in the past had held to the contrary). Carriers must be risked just like any other ships, to carry the war to the enemy.

Having said that much, Nimitz brought the meeting to an end with a final word. In the next two or three days, he wanted an operations plan from Pownall and Spruance which would indicate precisely how they intended to employ the carriers. They returned with the plan that Nimitz had expected: employment of the carriers in close support of the invasion force. So Nimitz, who had received permission from King to make the changes he wanted in the fleet staff, made changes that indicated his growing appreciation of the role of the carriers in the war. Admiral Towers was promoted to become Nimitz's deputy as commander-in-chief of the Pacific theater. Pownall, who was a good administrator, was shifted to Towers's old job as air forces commander. The job had developed into an administrative post, and Pownall was good at that. When Admiral Mitscher was appointed to become commander of the carrier force, throughout the navy the aviators cheered. It had taken the United States Navy two years to recognize what Japanese had known from the beginning, that carriers were the primary naval weapons of this war. But, at the beginning of 1944, the recognition was official. From that point on, the Pacific war would be fought by the Americans in a much more effective way than in the past. The operation against the Marshall Islands showed the change.

During January, 1944, Admiral Hoover's land-based aircraft moved into the Gilbert Islands and from there began a "softening up" campaign against the Marshalls. For the most part, they used the long-range bombers the army called *B-24s*, and the navy pilots developed new low-level bombing techniques that increased the effectiveness of heavy bombers. On January 29, Admiral Mitscher took four carrier groups, six fleet carriers, and six light carriers against the Marshall Islands of Wotje, Roi, Maloelap and Kwajalein. There was no holding back this time. They bombed and strafed everything that moved on the airfields, and when they came back they claimed they had knocked Japanese air power out in the Marshalls. On Roi, they smashed the hundred planes that had so infuriated Captain Clark. The American loss for the action was forty-nine planes, but that was a small price to pay for control of the air during the coming invasion.

The Marshalls invasion went off like an accurate alarm clock. The naval bombardment was careful and impressively intense. By the time the bombardment and accompanying air strikes from the carriers and jeep carriers ended, the Japanese were groggy, many of their guns were destroyed, and their whole defensive operation was reduced to fragments. Admiral Richard Conolly, in charge of the northern force that invaded Roi and Namur Islands, took his bombardment assignment so seriously that he told the ships to move in dangerously close to the islands, and thus earned the sobriquet "close in Conolly."

In two days Roi and Namur were secured. Then Kwajalein fell almost equally quickly. The Americans had suffered so few casualties they decided to move also against Eniwetok, and on February 22, all these islands were in American hands, and the Marshalls became an American base for further operations against Japan.

Meanwhile, following the new course of action, having pulverized Jap-

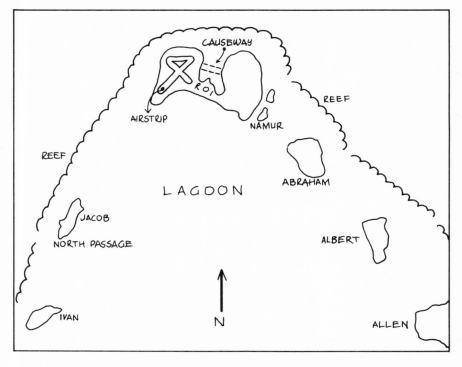

Kwajalein Atoll (northern section), March 1944

anese air resistance *before* the invasion, the fast carriers moved against Truk, the most important Japanese naval base in the South Pacific. Admiral Mitscher introduced some new tactical methods including the night attack. The carriers were accompanied on this operation by Admiral Spruance's battleships and cruisers, and the combined air and naval forces produced good results. There and at Jaluit, they destroyed 26 merchant ships, 6 warships, and 270 Japanese aircraft. But they did not find the Japanese fleet at Truk, where it had been only a few days earlier. On February 10, Admiral Koga, successor to Admiral Yamamoto as chief of the Combined Fleet, had gone to Tokyo to confer with the Imperial General Staff about the conduct of the war. The result had been a general pullback of the defensive line to Palau and the Marianas. That was one reason the Marshalls were not seriously defended. The Japanese were beginning to retract the tentacles of their empire.

22

Into the Empire

~~~~~~~

THE JAPANESE NAVY'S EVACUATION of Truk came as a surprise to Admiral Nimitz, but no more so than it did to the Imperial Japanese Army in the South Pacific. Japan's army and navy were so widely separated by internal differences that at the area command level the generals did not know, even at the end of 1943 that four important carriers had been lost at Midway. Then, in the battle for the Solomons, the light carrier *Ryujo* was also lost. The navy, entrusted with the aerial defense of this outlying region, had lost so many planes that it could not mount any sort of effective counterattack. The army had expected the navy at Truk to respond to American attack as successfully as it had done everywhere in the first months of the war, and when Truk was suddenly laid bare, the generals were shocked. Five days after the strike at Truk, the United States fast carrier forces hit the Marianas and blasted many army installations on Saipan and Tinian, which were major bases within the perimeter of the Japanese empire. This was something new. In the past, the places the Americans had struck were outposts. But thousands of Japanese people had moved to Tinian and Saipan. They had built Japanese-style houses and lived a Japanese life there. So when the carriers hit, they struck a vital nerve.

On Admiral Koga's hurried trip to Tokyo, he had informed the High Command of the true state of affairs in the south. Until this point, the army had considered the southern areas primarily the navy's problem. The army had seen the defeat at Guadalcanal more as an incident than a portent. But suddenly the army learned that the navy no longer had its old power. The only solution the army could see to the military problem was an enormous accel-

191

eration of Japanese air power plus seizure of defense responsibility for the inner empire by the army. This was done February 18, the day of the Truk raid. Imperial Headquarters established the Thirty-First Army to defend the Caroline Islands, the Bonins, and the Marianas. Two armies were transferred from Manchuria to the Gohoku—the region north of Australia and the Philippines. Premier Tojo made himself chief of the general staff as well as war minister and prime minister. The army, which had always demanded more than half Japan's aircraft production in spite of the navy's much heavier losses, refused to budge an inch in that respect. Distrusting the navy's ability to supply army troops in far places, the army actually began to build ships and submarines of its own. This duplication which indicated the almost total control of Japan's homeland by the army, led to further confusion in the defense plan.

The Americans had some of this sort of difficulty in the Pacific region. General MacArthur insisted to anyone who would listen that he should lead the American drive on Japan from the Southwest Pacific and the navy should be reduced to a support force. Admiral King said the navy plan would be far less costly in material and lives. This plan called for a drive through the Japanese mandate (the Marshalls and Marianas) toward Japan. The undetermined factor was the direction to be taken after the Marianas attack had breached the inner perimeter of the Japanese empire. Admirals King and Nimitz toyed with the idea of landing on Formosa. They also considered a landing on the China coast, with the intention of linking up with Chiang Kai-shek's forces, and then driving the Japanese off the Asian mainland. But these matters had to be left in abeyance, pending the direction of Japanese defenses and the buildup of American power.

The United States Army was not enthralled with the prospects of fighting the Pacific war under navy leadership. On the highest level, MacArthur continued to press for the supreme role. On a lower level, General Robert C. Richardson, commander of army forces in Hawaii, objected strenuously to the employment of army troops under a marine commander. He asked Nimitz to limit Marine General Holland Smith's role to command of marines and to put overall troop command under an army general. If Nimitz had any sympathy for this request, it was wiped out by General Holland Smith's report of the behaviour of the Twenty-Seventh Army Division under fire at the Gilberts. That division had not been adequately trained for the role it assumed, and its officers were unfamiliar with the marine way of doing things. Again, at the Marshalls, tired marines who had taken one island had to assist slow-moving army troops in the taking of another (Kwajalein).

Far more important, however, was the struggle for overall command of the Pacific effort. In February, General Sutherland, MacArthur's chief-of-staff, went to Washington to argue for the MacArthur theory of movement back through the Philippines. Admiral King resisted every argument. It was all right with King if MacArthur wanted to return in triumph to the Philippines but the essential effort against Japan must be launched from the China-Korea-Manchuria coast, using local people to establish the bases and thus assuring safe lines of communication without commitment of hundreds of thousands of American troops to rear areas.

Nimitz went to Washington in March, 1944, and came back with what seemed to be a firm commitment from the Joint Chiefs to the navy plan. At least the next step was clear: in June, the Central Pacific forces would launch the largest operation yet planned against the Marianas Islands. The South Pacific campaign was virtually over. Admiral Halsey's forces had moved up with one pincer to Emerau island and MacArthur's forces had moved to New Britain with the other; the twin drives had cut off the major Japanese base at Rabaul, isolating eighty thousand Japanese troops in the South Pacific. The local commanders were told that they could expect almost nothing, and the Japanese troops, once proud warriors, were reduced to gardening and foraging for food.

The attack on the Marianas was split into three phases. First would come the strike against Saipan by the Second and Fourth Marine Divisions. Once Saipan was taken, the Americans would move across the narrow channel to Tinian. The southern attack on Guam was to be made by the Third Marine Division and the First Provisional Marine Brigade. In reserve was the Twenty-Seventh Army division under Army Major General Ralph Smith.

This time there would be 15 Americans carriers, to protect an invasion force of 520 ships and 127,500 troops. Under the new doctrine the carriers were busy for weeks before the actual invasion, striking Japanese-held islands in the defense chain. What they would do at the time of actual invasion remained to be seen. The question was decided by the Japanese navy. On June 15, the marines landed on Saipan and began the hard fight. Once again the American intelligence system had come up with wrong answers. General Smith believed there were 15,000 defenders on Saipan. Actually there were 32,000.

As this difficulty began, the American fleet was steaming away from Saipan, to do battle with a Japanese force coming up from the Philippines and the Dutch East Indies. The Japanese navy had long been promising that "one decisive battle" would amend all the navy's difficulties and wipe out the striking potential of the American fleet. This battle was to accomplish that end, the Japanese admirals promised. The A-Go Plan, as they called it, was guaranteed to bring victory and buy Japan the time to consolidate her defenses.

Admiral Spruance moved cautiously. He held that his primary responsibility was to protect the invasion forces against attack by the enemy. As far

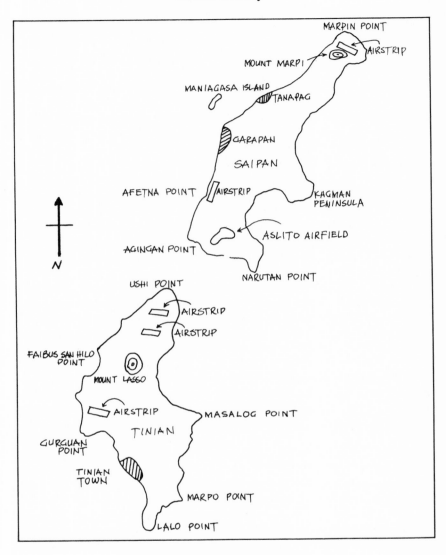

Saipan and Tinian Islands, July 1944

as he knew the Japanese fleet was coming in two elements, either of which might sneak around behind his back, if he moved out against the other, and then pulverize the assault force on Saipan. But still, a battle was joined on the morning of June 19, 1944, for the Japanese were as aggressive as Spruance was conservative.

Into the Empire

It began with Japanese air movement. The plan advanced by Admiral Toyoda, the new chief of the Combined Fleet (Admiral Koga had been killed in a plane crash) called for the Japanese naval pilots to shuttle planes back and forth from the Marianas Islands to the Japanese carriers, attacking the American fleet on each pass. But the fifteen carriers interdicted that plan. Admiral Mitscher's planes struck Guam, Saipan, and Tinian airfields repeatedly, knocking down planes that were in the air, taking off, landing, or sitting on the ground and burning the installations. Reinforcements were sent up from Palau and other islands, and they were treated the same way. The planes from Admiral Ozawa's carrier force tried to find the American fleet, met the American combat air patrols instead, and were decimated. The survivors headed for Tinian and Guam, and they were attacked in the air or on the ground. Virtually all the Japanese air power in this whole area was destroyed. In fact, finally, a submarine was sent down to Guam to pick up about fifty Japanese pilots who had no planes and save them before the invading forces could get to them because Japan was so desperately short of trained pilots.

Finally, the American air force from the carriers did find the Japanese fleet and sank the heavy carriers *Shokaku* and *Taiho*, the light carrier *Hiyo*, and two tankers. The distance was too great for Admiral Ozawa to launch a surface attack on the American fleet, and Admiral Spruance was too conservative to chase his enemy and seek a night action, so the fleets parted. The "decisive battle" had again been postponed.

But the land battle for the three major Marianas Islands proved to be a major struggle for the Americans. The Japanese had resisted stoutly at Betio and in the Marshalls, but these areas had been written off by the high command before the Americans attacked. The battle there was fought with a handful of guns and the weapons of foot soldiers. The battle on Saipan was on a much larger scale. The Japanese had heavy artillery in the mountains behind the beaches. They had tanks, and they used them. Almost immediately, after the initial easy landings, the Americans ran up against stiff resistance that was not to be stopped until the end.

Opposition was so heavy in the first few days of fighting that the army's reserves were committed to the action on June 22. The 106th Infantry and the 165th Infantry landed that day and went into the line. The Japanese had established a main line of resistance about a third of the way up the island from the south. General Yoshitsugu Saito had committed about fifteen thousand men here in rugged terrain, with the mountains rising up behind them. The 106th Infantry was sent to take a place called Hell's Pocket. But on June 23, the 106th failed to move, because the green troops encountered extremely strong opposition. The whole American advance was stalled since the 106th bogged down, and at the end of that day, General Holland Smith relieved General Ralph Smith, the commander of the Twenty-Seventh Division, and sent him back to Pearl Harbor. To relieve a general officer in the heat of battle was a

195

matter of such seriousness that Holland Smith knew there would be a repercussion, but he felt there was no other recourse. Once again, major differences between the army way of doing things and the marine way were revealed. The Twenty-Seventh Division was a New York National Guard Division, and the 106th Regiment was made up of officers from New York City for the most part. The division had never been properly trained for amphibious warfare, and the officers were not as aggressive as they ought to have been to be brought into this fight. After General Ralph Smith's departure, various other officers were also relieved, and finally the army troops got moving and kept on, making at last an enviable record.

For weeks, the Japanese had been cut off from supplies by the American air forces and the submarines of the Pacific Fleet. The naval bombardment and air strikes of early June had knocked out many supply dumps and some weapons. General Saito was committed by Imperial Headquarters to "fight to the death." By July 1, his headquarters radioed Tokyo that the officers and men had not eaten for three days. They were living on snails and roots, but fighting on. And they did fight on, as long as ammunition and strength lasted. But on the night of July 6, General Saito decided the end had come, and he ordered a mass attack the next day. The majority of the Japanese were holed up in the area once called Pleasant Valley, but now termed Death Valley by the Japanese and Hara-kiri Gulch by the Americans. Out of the holes and caves the Japanese came swarming the next day at dawn, and by sheer weight of numbers forced the Americans back toward the beach. But when United States tanks and artillery were brought up, the opposition soon melted away; most of these Japanese had very little ammunition, and some were armed only with sticks and clubs. And at the end of the day nearly all of them were dead, and Saipan was virtually secured. There was a mopping-up operation to be undertaken, to clear the northern tip of the island, but this was relatively easy. One of the great tragedies of Saipan was the death of many civilians, women and children, who had been so disciplined that they jumped off the cliff at the northern end of the island rather than surrender to the Americans.

The Saipan story was repeated on Tinian and on Guam. The marines performed very well, and the islands were soon secured.

But back at Pearl Harbor, decisions were being made that would affect the future conduct of the war, and at least part of the reason for these decisions must have been the open quarrel that had developed between the army and the marines over the question of command of ground troops.

That issue, of course, was minor in comparison with the truly great one: the future course of the war. But it underlay the whole attitude of the army. Generals, from Richardson on up to Marshall, were upset by the relief of General Ralph Smith, and rather than consider the real problem, they chose to regard the matter as a conflict between the marines and the army. The fact that almost certainly any army general would have been forced to do the same was submerged in emotionalism.

In this atmosphere, the argument about the future of the war continued. Admiral King was committed to the idea of bypassing the Philippines, now that they had reached the entry hall to the inner empire, and moving straight against Formosa. Here, King came straight up against General MacArthur's commitment, made so dramatically after he left the Philippines ignominiously in a PT boat in 1942. "I shall return," said the General sententiously. Now, with the capture of the Marianas, his chance to return had come.

The Joint Chiefs of Staff were divided about the future of the Pacific command because the fighting on Saipan, Tinian, and Guam had assumed a new character. In the earlier Central Pacific operations, the marines had seemed the ideal instrument, shock troops who stormed beaches and moved ahead swiftly with small weapons. But the battle of Saipan had assumed a character the army men knew well, the slogging broad-front struggle for territory. The future seemed really to belong to the army. Further, although King was committed to anything but capture of the Philippines, most of Nimitz's staff in Pearl Harbor felt the Philippines should be assaulted first, and their attitude was soon out in the open.

The Joint Chiefs of Staff could not make up their minds so the problem was thrown to the commander-in-chief of the American forces, President Franklin D. Roosevelt. In July, 1944, as the troops still fought on Tinian and Guam, President Roosevelt journeyed to Pearl Harbor. There he met General MacArthur and Admiral Nimitz, the two theater commanders. Admiral King showed up but was courteously informed that his presence was not desired any more than that of General Marshall would have been, and so King went grumpily off on an inspection tour.

In the confrontation, General MacArthur was at his best. He stood in front of the big Pacific situation map at Cincpac Headquarters and sketched his plan for the future of the war—move into the Philippines, reconquer the Dutch East Indies, and roll up the Japanese Empire from the south.

Admiral Nimitz, of course, had to argue to the King plan, but his heart was not in it, and when questioned he admitted that the Philippines seemed to him to be the logical point for the next major invasion.

The political overtones of a Philippine invasion were enormous, since this was American territory. Thinking as a politician, President Roosevelt concluded that MacArthur should take the lead. The fateful decision was made. With the invasion of the Philippines, the navy was to be reduced to a supporting role, and General MacArthur was to become the supreme commander of the war against Japan. This decision would permeate the entire war effort from that point on.

23

And MacArthur
Did Return

~~~~~~~

IF JULY AT PEARL HARBOR brought a major change in the outlook of the war, so did July in Tokyo. On July 18, 1944, a week after Saipan was declared secure by General Holland Smith, the Tojo cabinet in Tokyo collapsed. For months, General Tojo had asserted that no foreign troops would ever breach the inner defenses of the empire, and with the fall of Saipan that whole policy was in shambles. The distance from Saipan to Tokyo was twelve hundred miles, well within the range of the new American *B-29* bomber. Already bombers had flown the much greater distance from bases in west China to bomb Japan. The capture of Saipan and Tinian gave the Americans the advantage the Japanese had at the beginning of the war—island air bases. From this point on the Japanese high command knew that the bombing of Tokyo must be expected as a matter of course. The United States Army Air Forces began building a *B-29* airfield on Saipan on June 24, before the island was secured, and the first *B-29* raid on Tokyo was staged on November 24, when one hundred big bombers took off from Saipan.

After the fall of the Marianas, the Japanese believed the Americans might strike the Philippines, or Formosa, or the main islands of Japan, and their planning tried to take into account all these possibilities. Such wild schemes as "balloon bombs" were given serious credence by the army. Nine thousand of these were released from Japan, aimed along the prevailing winds at America. They were supposed to start forest fires, and explode everywhere in the American northwest, thus destroying American morale. Some bombs did start forest fires, but these were extinguished quickly enough, and the vast

199

majority of Americans never knew they were subjected to a "fright" campaign by the Japanese army.

During the summer of 1944, the American carrier forces ranged around the islands of the inner empire, attacking Chichi Jima, Iwo Jima, Yap, and Palau. They also hit the Philippines. In September, a small expeditionary force took Peleliu Island and Angaur and Morotai. These islands, east of the Philippines, were close enough to that archipelago to give the Japanese the idea that the American advance would next focus on the Philippines. Soon all these eastern islands sprouted American air bases.

After the capture of the Marianas, Admiral Nimitz created a new fleet, the Third Fleet; or rather, he perpetuated the command created in the South Pacific. Admiral Halsey and his Third Fleet headquarters were sent to sea in the same ships that had been operating under the name Fifth Fleet when commanded by Admiral Spruance. This change was not just semantic, although the propaganda effect was excellent and indicated even greater strength in ships than the Americans actually had. The real reason for the system was administrative. The ships—the carriers in particular—could be kept in almost constant service if they had a unified command. So while Spruance came back to plan the next landing operation, Halsey went afloat to do what he liked best, hit the Japanese and hit them hard. It was understood that the Philippines operation, to be carried out against Leyte, would be under the overall command of General MacArthur, and the landing operations would be conducted by "MacArthur's Navy," still another naval command, headed by Admiral Thomas Kinkaid. Halsey's Third Fleet would not be troubled with the demands of an amphibious force but would be free to range wide to support the landings and wipe out any air and naval power that appeared.

Halsey sailed at the end of August, and in his strikes in September he found Japanese air power surprisingly weak. Of course it was all relative. So great was the carrier power of the fleet that in one operation on September 12 and 13, Halsey's planes flew twenty-four hundred missions, destroyed two hundred Japanese planes, and shot up many merchant vessels, sampans, barges, and shore installations. Halsey was so contemptuous of Japanese power in the islands around the Philippines that he suggested the lesser invasions of September be cancelled as a waste of time, but the Palaus operation had gone too far, and Peleliu and the other islands had to be taken. One island, Ulithi, had a fine deepwater port, and Nimitz decided to make this his advanced base for supply of the fleet during the coming Philippine operations. The major result of Halsey's far-ranging carrier operations of September was the advance of the Leyte invasion by almost two months to late October, 1944.

The Japanese were as well prepared for the Leyte invasion as they could be. They were in the position of the hound with too many foxholes to watch.

Wherever the Americans landed, however, the Japanese navy planned to come forth with its remaining strength and seek that "final battle" that had been under discussion ever since the death of Yamamoto. The general plan, approved by army and navy, was called the Sho Operation. Following the events of early September, on the 22nd of that month the Imperial General Headquarters fixed the area of "decisive battle" as the Philippines, and guessing with great prescience, said it would come in the last week of October. General Tomoyuki Yamashita, who had captured the Philippines in the first place but had then been sent to the far more important area of Manchuria where he was First Army commander during most of the war, was recalled to the scene of his triumph as commander of the reorganized Fourteenth Area Army. He headed for Manila, to arrive just as the battle for Leyte began, before he could even make a tour of the command.

As Yamashita was on his way south, Admiral Halsey's carriers hit Formosa to knock out the Japanese pipeline of supply for aircraft. They destroyed five hundred Japanese planes on the ground and in the air. The Japanese attacked the fleet with everything they had left. The Japanese pilots were so determined on victory that they overestimated the damage they did and had Imperial Headquarters believing the American carrier fleet had been badly damaged. Actually, although the fleet was attacked by a thousand planes, only the Cruisers *Canberra* and *Houston* were seriously damaged, not the eleven carriers, two battleships, three cruisers, and a destroyer that Radio Tokyo said had gone to the bottom of the sea.

While the people of Tokyo were celebrating a great victory, the Americans struck. On October 17, Japanese observers sighted the United States invasion armada, heading for Leyte Gulf. Altogether, some seven hundred ships were employed in this invasion, not counting the Third Fleet's eighteen carriers, six battleships, seventeen cruisers, and sixty-four destroyers that were free to range the seas.

The next day, the Japanese put the Sho Plan into effect. One force left Lingga Roads, off Singapore, where it had been staying close to the base of oil supply. This force was led by Admiral Takao Kurita. A second force, led by Admiral Jisaburo Ozawa sailed from the north of Japan. This force was to be a sacrificial goat if necessary. It had in it what was left of the Japanese carrier fleet after the battle of the Philippine Sea at the time of the invasion of Saipan. These bare bones of the once mighty striking force consisted of the fleet carrier *Zuikaku* and the light carriers *Zuiho*, *Chitose*, and *Chiyoda*. Also in the fleet were two ships about which the Americans knew little, the old battleships *Ise* and *Hyuga*, which had been converted to carriers. They still had some of their guns and greatly foreshortened flight decks. But that did not make much difference because the whole carrier fleet of 6 carried only 116 planes—all that the navy could then muster and man with pilots who could

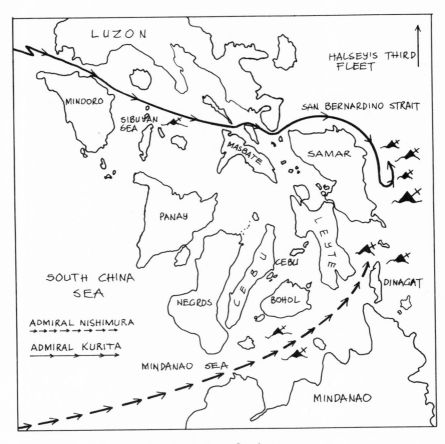

The Philippines, October 1944

operate from a carrier. No one expected that these carriers would come back, and Admiral Ozawa was also resigned to losing most of his surface force of cruisers and destroyers. But what he did hope to do was to lure the American carriers up north to meet him, while Admiral Kurita's force and one other smaller force led by Admiral Teiji Nishimura were to charge in among the ships of the amphibious command and destroy the landing on the beaches. Of course, if Admiral Ozawa could destroy some of the carriers it would be all to the good. On the night of October 24, Kinkaid's battleships and cruisers destroyed the Nishimura force as it came through the Surigao Strait, and Admiral Kinkaid was just relaxing when the word came that Admiral Kurita and his battleships and cruisers were bearing down on the invasion forces from the north. To protect the transports were eighteen escort carriers plus nine destroyers and fifteen escorts.

Admiral Kurita's battleships and cruisers came down like a wolf on the fold and soon had targeted the small carrier *Gambier Bay*. She was sunk, the only carrier during the war to be sunk by naval gunfire. But her planes, and those of the other escort carriers buzzed around the Japanese fleet and their bombs and torpedoes took their toll. Meanwhile the destroyers and escorts attacked so bravely that the Japanese aboard the battleships and cruisers thought they were facing American cruisers. Several of the other escort carriers were hit, but none sunk. But among the smaller ships, the destroyers *Hoel* and *Johnston* and the escort *Samuel B. Roberts* were sunk. The Japanese lost far more. The Nishimura force was decimated. The Kurita force was almost wiped out, and up north Admiral Halsey hit the Ozawa force hard. As a result of the series of three naval actions, the Japanese lost three battleships, four carriers, six cruisers, four light cruisers, and eleven destroyers. For all practical purposes, the battle of Leyte Gulf was the end of the Japanese fleet.

And, although Admiral Kinkaid was furious, and naval historians have continued to debate to this very day, Admiral Halsey's decision to go north and leave untended the San Bernardino Strait, which leads into Leyte Gulf, the results, on balance, justified his action. The loss of one escort carrier and three small combat ships was a very small price to pay. Halsey had always believed that all ships were at risk in a naval action, and the results of the battle of Leyte Gulf were the final answer to his critics: the war was not won without spilling blood.

24

But It Wasn't
Easy....

~~~~~

AT LEYTE the desperation of the Japanese began to show. It took a whole fleet to smash the carrier *Gambier Bay* and the three little ships of the destroyer force off Samar, but only one airplane, flown like a bomb by a suicide pilot, to destroy the escort carrier *St. Lo* that same day. October 25, 1944, marked a new phase of the Pacific war and the trials of the Pacific Fleet. It was the beginning of the Kamikaze terror. Even as the *St. Lo* was attacked, so were the *Petrof Bay* and the *Santee*. (The Japanese suicide pilots would always have a penchant for carriers.)

In the past, Japanese pilots whose planes were seriously damaged had often tried to make one last gesture to damage the enemy by diving into a ship. But during the invasion of Leyte, for the first time suicide diving became a national policy. It was invented by the navy out of sheer desperation. Admiral Ohnishi, who had helped plan the Pearl Harbor attack, had been moved to the Philippines to command the Fifth Base Air Force shortly before the American ships arrived at Leyte Gulf. What Ohnishi found was profoundly discouraging. Theoretically, the navy was entrusted with the mission of preventing allied landings, and the fifth Base Air Force on paper was equipped with hundreds of fighter and bomber aircraft. But in fact nearly all of these planes had been destroyed, either in the defense of the Marianas or in the series of carrier raids carried out by Admiral Halsey. If any defense at all was to be maintained, every plane must be made to count.

Ohnishi was much impressed by the undaunted patriotism of his young fliers and their willingness to sacrifice themselves for the war effort. Out of the pages of history came the idea. In the days of Ghengis Khan, the island

205

kingdom of Japan had been threatened. When the Khan's ambassadors were turned away without tribute and the Japanese refused to submit to Mongol rule, a vast armada was assembled on the China coast and dispatched toward Japan. The Japanese assembled all their military forces but given the size of the invading army and the Mongol ruputation, the leaders feared the end of independence had come. As the armada sailed, however, a terrible storm sprang up in the East China sea, and, by the time the ships reached the coast of Japan, it had developed into a hurricane. The storm did what the defenders might not have been able to do, it scattered the armada and sank many of its ships. Others were blown far afield, and the bodies of Mongol warriers washed up ashore for many weeks. So Japan had been saved by "divine intervention" in the form of a great wind, or "Kamikaze." This was the generic name given to the various units of fliers who volunteered to pilot flying bombs against the enemy.

During the first several days after the invasion of Leyte few planes flew. The rainy season was in progress, and the weather was particularly bad just then. But when it was possilbe to fly, the Kamikazes flew their one-way missions. On October 30, suicide pilots dived into the carriers *Franklin* and *Belleau Wood*. Both were seriously damaged and had to be sent to the new base at Ulithi for repairs. One day later, as Admiral Halsey's planes smashed Japanese shipping all around the Philippines, one American destroyer was sunk by a Kamikaze pilot, and four others were damaged. Four days after that the new carrier *Lexington* (named for the ship sunk at the Coral Sea) was hit. Admiral J. S. McCain, who had taken over from Admiral Mitscher as carrier commander for a few weeks, was forced to transfer his command to another vessel, and *Lexington* went back for repairs.

The Kamikaze threat, then, was extremely serious. If the Americans had not possessed enormous resources, the results might have been disastrous. One airplane loaded with high explosive could sink a big ship or put it out of action for weeks. And this was happening with alarming frequency.

The Americans countered in the only way they could: they set out to destroy all the aircraft they could reach in the Philippines and wipe out the bases. On the day that the *Lexington* was hit, Halsey's planes struck Luzon all day long, concentrating on airfields. They claimed to have destroyed 450 planes in a two-day strike, and while the figure was inflated as fliers' figures tended to be, the damage was indeed effective in slowing down Admiral Ohnishi's Kamikaze corps. At sea, the Americans wiped out one lone Japanese warship after another. One day planes found the cruiser *Nachi* and sank her. In the middle of November, the Japanese tried to bring reinforcements from Luzon to Leyte by transport, but carrier planes sank one cruiser, five destroyers, and seven transports, while shooting down eighty-four Japanese planes, and on November 25, they sank the cruiser *Kumano* as well. But the Kami-

206

kazes kept coming, concentrating when they could on the carriers. On the day that *Kumano* went down, *Intrepid* and *Cabot* both took Kamikazes, and both had to be sent back from the fleet for repairs. One of the major factors in saving these American ships from sinking was the new method of building by compartment, so that a big carrier could take an enormous amount of punishment and still remain afloat.

Another sort of Kamikaze also hit the American fleet in December. On December 17, Admiral Halsey was preparing to fuel, about five hundred miles off the coast of Luzon. The weather was acting up. To escape the storm, Halsey decided to move two hundred miles northwest before fuelling, but he was the victim of an error by his aerographer, who estimated that the storm was one hundred miles east and that it would soon strike an incoming cold front and turn northeast. In fact, by heading northwest, Halsey moved directly into the eye of the typhoon, and his fleet took a dreadful beating, all the worse because while new ships were constructed with ever-growing skill, the changes in the war and weapons had brought about modification of many older ships, especially destroyers, which received radar installations and other changes that affected their center of gravity. In a phrase, many of the fleet's destroyers were now top-heavy, and in this typhoon, the *Spence*, *Hull*, and *Monaghan* all capsized and sank like rubber boats in a bathtub; the wind and waves forced them over onto their sides, water went streaming down the stacks, and the ships gurgled and went down with nearly all their crews.

When the storm ended, had Admiral Ohnishi known, he could have rejoiced. For in addition to the three destroyers sunk, the carriers *Monterey, Cowpens,* and *San Jacinto* had all been so seriously damaged that they had to return to Ulithi. So were the escort carriers *Cape Esperance* and *Altamaha,* and twenty-two other ships of the fleet. About one hundred and fifty planes were also lost in the storm. It was the greatest loss to the fleet since the battle of Savo Island in the days of Guadalcanal. In January, 1945, Admiral Nimitz moved his headquarters to Guam. The reason was the change in the whole conduct of the Pacific War. General MacArthur, having seized the initiative from the navy, was not about to relinquish it. All the ships of the Seventh Fleet, which was commanded by Admiral Kinkaid, actually "belonged" to the Central Pacific forces by assignment. But when MacArthur got a ship he never let it go. As the ships remained in action, they suffered minor damage and attrition and needed to go back to major bases for repair. MacArthur stoutly resisted any attempts to move the ships out of his jurisdiction, and he remained firmly in control of the war in the Philippines. Nimitz moved his headquarters west to have better access to the MacArthur command. Further, while MacArthur was in charge at the moment, Admiral King had not given up his hope that the next show would be along the China coast and that the navy would run it.

Pacific Destiny

The United States' power to stage an enormous invasion was growing rapidly. As the war in Europe wound down to its end, the demands of the American armies in Europe decreased. The U-boat menace was largely under control, so the Pacific Fleet was able to secure most of the ships as they came off the ways. It seemed likely that the vast majority of ships could be committed to the Pacific in the next few months. Just now the navy had 89 carriers, including 13 of the 27,000-ton fleet class. By the end of 1945, as projected, the navy would have 2,500 ships. The keels for three 45,000-ton carriers had already been laid. It would take more than Kamikazes to destroy such a fleet.

With the invasion of the Philippines the war had changed character almost completely. Instead of fighting to drive a handful of Japanese off some island, the Americans were now fighting major elements of the Japanese army. There were, in November, 1944, an estimated two hundred thousand Japanese troops in the Philippines. By the middle of December, 1944, when the Americans captured the Ormoc base on the west side of Leyte, they also took most of the Japanese army's supplies for that island, so the campaign came to a close. General Yamashita was recommending the abandonment of the fight on Leyte and retreat to Luzon where the "major battle" would be staged. Although the American fleet was not given much credit, its activities in November and December played a large part in the changes in the Japanese plan. In November, the Japanese Southern Army headquarters was moved from Manila back to Singapore, a virtual admission on the highest level that the Philippines were lost. And this feeling was buttressed by the facts. By the end of 1944, the Japanese troop strength in the Philippines was reduced to 90,000. Admiral Halsey's campaign of sinking Japanese transports, destroying naval vessels, and knocking out air power had proved even more effective than the Americans then knew. Since the summer of 1944, by Japanese estimate, 80 percent of the ships sent south from Japan had been sunk.

Halsey's fleet struck hard in December and again in January. By this time, the army air forces had also built up fields on Leyte and Mindoro Islands, and were sending heavy bombers against Japanese lines of communications and strong points. On January 9, came the landings at Lingayen Gulf. In a month, the Americans were advancing on Manila. From that point on, it was a matter of taking ground, piece by piece, from a Japanese force that was isolated but not demoralized; the Japanese fought on with little food, less ammunition, and no hope. Still they fought, and the Philippines were not completely pacified even at the end of the war. On the day of surrender, Japanese troops were still holding out in the mountains above the Ashin river. This stubborn resistance put a serious crimp in General MacArthur's plans and gave the navy new hope that it would be put in charge of the drive across the Pacific once more.

But It Wasn't Easy. . . .

The next move, it was agreed in Washington, was to be against Iwo Jima. Perhaps Halsey was responsible for the decision; at least he had argued in the Pacific Fleet counsels for action against Iwo Jima after the Philippines. MacArthur still wanted to go into the Netherlands East Indies next, but his forces were tied up in the Philippines. The argument for Iwo Jima was settled when General Curtis Lemay of the *B-29* command said that his *B-29*s needed fighter protection if they were to be most effective against Japanese targets, and fighters based at Iwo Jima could do the job. So Iwo Jima was next.

25

The Desperate Days of Iwo Jima

~~~~~~~~~

NO ONE EXPECTED THE ASSAULT on Iwo Jima to be easy. This set of islands, located just north of the Tropic of Cancer, about halfway between Saipan and Honshu Island, is closer to Tokyo than Formosa. In 1945, it was, in fact, right in the heart of the Japanese empire. An assault against Iwo Jima was certain to bring forth every bit of Japanese resistance that could be managed, and long before the troops landed, General Holland Smith warned that this was going to be the most difficult operation his marines had yet tackled. There would be no army troops in the operation against Iwo Jima. In the first place, this campaign was of the sort the marines had carried out so well in the Central Pacific: attack on a small land mass that was heavily fortified and demanded shock tactics. General Holland Smith was confident that his marines could do the job ably and alone. There was another reason that the employment of army forces was not even considered. The press had stirred the Smith versus Smith controversy into a pretty stew. Not that the press was needed to do so; the ingrained rivalry between the army and the marines had always been held in check with difficulty, for the army had always been jealous of the marine corps's role as shock infantry. Holland Smith's relief of Ralph Smith at Saipan had rolled through the army like a tidal wave, and a tight-lipped General Marshall had so far lost his temper as to state flatly that never again in his time of command would army troops ever serve under a marine general. But for Iwo Jima, it was agreed that Holland Smith would be the commander. Smith's flat statements about the difficulty of taking Iwo Jima gave the conservative Admiral Spruance pause, but there would be no more easy victories. Having come so close to Japan, the Americans must

211

expect growingly ferocious resistance. General Holland Smith was so concerned about the state of Japanese defenses of this rocky island system that he asked Spruance for a ten-day naval bombardment. Logistically that was impossible. No ship could carry that much ammunition, and resupply of warships at sea with ammunition was too dangerous. Spruance argued that Iwo Jima had been bombed heavily for eight months. Further, he would make sure that for the seventy-two days that remained before invasion, Iwo Jima would be bombed every day. General Smith had to be satisfied with that compromise and was only allowed three days for the bombardment. He did not like it, because the Japanese had had a year to build up Iwo's defenses since the invasion of the Gilberts, but there was nothing else to be done.

The Japanese had, indeed, built up the defenses of Iwo Jima. After the invasion of Saipan, Imperial Headquarters concluded that Iwo Jima would be high on the American list of invasion points. The long-range bombers from Saipan needed fighter support, and Iwo Jima was perfectly located to provide it. Indeed, the Japanese had sporadically bombed American air bases in the Marianas from Iwo Jima in the last few months.

The Japanese strength on Iwo Jima had been increased to 17,500 men. Infantry, tanks, and artillery were all represented. In addition, navy personnel brought the defense force to 21,000. Lieutenant General Tadamichi Kurabayashi had supervised the rebuilding of the defenses. The shore guns and artillery were heavily fortified, the former built up with 6 feet of concrete all around to save them from anything but a direct hit. The anti-aircraft guns were similarly protected, placed in pits which were half covered over. The various pillboxes and defensive points were interconnected by a hive of tunnels.

The more General Holland Smith learned about the Japanese defenses from aerial photographs, the harder he fought for more bombardment time. But Spruance was adamant; he could only allot three days.

Spruance wanted a strong carrier strike on Tokyo just before the landings. He estimated that the strike there at that time would preoccupy the Japanese at home and keep them from sending planes down to Iwo Jima. He hoped to concentrate the air strike on the Japanese aircraft industry. Obviously Spruance did not know much about the Japanese aircraft industry of the methods of bombing heavy industry if he expected carrier bombers to do a great deal of damage. But he hoped.

On February 8, the American fleet, named Fifth Fleet again since Spruance was in command, sailed toward Japan, and on February 16, the fast carriers reached a point only 60 miles off Honshu. They launched their strike from that point. The carrier bombers performed as demanded, but did far more damage against Japanese planes in the air and on the ground than they did to the aircraft industry. The Japanese aircraft plants were virtually unhurt

212

and continued to pour out planes at the rate of seventeen hundred a month. The planners called for thirty-three hundred planes a month, but the aluminum, the copper, and the steel were just not available to produce so many.

But there were aircraft to throw into the Japanese island pipeline, and they kept moving out, to the Philippines and to other islands. In fact the Japanese defense effort was still formidable.

What had now become the usual team was selected by Admiral Spruance for the Iwo Jima operation. Admiral Richmond Kelly Turner was by this time the world's leading expert in amphibious operations, and he would command until the troops were safely ashore and the beachhead established. His principal assistant, as at the Marshalls and Marianas, was Rear Admiral Harry Hill. General Holland Smith was commander of the expeditionary troops, and under him came the V Amphibious Corps of Marines, with Major General Harry Schmidt in charge. Rear Admiral W. H. P. Blandy would command the bombardment team.

In the planning of this assault, at first the admirals and generals considered Chichi Jima, a larger island in the Bonins north of Iwo Jima, but the aerial photographs showed that it was even more heavily fortified than Iwo. What began to worry them was a report on the nature of the beaches here—black volcanic cinder. One day one of the aerial interpreters noticed that a beached Japanese vessel on one of the Iwo Jima beaches had sunk several feet into the sand since the previous picture taken a few days earlier. This gave everyone pause; the amphibious command's solution was to rig up sections of light weight steel framework called Marston net, which had been used successfully to substitute for paving on muddy airfield runways.

Besides the sand and the heavy fortification of the island, General Holland Smith worried about the terrain. Iwo Jima was topped by a live volcano, Mount Suribachi. It had not erupted during the war, but Americans knew little about its behavior before that because the Japanese had been so secretive about all their territory. The photographs told them, however, that Mount Suribachi still spouted steam and sulphur, so she might go up at any time. Overshadowing all difficulties was the fact that the Japanese had completed two airfields on Iwo Jima and started a third to increase their bombing of Saipan, 625 miles away. Three days after the first B-29 raid on Japan in November, 1944, when the American crews were loading up the B-29 Superfortresses for another raid, two twin-engined bombers came in low over the airfield, and when they left, one B-29 was destroyed and eleven were badly damaged. The same day, a dozen Japanese fighters came in around noon, destroyed three more B-29s and damaged another two. All these planes had come from Iwo Jima.

So it was not only necessary that the island be captured if the B-29 raids were to be successful, but that until it was captured, it be neutralized. In

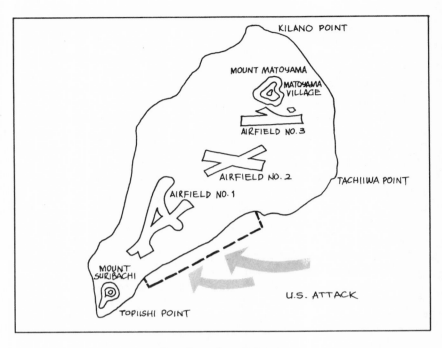

Iwo Jima, January 1945

December, the *B-24* squadrons of the VII United States Army Air Force were assigned to make daily bombing raids on Iwo's airfields, but the raids were not effective. On Christmas eve, the Japanese flew another mission to Saipan; twenty-five planes came in and destroyed another *B-29* and damaged three more so badly they had to be junked for parts. Naval bombardments, *B-24* raids, fighter raids, and carrier bomber raids had all done damage, but had not penetrated into the deep defenses. Further, Iwo Jima was a perfect example of the effectiveness of the Japanese island-hopping system. A raid might knock out every plane on the island one day, but by the next day, the force was totally reconstituted by planes flown from Japan and Formosa.

Although Japan's fleet was in a shambles, and American ships and planes ranged the air and waters all around the empire, and American submarines penetrated even into the Inland Sea, the stout defenses of the inner empire showed just how difficult the attack on Japan itself was going to be. Urged by General Holland Smith, the American raiders became even more persistent. By the end of January, 1945, the fleet had bombarded Iwo Jima three times, and Superfortresses had diverted from Japan to hit the island

214

twice. In the first two weeks of February, the island was bombed day and night. Still, after each raid the defenders repaired the damage and continued to build deeper into the mountain. And after each raid, more aircraft from Tokyo were flown in.

General Kuribayashi intended to make Iwo Jima absolutely impregnable. Studying reports of past American invasions the general saw that he could not hold the beaches against the pressure the Americans could apply from sea and air. Nor could he hold the airfields, after the American fleet and the carriers arrived to ring the island. So he concentrated his defenses around Mount Suribachi in the south, and around Motoyama village just above the center of the pear-shaped island. Kuribayashi's naval advisors protested against this defense. It was naval doctrine to defend every inch of the land—the navy still believed it could drive the landing force into the sea. So the general let the navy men have their way. The navy fixed the coastal guns so they could fire along the length of the beaches. The navy built a system of pillboxes just above the beaches, and connected them with tunnels. They built concrete blockhouses to shelter the infantry from bombs and bombardment.

Since the navy did this work, General Kuribayashi's army troops could concentrate on the sort of defense found most effective at Peleliu and Leyte. The slopes of Mount Suribachi were dotted with artillery, mortars, and machine guns, all of them protected by concrete and connected by elaborate systems of caves and tunnels which were supplied with food and ammunition. A defense line was built across the island near Motoyama, between two airfields, consisting of more trenches, tunnels, and caves, five levels in some places. Even the tanks were dug in so that only their turrets projected. All was camouflaged so cleverly that the aerial photos and the observers missed most of the strong points. The marines would see them only when they were ashore and the Japanese opened fire.

All this construction had been proceeding feverishly since September. General Kuribayashi accepted the decision that Iwo Jima must be fought to the last, in the hope that the enormous losses inflicted on the Americans would make them stop moving into the Japanese empire. This was the military rationale of the policy of no surrender. By January, with the landings at Lingayen and the increase in allied activity everywhere, Imperial General Headquarters knew that even these tough defenses would not stop the allies and was planning defense of the Japanese homeland itself. Training of Kamikaze pilots and production of one-way aircraft became the order of the day. The new planes were fitted with disposable landing gear, which were to be jettisoned after take off to lighten the plane and streamline it. Miniature submarines were produced by the hundreds. A plywood motorboat with a bomb in the bow was developed and thousands of them were built. Mines were stacked up for sowing on the beaches, and the civilian population of Japan was exhorted to prepare for the day when every man, woman and child would have to fight.

The coming battle of Iwo Jima was used to show the Japanese the reason they must prepare to sacrifice all. The propagandists pulled out all the stops.

The battle for Iwo Jima opened with a 16-carrier air strike against aircraft factories and airfields on February 16 and 17. The attacks were not very successful; the pilots claimed to have destroyed more that 500 Japanese planes; the real figure was far less. They lost 78 American planes. They sank a few ships, the largest of them a 10,000-ton merchantman. Then they went back to stand off Iwo Jima in support of the landings.

Admiral Spruance had told General Holland Smith he might get a fourth day of bombardment, depending on the decision of Admiral Blandy, who was in charge of that phase of the operation. Blandy had six battleships, four heavy cruisers, a light cruiser and sixteen destroyers for the task. But the weather was bad and the spotters could not find their targets, so artfully were they concealed. On February 16, a sweep of the airfield by planes from the dozen escort carriers provided little more information about targets. The most effective work that day was done by the minesweepers and frogmen, who were checking on underwater explosive devices and obstructions. The next day the weather was better. The bombardment continued, with some effect on Japanese guns that were firing on the minesweepers. But the Japanese hit back and put half a dozen shells from six-inch guns into the cruiser *Pensacola,* causing 115 casualties. The *Pensacola* withdrew from the fight temporarily. The underwater demolition teams were sent in that day to the beaches to check for obstructions. The Japanese decimated the landing craft that brought them in, killing and wounding about 200 men. The frogmen did their job, however. They found no obstacles around the beaches.

The first two-days' bombardment had not been very impressive, but the guns had destroyed camouflage around some Japanese positions, and someone had convinced General Kuribayashi that the UDT teams meant the invasion had started, and he ordered a number of his hidden guns to unmask. So the fire on the fortifications did produce some direct hits.

The Japanese reacted with an air raid on the ships, and two destroyers were put out of the Iwo Jima fight. Admiral Turner arrived at six o'clock on the morning of the fourth day. There was no talk of more bombardment, for Admiral Blandy had not even used up the shells allocated for the three days. The ships had just not found enough targets. When General Holland Smith learned this, he was more than usually depressed. Smith's constant complaint did not please Admiral Turner, commander of the invasion, who this morning said he was going to conduct the heaviest pre-invasion bombardment of the Pacific War. And he did. Seven battleships, ten cruisers, and a handful of destroyers stood off the island and pumped shells into the land. An hour and a half later the barrage was lifted so that carrier planes could strike the island with rockets, bombs, strafing, and napalm. The navy was clearly trying to do its best, given its limitations. General Holland Smith was both right and wrong; the bombardment was not enough to knock out the defenses, but given the depth of those defenses it seems improbable that any amount of bombing and bombardment would have. General Kuribayashi had done his job very well.

Holland Smith's constant reiteration of the dangers, and his constant reminders of the poor job the navy had done at Tarawa got on everyone's nerves. Admiral Spruance rejected Smith's pleas for longer bombardment, and Admiral Turner virtually put Smith in isolation aboard his flagship. It was hardly an auspicious beginning for the invasion.

Under the amphibious doctrine of the United States Navy, the amphibious commander was in complete charge of the operation until the troops were ashore and their lines of communication established, and the beachhead declared "secure." So in effect Turner was his own general, and his relations with Smith had become so strained that the latter spent most of his time in his cabin playing cribbage.

When the landings began, General Smith's worst fears were realized. The first assault wave made it to the beaches, but there men and vehicles bogged down in the soft black volcanic cinder. The Japanese field artillery and mortars began to find the amphibious tanks, and soon the beach was littered with damaged vehicles. In the beginning, the Japanese fire was fairly light, because most of the troops had been deep underground during the bombardment. But when the ships stopped firing, the defenders emerged to man their weapons. After the first half hour the firing became intense and the amphtracs bogging down on the beach were hid. Four tank-laden landing ships came ashore at 9:44 A.M. and were immediately damaged by mortar shells.

The "beach" at Iwo Jima consisted of a series of terraces leading up to Mount Suribachi. The marines came ashore and tried to make their way up the steep hillside, terrace by terrace. They soon discovered the depth and extent of the Japanese defenses. Many of the pillboxes were not discernible from the sea because they were built flush to the earth, with only a firing slit uncovered. Such installations were impervious to anything but a direct shell hit, and it took a big shell to knock them apart. The alternative was for the marines to throw grenades, satchel charges, and flame into the aperatures. To do this the men had to get in close, and that meant taking casualties.

Altogether, the marines landed on seven designated beaches, the 5th Division on one side of the island and the 4th Division on the other. As they progressed, frequently they called back to the ships for fire support against specific targets. The ships responded, zeroing in on targets they could not spot before and blasting them with direct armor-piercing fire that blew apart one blockhouse after another. But this was slow work, and it cost heavily in casualties. Tanks came in, but they also became prime targets for the Japanese artillery as they labored up the slopes of the terraces, and many of them were knocked out. The primary weapon remained the marine on foot, but there was a difference between this and any previous invasion. The foot soldiers *needed* the ships all the way. Each marine battalion was given one destroyer on which it could call for direct fire support on specific positions, and the larger ships opened each morning with a barrage and then stood by to hit targets the destroyers could not destroy.

General Schmidt was in charge of the land operations almost from the beginning. Admiral Turner would not allow General Smith to go ashore except for "inspection" trips. Commander of the marine force though he was, he was not allowed to command. He remained on board the flagship and continued his cribbage.

Ashore the days went with painful slowness. Some had predicted that Iwo Jima would be cleared in four or five days. On February 23, the fifth day, the marines raised the American flag atop Mount Suribachi, and the event was duly recorded by Associated Press photographer Joe Rosenthal in a picture that soon had captured the imagination of all America—but for the wrong reason. As a photograph it was supreme. As an indication of what was happening on Iwo Jima it was most misleading. The Japanese were far from defeated and the Americans were far from in control of this island. The Americans were on top of Suribachi, but the Japanese were deep inside. The village of Motoyama and the airfield called Airfield Number 2 were not captured and secured until March 1. On March 4, Admiral Turner said he had to leave, to prepare for the coming invasion of Okinawa, and he sailed away, having transferred General Holland Smith to Admiral Harry Hill's flagship, with instructions that he was to continue his cribbage and remain out of the action. Admiral Hill felt so sorry for Smith that he spent his free time playing cribbage with the general.

But the fighting on Iwo Jima continued unabated. On March 16, the marines declared the island "secured" but for the next week they fought to secure it. General Kuribayashi was still alive and still directing his troops, although on March 21, he radioed a subordinate on nearby Chichi Jima that the troops had not eaten for five days and the end was near. "Goodbye" said General Kuribayashi. And shortly thereafter he committed suicide.

General Schmidt announced on March 26 that the Iwo Jima operation was ended, and he took his command post aboard a boat and left the island. Airfield Number 1 was already landing and sending off fighter planes to escort the *B-29*s on their missions against Japan. The army's Major General James E. Chaney became commander of the garrison that would man the island from this point on—and the fighting continued. Small groups of Japanese holed up and then came out to harry the Americans. In April and May, sixteen hundred Japanese were killed and eight hundred and sixty prisoners taken, largely through the efforts of the American Nisei, who persuaded the Japanese to surrender. But many did not, and the fighting was not just a matter of picking off stragglers. One night in April, two hundred Japanese staged a Banzai charge against an infantry outpost, and although the Japanese were all killed, they did blow up a dynamite dump, and the explosion of six thousand cases of dynamite shook the entire island.

It was June, 1945, before the resistance on Iwo Jima ended. And when it was all over, the United States casualty figure was high. Admiral Samuel Eliot Morison, visiting Iwo in April, had counted fifty-three hundred crosses in the marine cemetery. That was only the dead. Thousands of men were wounded, and thousands of men aboard the warships were hurt or lost. So the casualties at Iwo were more than twenty thousand. Some elements of the American press began to complain that the price was too high, but the fact was that Iwo Jima, or another Bonin Island was desperately needed to provide air bases for the fighters that would protect the bombers that would bomb Japan. Had the marines chosen Chichi Jima the going would have been worse because it was a larger place. But the casualties at Iwo Jima were just a taste of what was to come if the Americans plowed on and staged the final assault against Japan.

26

Assassins
at Okinawa

~~~~~~~~

IWO JIMA MARKED THE END of General Holland Smith's battle career. He
went back to America to a training command, victim of the quarrels between
navy and army over the employment of troops, and his own quarrel with the
navy over bombardment. His many achievements could not be denied, but he
was never to have another chance to perform in action. The politics of war
became as vital as the politics of peace had ever been.

The quarrel over bombardment was never resolved. Unwittingly, as Iwo
Jima proved, General Smith had called attention to one weakness of naval
doctrine in the middle of the twentieth century: the weapons were not adequate for the task. Naval bombardment at Iwo Jima was effective in direct
relationship to the accuracy of fire. The old idea of a general barrage was not
effective. General Smith's position was that of the messenger bringing bad
news to the king. The one positive result of the Smith versus Smith quarrel
was a warning to the army to prepare its troops better for combat, and that
lesson certainly was learned. It had to be learned, because the next attack,
which was to be against Okinawa, involved an island twenty-five miles long
with an area of nearly five hundred square miles. On Okinawa there was
plenty of room for military maneuver. Here the Japanese could be expected
to use crack troops with tanks and heavy artillery. Okinawa was to be much
more like the battle for Japan would be than like the battle for those Central
Pacific atolls at which the marines had so excelled.

Okinawa first came into Pacific Fleet consideration in the summer of
1944. After Admiral Halsey was detached from duty in the South Pacific, he
returned to Pearl Harbor where he was told to start planning for the future.

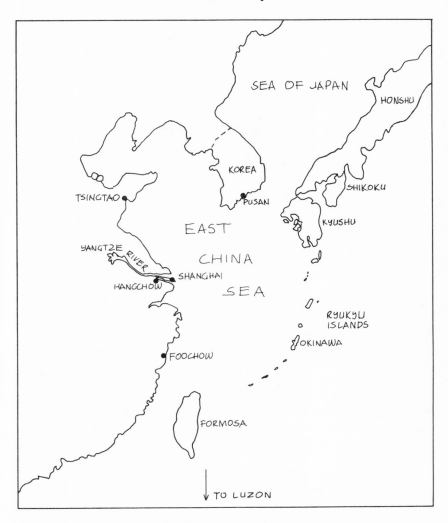

The Japanese Innermost Empire, 1945

That summer the Joint Chiefs of Staff were talking about the route to Tokyo. In the staff conferences that followed King asked Nimitz for ideas, and Nimitz asked his admirals, and Halsey suggested Okinawa. The idea took hold. By September, 1944, Nimitz was talking about an attack the following March on the Nansei Shoto, as the Japanese called these islands, or the Ryukyus, as they were known in English. These islands, of which the largest was Oki-

222

nawa, form part of the eastern wall that protects Japan proper and the East China Sea. As far as the navy was concerned, the point of attack had to be from either Formosa or Okinawa. and Formosa was ruled out because it was expected it would be far too expensive in casualties. Much of the highly praised Kwantung Army from Manchuria had moved to Formosa as the Japanese half expected the major attack there. But Okinawa was equally important; it was only 340 miles from Japan, and it offered an excellent staging point for invasion of the Japanese home islands.

At the end of 1944 the Japanese made a bad guess. They decided that the focal point of the next major invasion would be Formosa, and they moved in new troops, among them the 9th Division which had been stationed on Okinawa. Lieutenant General Mitsuru Ushijima, commander of the 32nd Army, which defended Okinawa, asked for a replacement but it never came. In Japan the Imperial General Staff was gearing up for the expected assault on the Japanese home islands, and all major moves were viewed in light of that need. Okinawa was to be defended if attacked but not in the traditional way. Rather, the high command projected the use of an entirely new technique to support the troops on the island. A thousand planes of the new *Tokko* air force would be used to strike the enemy. The *Tokko* force was the result of Admiral Ohnishi's desperate measures at Leyte to try to stop the Americans. The Americans had not been stopped but enough damage had been done in the Philippines to the American naval forces to persuade the Japanese high command that suicide planes were an important weapon, and they came at a time when Japan was desperate for weapons. It is ironic that, at long last, the Imperial General Staff had accepted the doctrine of Admiral Yamamoto: create a climate in which the Americans would settle for a negotiated peace. The only hope by the beginning of 1945 was to make a United States victory too costly.

Reluctantly, Admiral Nimitz prepared for an entirely new sort of battle. He was not eager, for Nimitz, like Admirals King and Leahy (President Roosevelt's naval aide) believed that the Japanese could be brought to their knees through sea power alone, and there was no need to sacrifice so many lives. This navy point of view was buttressed in the beginning of 1945 by the growing success of the submarine force and the carrier force in interdicting supply ships bound for Japan with raw materials. But the army and air force members of the Joint Chiefs of Staff would never accept this view. The airmen said air power would do the job. The army men said "you have to seize the territory." So the Joint Chiefs prepared for the final assault against the Japanese homeland, and Okinawa was to be both a staging point and a testing ground.

The invasion of Okinawa called for the employment of a field army. There was no chance that an army was going to serve under a marine general. Not after Smith versus Smith. Recognizing this reality, Admiral Nimitz planned for the employment of an army general under the command of Admiral Spruance. He would be Lieutenant General Simon Bolivar Buckner, Jr., and the army would be known as the Tenth Army. This time, the marines—the III Amphibious Corps—were to serve in the Pacific under an army general. This force included the First Marine Division and the Sixth Marine Division, plus the XXIV Army Corps, whose components were the Seventh Division and the Ninety-Sixth Division. The reserve was to be the Twenty-Seventh Division once again.

By the spring of 1945, the Americans estimated Japanese strength on Okinawa to be about sixty thousand men, with most of the troops in the southern half of the island.

When the operation began, Holland Smith's shade lingered on. Admiral Blandy, who was to deliver bombardment and fire support on Okinawa as he had on Iwo Jima, was ordered to give eight days of bombardment to soften up the defenses.

From March 18 to March 31, the fast carriers of the Pacific Fleet struck Kyushu Island airfields. By the time the Americans came to invade, Okinawa's four airfields had been hit so hard that all fields were unusable, and no Japanese planes were operational.

Operations against Japanese fields brought higher casualties to the carriers than they had been used to in the past. On March 18, the carriers bombed Kobe and Kure, and damaged the battleship *Yamato* and the carrier *Amagi,* but not seriously. They bombed airfields but did not find many planes. The enemy planes were simultaneously attacking the United States carriers. One dropped a bomb on the *Enterprise*'s flight deck. Luckily it was a dud. Another bomber tried to crash on the flight deck of the *Intrepid* and came so close that the explosion killed two Americans and wounded forty. The *Yorktown* took two bomb hits that day, too.

On March 19, the *Wasp* was bombed and suffered three hundred and seventy dead and wounded but continued to operate. The *Franklin* was hit so hard that a thousand men were killed and the order was given to abandon ship. More than seventeen hundred men were rescued from the water. The captain stayed aboard and managed to save her. Still she had to be sent back for major repair.

That same day, the carrier *Hancock* was attacked by a Zero pilot who either was flying a Kamikaze mission or had been hurt and intended to do as much damage as possible (at this point it was hard to tell the difference). The plane missed the *Hancock* but hit the destroyer *Halsey Powell* and very nearly sank her. So the opposition was getting stiffer.

The Americans had not seen the worst yet. On March 21, the carriers found a group of "bogeys" about sixty miles away, and when the fighters went out they encountered forty-eight Betty bombers and Zeros. The bombers

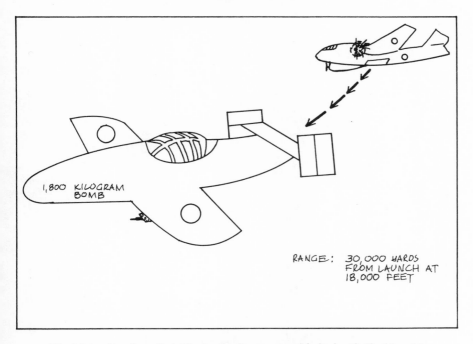

1,800 KILOGRAM BOMB

RANGE: 30,000 YARDS FROM LAUNCH AT 18,000 FEET

The Flying Bomb, called *Oka* by the Japanese and *baka bomb* (fool bomb) by the Americans

were carrying new weapons, flying bombs, or *Oka* they were called by the Japanese. Each *Oka* consisted of a 4,700-pound winged projectile with a pilot's compartment and a rocket propulsion system. They were capable of six hundred miles per hour and they moved and turned so swiftly that they were almost impossible to shoot down. On this first day, the Americans caught the bombers off guard. Carrying the heavy bombs, the Bettys were almost incapable of defensive maneuver. One after the other the bombers were shot down, their *Okas* still attached. The Americans labelled them "baka"—fool bombs—but as the next few days showed, "baka" was a misnomer.

While the carriers of the American fleet and a group of four carriers, two battleships, and five cruisers of the new British Pacific Fleet softened up the Japanese for the Okinawa invasion, Spruance was preparing at Ulithi. The hundreds of ships that lay in harbor began sailing for Okinawa on March 14. Before the attack, Admiral Turner's forces occupied the Kerama Retto, a small group of islands west of Naha, very luckily as it turned out, the biggest city on Okinawa. Admiral Turner had wanted the islands as a harbor for

225

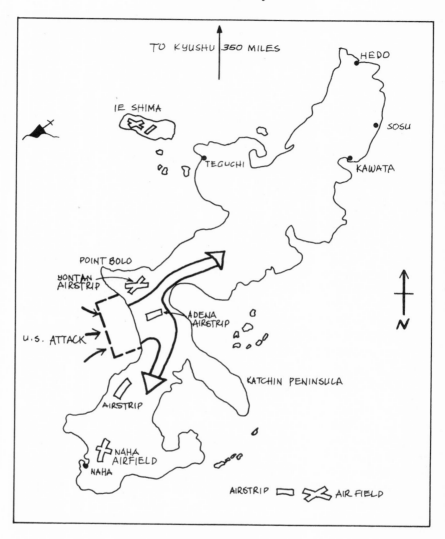

TO KYUSHU 350 MILES

HEDO

IE SHIMA

SOSU

TEGUCHI

KAWATA

POINT BOLO

YONTAN AIRSTRIP

ADENA AIRSTRIP

U.S. ATTACK

KATCHIN PENINSULA

AIRSTRIP

N

NAHA AIRFIELD

NAHA

AIRSTRIP ☐ ✈ AIR FIELD

Okinawa, March 1945

refuelling and transfer of ammunition in bad weather. He did not know that they were Japanese suicide boat bases. After the occupation, the Americans discovered 250 of these craft, each 18-feet long, each carrying 500 pounds of depth charges. The mission of the operator was to steer into the side of an American ship with the result of a well-placed torpedo. How many lives were saved by this offhand decision to take the Kerama Retto no one knew, but from what followed it is apparent that many were. Next, the Americans took Keise Shima, an island group about 10 miles off the southern coast of Okinawa which commanded the town of Naha from an artillery point of view. The XXIV Corps landed 155-millimeter artillery pieces to support the infantry drive on Naha.

The invasion preparations continued in a tantalizing, slow-motion way. Fleet tankers arrived in the protected waters of the Kerama roadstead. Repair ships came in. For this battle, the navy would have the equipment to make some repairs so that ships did not have to disengage after suffering damage. This was, of course, undertaken for more reasons than one. Admiral Nimitz was looking ahead to the invasion of Japan. Kerama Retto and Okinawa would become the Ulithi of the China Sea, the new advanced base.

The Americans outdid themselves with the bombardment. This time ten battleships, seven heavy cruisers, three light cruisers, twenty-four destroyers, and eight destroyer escorts were to lay down the barrage. The barrage would be more important than it had been at Iwo Jima, because no landbased aircraft except *B-29*s could reach this far, and General Curtis LeMay, commander of the 20th Air Force, did not want to use his *B-29*s against "tactical" targets. The ships and the carrier aircraft would have to do the job.

As the bombardment began on March 26, the ships had their first run-ins with the Kamikazes. Seven suicide planes attacked and one hit the battleship *Nevada,* knocking out her forward turret guns and killing or wounding 60 men. One suicide plane hit the cruiser *Biloxi.* The bomb did not explode, but the damage was still such that the cruiser was hurried into Kerama Retto for repair. In a night attack, the destroyer *O'Brien* was hit squarely and suffered 126 casualties and such severe damage that she was sent back to the West Coast.

This first day of the effort against Okinawa was an indication of the sort of trouble the navy could expect. The Japanese had been more thorough in preparing their defenses on land and at sea here than anywhere else the Americans had encountered them. The minesweeper *Skylark* moved in close to the beach, struck a mine, and sank in a few minutes. That same day, underwater demolition teams swam in along the Hagushi beaches, where the troops would land, and found wooden posts driven into the coral to impede the progress of landing craft. But there were no mines or traps so these posts were wired and blown up in the next two days.

From the air and from the sea both Okinawa and little Ie Shima just off the Okinawa coast appeared to be completely deserted. The men of the ships looked at the quiet land, for they had been told that somewhere out there were at least sixty thousand Japanese soldiers, and they saw absolutely nothing moving. On March 31, the sixth day of the bombardment, Admiral Spru-

227

ance's flagship, *Indianapolis,* was hit by a Kamikaze, and damaged so badly she had to go to San Francisco. In retrospect it was symbolic of the difficulties to come that the flagship was the first big ship to be put out of action, by one man with one bomb.

On April 1, eight waves of small boats swept in to four landing areas on the southern beaches. The landing operation had an eerie quality, for the craft went storming to the shore, guns ablaze—and landed against virtually no opposition. A few mortars fired, and that was all. Tanks moved swiftly up the slopes from the beaches, and the troops came along behind. The landings began at 8:32 in the morning; at ten o'clock the marines reported from the edge of Yontan airfield that they had not suffered any casualties. Half an hour later troops reached the edge of the Kadena airfield, again without opposition. The word came: Yontan and Kadena airfields, for which Admiral Spruance had expected to fight fiercely, were in American hands. They were not expected to be captured for three days.

All day and all night long the transports disgorged passengers and supplies. It was almost as quiet as if they were in San Diego harbor. Fifty thousand troops were landed, no enemy troops were seen and only a few Japanese aircraft, most of which appeared at dusk. The Japanese sent a few Kamikazes from Kyushu, and one crashed into the battleship *West Virginia,* killing or wounding twenty-seven men but not hurting the ship's capability. Actually, a small force of Americans sent to the south coast of the island to simulate a landing and draw fire suffered more than the landing force. Kamikazes struck that diversionary force, and one crashed into an *LST* and another into the transport *Hinsdale.* Eight men were killed or wounded, the highest casualty figure to the landing force for the whole day's operations.

Where were the Japanese? The Americans talked about sixty thousand men. Actually, including the Okinawan home guards there were one hundred thousand—but where were they? They had moved into the interior, north and south. General Ushijima wanted to draw the United States troops inland, away from the cover of the naval and aerial bombardment. He had made one important miscalculation in his hurry when the landings began—he had neglected to destroy the airfields. On the second day, the Americans made the airfields operational, and thereafter would have land-based air support.

On April 2, when the United States troops moved north, the battle began. The Kamikazes came out at evening and did a certain amount of damage. Two transports were hit and had to retire for repairs. The destroyer *Dickerson* took a Kamikaze which damaged it so badly the ship had to be scuttled. The transport *Henrico* was hit.

The tempo of air attack picked up on April 3. A Kamikaze exploded off the side of the escort carrier *Wake Island* and blew a hole in the hull eighteen by twenty-five feet. She had to go back to Guam. It did not even take a direct hit to wreck a ship, and that was an entirely new problem for the fleet. There was no real solution. To be sure the Americans could and did remain watchful. They began shooting at anything that appeared in the sky (a number of American and British planes were shot down by mistake by their own gunners). They stationed picket ships all around the outskirts of the fleet to give warning of the coming of Kamikazes. But these determined young Japanese, willing to give their lives to strike an American ship, many times managed to succeed. And the effects were too often disastrous. In the first few days of April, the extent of the threat to the fleet was not apparent because the previous week's *B-29* and carrier raids on Japanese airfields had denuded the airfields of Kyushu of aircraft. But planes from the north began moving down to Kyushu on April 1 and planes from the aircraft factories were diverted to the fields where Kamikaze pilots were stationed and waiting only for weapons.

Admiral Toyoda, chief of a Japanese Combined Fleet that virtually no longer existed, was entrusted with the major Japanese air effort against Okinawa. It was part of the plan called *Ten-Go*. By April, he had amassed seven hundred aircraft, more than half of them Kamikaze flying bombs. On the afternoon of April 5, he sent the first wave against the Americans.

They came in just at dusk, low over the water, the Kamikazes or *Kikusui* escorted by Zeros and other fighters whose task was to get the suicide pilots to their destination and draw fire so the attack of the *kikusui* (floating chrysanthemum) could succeed, and finally, to bring home to Toyoda reports of the results. They attacked the destroyers *Newcomb* and *Leutze*. *Newcomb* was hit by three Kamikazes, and yet she managed to survive and later was repaired. The actions of her crew and of that of *Leutze,* which came to her rescue and took a Kamikaze herself, were nothing short of heroic, but the fact was that the Kamikazes had accomplished their purpose.

It seemed impossible that a ship could survive if attacked by a number of ''floating chrysanthemums.'' The picket destroyers, stationed out ahead of the fleet, took the worst beating. At two o'clock on the morning of April 6 the mass attacks began. First in came a group of regulation bombers, which bombed the destroyer *Bush*. All bombs missed. This failure was reminiscent of American performance in the early days of the war, and the reason was basically the same: Japan had virtually run out of trained pilots and some of these men flying bombers were fresh out of flying school. But the bombers were not alone. At three in the afternoon, fifty planes came in on *Bush* and the destroyer *Cassin Young*. *Bush* took a Kamikaze and soon went dead in the water. The destroyer *Colhoun* came to her rescue, and she took a Kamikaze, and then a second one. In two hours the two destroyers were hit by six different attacks. Although the ships were afire and *Bush* appeared to be sinking, the gunners continued to man the guns and shot down a number of planes, some of them obviously suicide planes. Before the end of the day, they were struck again by Kamikazes, and both ships sank. Altogether thirty-five men were killed aboard *Colhoun* and ninety-four aboard *Bush*.

The radar picket stations saved the fleet. The sixteen picket ships suffered a good deal: destroyer escort *Witter*, destroyers *Morris, Hyman, Howorth, Mullany,* and destroyer minesweepers *Rodman* and *Emmons* were put out of action. *Emmons* was sunk after five Kamikazes hit her almost simultaneously.

That day the Japanese launched one raid after another. One raid was directed against the Kerama roadstead, which was virtually alive with ships. First the Kamikazes attacked an *LST* and two ammunition ships. The ammunition ships drifted, giving off fireworks for two days. No one could go near them. In view of the fact that the Japanese sent 355 Kamikazes and 341 other planes against the American fleet the American defense was remarkably good. The damage was nothing like the claim by the Japanese of 120 ships hit and 60 sunk, including two battleships. The Americans actually lost 6 ships and 10 more were seriously damaged. Still, the damage was serious, although the ships and planes destroyed 250 Kamikazes. On April 6, a new batch of Kamikazes and bombers was ready, and the attacks began again. The suicide planes hit the battleship *Maryland,* and the destroyers *Bennett* and *Gregory D. E. Wesson.* After two days of action, the roadstead at Kerama began to crowd up with injured ships, and the action also took a serious toll of the planes and pilots of the American escort carriers since the most experienced of the Japanese pilots were assigned to fly fighter cover for the Kamikazes and ordinary bombers. Admiral Spruance became so worried that he asked Admiral Nimitz to speed replacements, even use escort carriers as transports, because there was no time to follow the usual routine in which a carrier moved back to a base to pick up planes and pilots.

At Okinawa the Japanese navy had its last moment of glory, if it could be called that. Admiral Yamamoto would never have done it—but Admiral Toyoda sent the super battleship *Yamato,* once Yamamoto's flagship, the light cruiser *Yabagi,* and destroyers on a suicide mission. The ships were dispatched *with only enough fuel to get to Okinawa.* There they were expected to engage elements of the American fleet and go down gloriously, taking many of the enemy with them.

American submarines reported this fleet just after it sailed, and Admiral Mitscher's carriers were put on the alert. At eight o'clock on the morning of April 7, a plane from the *Essex* spotted the Japanese ships not halfway to Okinawa. By midafternoon the *Yamato,* the *Yahagi,* and four destroyers were at the bottom of the sea, and four destroyers had turned around and sped back to Japan, all of them damaged. The suicide fleet had not made contact with United States ships at all. From all angles, the mission had to be adjudged a miserable, disastrous failure.

Assassins at Okinawa

The British Pacific Fleet, operating off the southern group of islands of the Nansei Shoto, also received some attention from suicide planes. The carrier *Indefatigable* took a Kamikaze on the flight deck, but instead of creating havoc, as a Kamikaze usually did when it struck squarely on an American wooden flight deck, this one put flight operations out for only half an hour. The British built their carriers with steel decks, an enormous advantage as the next weeks showed. The Japanese launched another mass attack on the United States fleet on April 11. One Kamikaze struck the battleship *Missouri*. Two more hit the carrier *Enterprise*. The *Missouri* was fully armored, and the damage was confined to scorched paint. *Enterprise* operations were shut down for forty-eight hours while the damage repair parties worked to control fires.

With this second wave of 185 *kikusuis* this invasion was going to be the most costly yet. Concurrently the Japanese ashore had suddenly stiffened their lines of resistance against the marines in the north and the army troops in the south, and the United States ground forces had taken almost four thousand casualties. The naval forces had suffered thirteen hundred casualties, a very high ratio in relation to past campaigns. The Americans had control of the air and control of the sea, but they did not have the island and could see that they were going to pay a high price to take it. The Japanese knew as well as Admiral Nimitz that once Okinawa was gone the next step would be attack on Japan proper.

April 12 turned out to be a day of horror for the invaders. The Japanese launched a flight of three hundred planes, half of them *kikusui*. Sometimes the sacrificial urge overcame even the escorts. One plane that came down, apparently undamaged, hit one destroyer and lodged in its cockpit in the fire room was found to be an ordinary Zero, with plenty of gas in its self-sealing tanks and an ordinary instrument panel. On this day, the Japanese suicide pilots damaged or sank eleven ships, and the piloted *baka* bombs, released from Betty bombers, hit two. The *baka* bombs were deadly but the Americans learned that they were easier to outmaneuver than the ordinary suicide craft. The very speed of the *baka* meant that the pilot had to commit himself almost immediately after launching and once his course was set, it was difficult for him to maneuver. For example, one *baka* pilot came in at the destroyer *Stanly* at five hundred knots, so fast that the gunners of the destroyer could not track him, but he miscalculated. The bomb passed over the ship so close it ripped the flag from its staff, but when the pilot tried to bank, he was too low and moving too fast, and the *baka* hit the water, bounced, and blew up.

But in all, the Kamikaze system turned out to be the most serious menace that the American fleet had yet faced. For the first time in the war, the navy became less than candid about casualty figures to ships and men for the consumption of Americans at home. The reason given was military security—it could only encourage the enemy to learn how effective their attacks were. But it was indicative of the seriousness with which the highest quarters considered the Kamikazes that the policy of total honesty was sacrificed. By the end of May, the Japanese had launched eight mass *kikusui* attacks. So concerned were the naval authorities that they established a special office on the American mainland to study the suicide planes and the best methods of counteracting them. (The office never came up with an answer, and after the war ended, none seemed to be needed, so the special section was disbanded.)

The land battle for Okinawa was also extremely costly. On April 19, for example, three divisions of Major General John R. Hodge's XXIV Corps attacked southward along a line across the island just north of Naha against Japanese holed up in deep caves. The day began with naval gunfire delivered by every ship available, six battleships, six cruisers, and eight destroyers. At the same time the area was blanketed by nineteen thousand rounds of shellfire from the artillery. Nearly seven hundred bombers and fighters added their destructive force. The infantry then advanced, confident that the barrage would have knocked out the enemy. They could not have been more wrong. They were stopped completely, for the Japanese came up out of their deep caves to man the guns that had been artfully concealed and carefully protected by fortification. For five days, progress of the XXIV Corps advance was measured in yards. Every position had to be taken by tanks, flamethrowers, and engineers with demolition charges. And when, at the end of a week, the line was penetrated in several places, General Ushijima ordered a withdrawal to the next set of prepared defenses. This was done quickly and efficiently through the caves. The Japanese moved out on the night of April 23. On the morning of April 24, the Americans charged in again and found only a handful of stragglers to impede their progress. Then they had to go against the second line.

The land battle continued until mid-June. The Americans thought they had cleared all the little islands around Okinawa of aircraft but this was not true. One evening a ship limping back to Kerama Retto after taking a Kamikaze aboard, passed near little Ie Shima, which was supposed to be deserted. There members of the crew saw a Japanese plane land, and a ground crew come up casually and fold its wings and put it into a hidden revetment. When this news was reported to Admiral Turner he decided that Ie Shima, which was scheduled to be occupied some time in the future as a matter of course, would have to be taken immediately. No one expected much of a fight, but when the invasion came on April 16 after three days of bombardment, the American soldiers of the Seventy-Seventh Division found that the Japanese here were almost as well ensconced as those on Okinawa. The fighting here was also difficult and costly: a thousand Americans fell in the struggle, including the correspondent Ernie Pyle, who had covered the European war almost to its end for the Scripps-Howard newspapers had come to the Pacific

232

to write his stories about ordinary soldiers and sailors and the war they fought. Neither Ernie Pyle nor any others had expected what they got on Ie Shima. In a way his death was a symbol of what would happen once the Americans began the attack on Japan.

General Ushijima could not hold out forever, however, because the only support he received from Japan was the shower of "floating chrysanthemums." By mid-June his army was almost wiped out. He sent his last messages, and on June 22 committed suicide, begging the emperor's pardon for having failed. It was July, however, before Okinawa was declared secured. When the cost was finally assessed, the navy had lost 30 ships and suffered damage to 368, mostly from Kamikaze attacks. The fleet lost 800 planes and the British Pacific Fleet lost many more. Nearly 10,000 navy men were killed or wounded. The Tenth Army had suffered 65,000 casualties. Of course the Japanese had suffered more. They had committed 4,000 suicide planes to the battle and the remnants of the fleet, including the mighty *Yamato*. They had lost 80,000 trained troops. But the battle showed the future.

In Japan the war cabinet and Imperial General Headquarters were talking of the whole nation as an "army." Propaganda was involved, of course, but also the national feeling that Japan must not surrender. And when Admiral Nimitz and Admiral King looked at the figures, it was enough to make them wince: the Japanese army numbered 5,500,000 officers and men with 9,000 aircraft in service, and more coming from the factories. Suicide planes, suicide boats, and suicide troops would take a heavy toll. The United States casualties, based on the record at Okinawa could be in the *millions*.

27

The War Ends

LATE IN MAY, Admiral Halsey relieved Admiral Spruance so that the latter could go to Guam to confer with Admiral Nimitz about future American naval operations. During June and July, Spruance helped draw a plan which would have split the American naval forces into two fleets. The enormous power—ships and planes—would be ready by autumn. Then Admiral Spruance would take the Fifth Fleet to Kyushu to support the landing of the American Sixth Army and the marines of V Amphibious Force. Admiral Halsey's Third Fleet would land the Eighth Army on the Tokyo plain. Admiral Kinkaid's Seventh Fleet would take the XXIV Corps to Korea. Admiral Frank Jack Fletcher would at last be able to get back into the shooting war, to bring his North Pacific Force and army troops to invade Hokkaido.

Meanwhile the war at sea continued. By the summer of 1945, American submarines had so scoured the seas between Japan and the Asian mainland that targets were hard to find. One by one the remaining Japanese naval vessels were picked off by submarines and air strikes. The carrier *Junyo* had been damaged so badly as to be taken out of action in December. The new carrier *Unryu* was sunk by the submarine *Redfish* that same month. Month after month, the submarines sank freighters and tankers until Japan was sorely hurting for lack of rubber, tin, and petroleum. By spring, the submarines were reduced to attacks on patrol craft and small ships that would have seemed hardly worth the effort six months earlier. In June, the American submarines even invaded the Sea of Japan, which was similar to having Japanese submarines in San Francisco Bay. But by this time, the submarines had taken on a new duty that was at least as important as chasing after miscellaneous vessels; they were used in the "lifeguard service." As the *B-29s* pursued their attacks on Japan and the Japanese fighters swarmed up at them, many were hit and some had to ditch en route back to Saipan and Tinian. Beginning at the Gilberts operation, the submarines had been used to pick up downed fliers. The system was so successful that it became a definite part of the bombing program. At least three submarines were sent out to stations along the route of each *B-29* mission. During the last eight months of the war, eighty-odd submarines rescued nearly four hundred aviators. It was a comfort to the fliers to know that at any point on their route they could expect rescue from the sea within hours.

But though the war was drawing to a conclusion over Japan, pilots began ramming *B-29s* when they failed to shoot them down with guns. And in July, the American cruiser *Indianapolis,* sometimes flagship for Admiral Spruance, was sunk by a Japanese submarine.

Admiral Halsey was speeding the destruction of the Japanese war effort that summer in spite of running into another typhoon that caused considerable damage in the fleet (but no lost ships). The fleet operation plan gave Halsey the authority to range wide in his attack on Japanese naval forces, air forces, shipping, shipyards, and coastal objectives—which meant just about anything Halsey wanted to do. He was also to support the naval forces around Okinawa, but as the campaign there drew to an end, the Japanese stopped sending suicide squads against the ships, and the ships began to disperse, preparing for future action. So by July 1, Admiral Halsey was free to roam.

The Third Fleet then consisted of nine heavy carriers (one hundred planes) and six light carriers (thirty-five planes) plus the fast battleships, cruisers, and destroyers. It was capable of air strikes and surface bombardment of Japanese targets. Halsey intended to do both against Japan itself.

On July 10, Halsey ordered the fleet to hit Japanese airfields on the Honshu coast. When the pilots came over the coast, they were nearly bewildered by the number of targets. From five thousand feet, anyone could see at least a dozen airfields in this area. There were no planes in the air nor did any come up to meet them, and as they flew low across the runways and looked down they saw nothing but wrecks. But back on the carriers photo intelligence officers checking the pictures taken found hidden Japanese planes sometimes as far as a mile from the airfields.

What opposition the Japanese seemed to lack in aircraft was more than made up by heavy anti-aircraft fire around these fields. The Americans did destroy some aircraft but there were still far more left than anyone in the fleet knew. The Japanese were waiting for the last desperate days.

On July 14, the American fleet hit Hokkaido and northern Honshu, areas that had so far been safe from exposure to the war. Again there was no air opposition, although the fliers zoomed across the airfields and shot up planes,

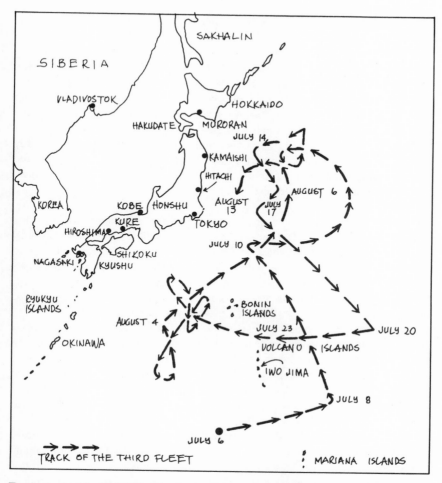

Track chart of the Third Fleet in the last days of the Pacific War, July–August 1945

when they could find them. Again, the Japanese air forces were waiting. Since there were no air targets, the fleet air force turned its attention to inter-island shipping and the few naval vessels they could find. They damaged one destroyer and sank another. They also sank several escort ships and a number of small merchant ships and ferries that operated in inland waters. After the United States fleet was gone the Japanese found that they had no craft left to operate their Aomori-Hakodate car ferry system, which meant that Hokkaido was virtually cut off from Honshu.

237

Halsey had promised to carry the war to Japan, and he did, with a vengeance. That same day, he sent Rear Admiral John F. Shafroth with a bombardment force of battleships, cruisers, and destroyers to strike the Japan Iron Company's steel plant at Kamaishi. For two hours the ships fired everything they had at the steel works. The sixteen-inch shells of the battleships did much damage, resulting in a series of fires in the residential districts. Cooking fires in Japanese kitchens spread to straw mats and paper screens of the houses. The damage to the town was greater than that to the factory. As far as the plant was concerned, the bombardment added to the problems already created by the American submarines and *B-29*s, which had already cut the factory's production by interdicting the supplies of raw materials. The Shafroth bombardment was later estimated to have cut factory production by a quarter.

The Americans had no fear of going anywhere in Japanese waters. That same night of July 14, Halsey sent his cruisers and destroyers on an antishipping strike along the coast of Honshu. They found nothing at all—so much already had been destroyed. Halsey had such enormous strength at his disposal that he did not always use the same ships for strikes. On July 15, Halsey sent another bombardment force against the Wanishi Ironworks at Muroran, Hokkaido. Again the damage done was substantial.

Halsey's fleet went after every sort of target. Using techniques developed in the Atlantic, an escort carrier and a pair of destroyer escorts went looking for submarines. They found and sank the *I-13*. This sort of attack, in Japanese home waters, would have been unthinkable even six months before, but the character of the Pacific War had changed completely with the occupation of the Philippines and the almost total destruction of the Japanese fleet at the battles of Leyte Gulf.

On July 18, Rear Admiral Oscar Badger's bombardment unit, the battleships *Iowa, Missouri, Wisconsin, North Carolina* and *Alabama,* and a number of cruisers, hunted targets along the coast. They hit the industrial city of Hitachi, not a hundred miles from Tokyo, and bombarded six different industrial plants. They were accompanied by the *King George V* and other elements of the British Pacific Fleet, which bombarded another plant north of the city. The result of this and the *B-29* raids of that day was to cut off rail service, electricity, and water from Hitachi. To the Japanese civilians, air and naval bombardment was bringing the war home. The carriers struck the naval base at Yokosuka in the heart of Tokyo Bay, sinking a submarine, a destroyer, several smaller vessels, and damaging the battleship *Nagato,* one of the handful of remaining Japanese capital ships. That night the cruisers swept around the peninsula southeast of Tokyo, but there were no ships to be seen and they bombarded shore stations.

By this time the American fleet was able to go anywhere. On July 21, the carriers and their support ships were fuelled on the high seas in Japanese home waters. For two days they operated without their normal protection— sitting ducks one might call them. At least that was how Frank Jack Fletcher had referred to his carriers when refuelling. But the American strength was now so great that these old considerations were no longer binding. Further, there was not any Japanese air or surface opposition to worry about. It was almost as if the war was over for the navy.

Consider the week of July 24: Admiral Halsey decided to go after what was left of the Japanese navy. These ships were located mostly at Kure and Kobe, and they were hidden in coves for protection from bombers. The carrier planes sank the battleships *Haruna, Ise,* and *Hyuga,* the heavy cruisers *Tone* and *Aoba,* and two old ships that were used as station vessels. The carrier *Katsuragi* was wrecked. The carrier *Amagi* was badly damaged. The cruiser *Kitagami* and five destroyers were damaged. And in doing all this the American planes did not meet any Japanese air opposition.

But the fact was that the Japanese planes were down there, still waiting as the American fleet raged around Honshu. Early in August, Admiral Nimitz's intelligence system reported that the Japanese had massed bombers and soldiers in northern Honshu, preparing for a major suicide strike. They would load the troops aboard the bombers and fly to Saipan and Tinian where the bombers would crash land on the *B-29* fields and the soldiers would charge forth and destroy the giant planes that were wreaking such dreadful havoc on Tokyo and other Japanese cities. Admiral Halsey went north. As he did so, from one of the Marianas bases a *B-29* took off bearing an entirely new weapon, an atomic bomb, and on August 6 dropped this bomb on the city of Hiroshima. In one move thousands of people were killed, an area of four square miles was totally devastated, and one hundred and seventy thousand people were made homeless. The water system, electricity, everything that made a city tenable, was wiped out in that one minute. The estimates on the number actually killed at Hiroshima vary. Hiroshima was a war base and a busy port and no one knew how many people were in the central district at the time of the bombing. A recent estimate put the total who eventually died from the bomb at sixty thousand.

The Halsey strike was successful; several hundred planes that had indeed concentrated in northern Honshu for a suicide strike on the *B-29* bases were destroyed and the attack was never staged. That same day the second atomic bomb was dropped on Nagasaki, virtually repeating the Hiroshima story.

The combination of events—the firebombing of Tokyo, by *B-29*s, which had destroyed miles of the capital, the loss of the fleet, the loss of most merchant shipping, and the inability of the government to guarantee food and supply, and the new ease with which the American fleet could strike any point in Japan had brought responsible leaders to the point of surrender. The atomic bomb was the clincher in their minds. Yet it was not certain, even after the Nagasaki bomb, that Japan would actually surrender. Halsey continued to hit airfields and other installations on northern Honshu. On August 12, his planes struck the Tokyo area, and they repeated that performance on August 13.

Quite incidentally, these air strikes gave authority to those who were struggling on the ground in Japan to bring peace. All the Americans had done was capped for Japan by the declaration of war from Soviet Russia. Soviet troops began marching down through Manchuria and Korea, and since the Japanese had denuded the Kwantung Army and other forces in the north to replace and resupply those of the south, the Russians had easy going. There was fear in Japan that they would march all the way to Tokyo.

In meetings at Potsdam that summer the Americans, British, Chinese, and Russians had agreed on terms of a Japanese surrender, which were in effect no terms at all. The Americans, however, held out (under pressure from former Ambassador to Japan Joseph Grew) for retention of the imperial system. Had they not done so, probably the war would have gone on for months and the casualty list of human beings of all nations involved would have been enormous. For no foreigners understood the depth of the feeling that was ravaging Japan when talk of surrender entered the air. The army and navy leaders opposed surrender initially and then insisted on surrender with dignity. The emperor would be retained. The Japanese must disarm their own troops and bring them home. "War criminals" must be prosecuted in Japanese courts. Only a token occupation would be permitted. General Anami, the war minister held out for all this. He was joined by General Umezu, the army chief of staff, and Admiral Toyoda, now navy chief of staff. They insisted on these conditions even in meetings at the Imperial Palace. Finally, the matter was taken to the emperor himself for a direct decision—something unique in the annals of Japanese government. Having heard the arguments, and recognizing that the Allies would never accept the conditions, the emperor said that the war must be ended to save the Japanese people from "unbearable distress." In Japan the emperor's wish was law, and without further discussion the prime minister set about arranging terms for surrender. But at this point the army and navy chiefs did what had been unthinkable since the Maiji restoration. They balked, and another meeting was held on August 14. The cabinet shrewdly insisted that the Americans could not have more than another bomb or two (this was true) and that Japan could continue to fight on. Enormous caches of food and ammunition had been stored around Japan for just such an emergency. There were still five thousand Kamikaze planes available, and more on the production line. Thousands of suicide pilots were undergoing training. The navy had equally desperate plans: thousands of suicide boats, and hundreds of *kaiten* midget submarines. The war party insisted that Japan could fight on and make the invasion so costly that the Allies would have to reconsider their surrender demands. And they were supported by millions of people. That night a rebellion was staged within the army. Officers called on Lieutenant General Takeshi Mori, the commander of the Imperial guard and demanded that he seize the Imperial palace and make the emperor prisoner of the army. Mori refused and was killed. The plotters forged orders and set out to capture the palace, but General Tanaka of the army, who commanded troops in the Tokyo area, heard of the rebellion and suppressed it.

Yet Japan came very close to continuing the war in spite of the atomic bomb. The bomb's destructive power was not underestimated, but neither was it overestimated.

On August 15, Admiral Halsey's carriers launched another air strike against Tokyo. The first air strike was actually over the city, bombing and strafing and a second strike was approaching the coast when Halsey received a message from Admiral Nimitz to suspend operations because word had been received that Japan would surrender. Even as this word came in, Americans were engaged in a desperate air battle over Tokurozama airfield near Tokyo. Nine Japanese planes were shot down and four American planes were destroyed in this last battle, while a number of Japanese planes also attacked the fleet.

Then came the Imperial Rescript, the emperor's statement to the Japanese people and the world that by accepting the allied surrender terms he was ending the war. So overwhelming was Japanese patriotic emotion that millions of people simply did not believe it. Many expected that when the Allies landed in "occupation" they would be greeted by an army ready to fight, that the Imperial Rescript was a clever trick to win the war. There was still an important segment of public opinion that did not recognize or accept defeat and prepared to continue the battle. The emperor understood this feeling so well that he personally sent members of the royal household to various military commands. Their task was to inform all concerned that the surrender came from the emperor's free will and his own judgment, and that it must be accepted. Prince Takamatsu, the younger brother of the emperor, went to Atsugi airfield, a major Japanese air base, and personally restrained the Kamikaze corps there from carrying out their plan: they had made all preparations to take off as the allied warships entered Tokyo Bay and destroy as many as possible. They would start the war all over again.

The emperor and the imperial family then in these querulous days took the strongest direct action in government that they had ever taken, and through their intervention the surrender was accomplished. On September 2, the Japanese delegation led by Foreign Minister Mamoru Shigemitsu boarded the USS *Missouri*. General Umezu, the army chief of staff, had first refused to come to the ceremony and had decided to commit suicide. Only the emperor's personal message persuaded him to fulfill this onerous duty.

On the deck of the *Missouri,* the proud victors crowded around the simple green-covered table where the surrender document would be signed. Invitation to the ceremony was a status symbol among United States senior officers; they had fought for nearly four years to see this day. Finally it was done. General Douglas MacArthur, who had already been chosen to head the occupation of Japan, took a role as senior spokesman and made a ringing speech in which he called for a better world to come out of this holocaust. The Pacific War of 1941–45 was ended.

28

The Wiles
of the Communists

~~~~~~~~

GENERAL MACARTHUR'S BRAVE NEW WORLD never existed except in the minds of some men, most of them apparently Americans. The 1945 transition was not from war to peace, but from war against the Rome-Berlin-Tokyo Axis to an uneasy detente between the West, as exemplified by the Americans, and the East, as exemplified by the Soviet Russians. The "peace" was further complicated by forces unleashed by Japan in the war years: the Greater East Asia Co-Prosperity Sphere may have been a ploy of a colonial-minded Japan to conquer Asia and the Pacific, but the ringing promises of freedom and independence were echoed by the Western world in the Atlantic Charter, and the colonial peoples of Asia and Africa believed. It was also a truism that power abhors a vacuum, and in the immediate postwar days the world was filled with vacuums, politically speaking. But in spite of a need to retain a strong military presence in the Pacific, the political demands of America were for reduction of the armed forces. "Bring the boys home," cried the mothers and daughters, and the politicians in Washington heard and heeded. The occupation of Japan began in September, 1945. Korea was also occupied, below the 38th parallel by the Americans, and above the 38th parallel by the Russians. The Americans set up a military government in South Korea. The Russians, far more astute, set up a "Poeple's Republic" in North Korea, as the Americans fumbled trying to create a government that would satisfy the United States political demand that it be non-communist and the popular demand that it represent the Korean people. The result was the return of Dr. Syngman Rhee, a legendary figure famous for rebellion against the Japanese, who had been in exile for years, mostly in America. Meanwhile, the Americans and Russians were encharged by the Yalta agreement to agree on one government for one Korea. But it was not possible that the Americans and Russians would agree, given such diametrically opposite political and social systems as they had plus a growing sense of antagonism that by 1947 had divided the world into two camps.

The Pacific Fleet's war role ended and its resources dwindled, but its peacetime role was greater than even before. A force was maintained in Japan, but gradually the ships slipped away to go into mothballs in the estuaries of San Francisco Bay. By December, 1945 an LST was the station ship at Inchon, the harbor for the capital of Korea, and its commanding officer was a lieutenant in the naval reserve. A destroyer made the rounds: Japan-Shanghai-Tsingtao-Inchon, carrying the mail and bringing the occasional replacement. The marines occupied North China with what were token forces, because the Americans had not really made up their minds which side to support in the developing Chinese Civil War. The constructive role of the fleet was to build bases in the Pacific: Guam, Okinawa, and other islands of what came to be called Micronesia. The command soon changed. Admiral Nimitz went home to a Washington job and then retirement in California. He was replaced by Admiral Towers, who finally achieved his ambition for a major command. Admiral Halsey retired and so did Admiral Spruance, who served as ambassador to the new republic of the Philippines for a time.

And yet the United States Navy and the Pacific Fleet did play a war role of sorts. President Truman decided first to try to mediate the struggle between Chiang Kai-shek's Republic of China forces and Mao Tse-tung's Chinese Communists. During the Pacific War, the Communists had taken over huge portions of territory in North China. If the Japanese moved a major element in the Communist forces melted away. But if the Japanese relaxed, the Communists were back again. Thus at the end of the Pacific War, much of China was in Communist hands, and when the Russians occupied Manchuria, they passed political and military control to the Communists, while looting the factories and the cities to replace with Japanese material what had been destroyed by Japan's German allies in the USSR. By the summer of 1946 peace efforts in China were in shambles. General Marshall was sent to Peking as President Truman's personal ambassador, to try to bring about compromise. He failed, for both the Nationalists and the Communists were unwilling to work together. Seizure of Japanese arms in the northeastern provinces had given the Communists a satisfactory arsenal, and their armies massed in Harbin and Tsitsihar under General Lin Piao. In 1947, they began to march and stalemate became war.

In all this, the Pacific Fleet played a role far more important than was generally realized at the time. When the war ended, the United States was committed by the Yalta and Potsdam Agreements to assistance of the Chinese Nationalist Government in regaining control of the areas of China held by the

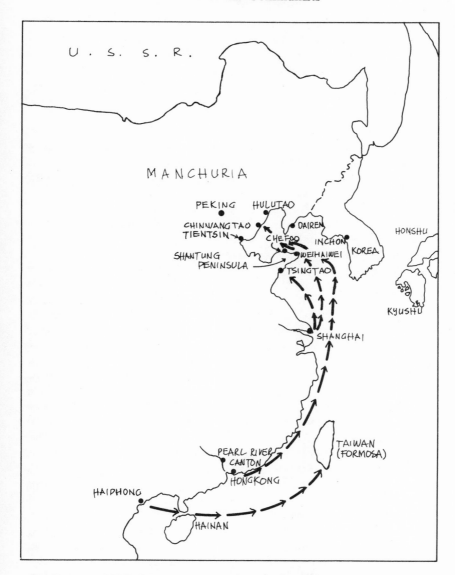

Involvement of U.S. Forces in the first days of the postwar Chinese Revolution

Japanese. The Russians were already in Manchuria, having marched in the last days of war. They intended to remain there until they had achieved their ends. A minor confrontation between American naval forces and Soviet army forces occurred when Admiral Kinkaid's Seventh Fleet ships showed up at

Dairen to evacuate a number of civilians who had been held by the Japanese during the war. Planes from the carriers *Antietam* and *Cabot* were fired on by Russian aircraft. Since also an American *B-29* airdropping supplies to a prisoner of war camp in North Korea was shot down by Russian fighters at about this time, the general air of tension grew. It was not helped by constant confusion over the role the United States fleet was to assume in this intensely political situation in Asia.

The political factor came into play almost immediately. In September, Rear Admiral T. G. W. Settle took the Japanese Imperial Navy's surrender at Tsingtao and then went to Chefoo to occupy the fort in behalf of the Chiang Kai-shek government. The Sixth Marine Division would soon follow. As this was done, the Nationalists applauded and the Chinese Communists complained. Their Eighteenth Army Group already controlled most of the countryside. Why were the Americans coming at all? It was the sort of question a military commander could not answer.

This Chinese Communist opposition to American occupation of any part of China was understandable; they knew such a move would have to turn the territory over to the Nationalists. When it was announced that American marines would occupy Peking, Chou En-lai, the number two man of the Communist party, protested loudly in a meeting with the marine commander who had already landed at Tientsin. An American occupation would prevent the Communists from taking control of Peking, which would have been very easy since they occupied the whole countryside around the city. And this was an immensely important matter of prestige since Peking was the old imperial capital and the city the Communists intended to use as a capital once again. When the marines did march to Peking that September, Communist forces resisted and three marines were wounded in a fire-fight.

On consideration, the Americans decided not to occupy Chefoo. They did land marines at Tsingtao but they promised to refrain from interfering in any conflict between Nationalist and Communist forces and did. Yet the American presence in North China was much resented by the Communists, particularly when under its cover Chiang Kai-shek moved two armies into Peking and Tientsin to establish Nationalist control.

The fleet's attempts to remain neutral in the political and military struggle in China came to nothing when President Truman ordered the navy to land Chinese Nationalist troops at Dairen. Truman had been convinced by Nationalist representatives in Washington that unless this were done, all Manchuria would soon fall into Communist hands. Admiral Daniel Barbey, who went up to Manchuria to investigate, reported that the United States Navy ought not land any Nationalist troops in a Communist-controlled port unless the United States was prepared to become involved in the China civil war, which seemed doubtful at that time. Finally, early in November, a division of Nationalist troops was transported in American ships to Chinwangtao, and other troops followed shortly after.

On the Shantung peninsula, the Communists and the Nationalists battled frequently. The American marines did not participate in these fights, but they did supply the Chinese Nationalist troops with ammunition and this infuriated the Communists and convinced them that United States policy was a sly attempt to support the Nationalists without admitting it. The fact was the United States policy was thoroughly confused and operating at cross purposes on several levels. Most important was a commitment made at the presidential level before the end of the Pacific war to Chiang Kai-shek, leader of what was then regarded as the legitimate government of China, to move Chinese troops to reoccupy parts of the countryside that had been in Japanese hands. That was the primary reason for American involvement. When the commitment was honored, the Chinese Communists regarded the American move as interference. The Nationalists were not above misusing their American connection.

For example, on October 19, after the Seventh Fleet had decided not to occupy Chefoo since there were no Japanese troops in the city to be disarmed, a group of eight small steamers and four junks arrived in that port, as Admiral Settle's flagship, the USS *San Francisco,* did. An officer came aboard the flagship and identified himself as Colonel Sun Chen-hsien, chief of staff to the Nationalist Shantung army. He wanted the Americans to provide gunfire support while his troops invaded Chefoo. Settle said no and left the harbor for Weihaiwei to avoid being drawn into an incident. Colonel Sun remained, and brought in more junks filled with troops and several motorized craft. They attacked a number of Chinese Communist vessels and captured them, killing some crewmen. And, it was discovered later, as they did this, some of the Nationalist soldiers were wearing American uniforms and American insignia.

When Admiral Kinkaid learned of this violation of United States regulations, he ordered all American units in Chinese waters to observe strict neutrality in the struggle, yet without recognizing that the Communists had any authority. He also sent word to Colonel Sun demanding that he stop using the American flag for any purpose whatsoever. Yet the Communists ashore, who controlled Chefoo, drew the inference that American support of Colonel Sun was specific and official. It would have taken more than a message to change their minds, given the evidence they had. In fact, the Nationalist force was defeated soon after, and Chefoo remained in Communist hands to become an important staging point for movement of Communist troops into Manchuria. By the summer of 1946, the Communists were running steamships between Dairen and Chefoo, and Chiang Kai-shek became so concerned that his forces attacked the city. His equipment included a group of LSTs that the United States Navy had handed over to the Chinese rather than become further involved by transporting more troops. Chefoo was captured by the Nationalists in the summer of 1947 but it was too late: the Communists had already taken full advantage of the port's usefulness to augment their forces in Manchuria.

American naval vessels did carry out a "sealift" for the Nationalists in the fall of 1945. They landed troops on Formosa and at Chinwangtao. They landed the Thirteenth Chinese Nationalist Army at Formosa and the Fifty-Second Chinese army at Chinwangtao, and also the Eighth Chinese Nationalist Army at Tsingtao. These latter troops began pushing inland to fight the Communist Eighth Route Army and take over control of Shantung province. The Eighth Nationalist Army ran out of ammunition, and General Albert Wedemeyer, the American commander in China, ordered the Sixth Marine Division at Tsingtao to supply the Nationalists. This move did not sit well with the Chinese Communists either.

As 1945 came to an end, the United States Seventh Fleet showed considerable reluctance to continue its role in China. Navy transports were heavily occupied in two other tasks: ferrying Americans home from the Pacific and ferrying four million Japanese from China, Manchuria, Formosa, and Indochina, back to Japan. But Chiang Kai-shek kept up the pressure for American aid, and so another sealift was begun. Five Chinese armies were brought up from the south to Hulutao. Manchuria was to be a focal point of the civil war, and Chiang insisted that he could not retake the Manchurian provinces, so long separated from China, without American assistance. All this was definitely American aid to the Nationalists, and yet that fall of 1945, the Seventh Fleet also assigned ships to bring United Nations Relief and Rehabilitation Administration supplies up to Chefoo to the Communist Eighth Route Army. American policy was indeed ambivalent. But what else was to be expected as an aftermath of the peculiar way in which the war against the Japanese was conducted in China? The story of the East River Column illustrates in microcosm the greater dilemma.

The East River Column consisted of two detachments of Chinese guerillas who operated against the Japanese behind the lines in the East River area near Canton, following the fall of that city to the Japanese in 1938. The first group, called the Wang detachment, was for a time accepted by the Nationalists as part of their force. But the leader, Wang Tso-yao, proved too independent, and later Chiang's forces demanded that the group be disbanded. Wang paid no attention and continued to fight the Japanese. A second unit, led by Tseng Sheng, was organized as the Seaman's Guerilla Column, and later as the Third Independent Guerilla Column. In 1939, these units joined, Tseng became commander and Wang the chief of staff. They soon disagreed with Nationalist policies, particularly when Chiang Kai-shek refused to prosecute the war vigorously in Southeast China and turned to the Chinese Communists. But they also rescued so many downed American aviators and assisted the American intelligence operators on the Chinese coast so well, that they had commendations from General Joseph Stilwell, commander of the China theater in 1944, and General Claire Chennault, the commander of the 14th Air Force. All this while, they were not only fighting the Japanese, but the Nationalists. By the war's end they were quite openly allied with the Communists. Chu Teh, commander of the Communist armies, ordered the Japanese to surrender in the Kwangtung area to the East River Column. The Nationalists in the fall of 1945 set out to drive the East River Column out of the Kwangtung area, and the fighting continued in 1946. It was inconclusive. General Marshall was then trying in Peking to bring about a political accommodation between Nationalists and Communists, through the Executive Headquarters which represented both sides and the Americans. At Peking, one American representative at Executive Headquarters suggested that the problem in Kwangtung could be solved by moving the East River Column up to Chefoo which was Communist territory. All concerned agreed to the plan. In May, 1946, the East River Column's twenty-seven hundred guerillas marched to Byas Bay, forty-five miles northeast of Hongkong, and three LSTs of the Seventh Fleet, guarded by destroyers, brought the column safely to Chefoo. There, the force was augmented and renamed the Kwangtung-Kwangsi column. The American movement of these Communist troops measurably strengthened the Chinese Communist forces in Chefoo.

Throughout the war, the United States fleet had a strong interest in events in China. Captain "Merry" Miles maintained an organization of intelligence operators on the coast throughout the war. Admiral King had wanted eventually to land on the China coast, so during the war when Chiang Kai-shek had requested that the Americans train a Chinese navy he had agreed. He thought perhaps a Chinese navy could help in the war against Japan. The Chinese Nationalist government then said it had available sufficient trained personnel to man a small force: two cruisers, a destroyer squadron, and smaller vessels. Admiral H. E. Yarnell, who had spent several years in the Asiatic Fleet before he retired, suggested that the Nationalists would be up against a civil war once the Pacific War ended, and that it was in the American interest to guarantee a strong and viable Nationalist government. The development of a navy would help. Actually, however, American preoccupation with the Pacific war prevented such a program, and the Chinese naval training in America was confined to a handful of university students learning theory. At the end of the war, the Nationalists did have a small navy, centered around the former British cruiser *Aurora* and the British destroyer *Mendip*. The British, in other words, provided the backbone of the infant Chinese navy, not the Americans. The British also trained the crews of these vessels before turning them over to the Nationalists in 1948. By the time the ships came on the scene, the Nationalists were losing the war, and the major naval task was to cover the withdrawal of Nationalist troops from Manchuria, where General Lin Piao had been constantly moving forward. The *Aurora,* renamed *Chungking,* suffered from a high rate of desertion as Nationalist morale collapsed. On January 21, 1949, when affairs had become so chaotic that Chiang announced his retirement as President of the Republic, the *Chungking* disappeared, to turn up in Chefoo. Her captain and crew had defected to the Communists. The Nationalists tried to persuade the British and the Americans to sink the *Chungking* as a threat to Chinese Nationalist merchant shipping. Both navies declined. Nationalist air force planes tried to find her and bomb her, but she moved on to Hulutao in Manchuria. They found her there on March 19 and sank her after three days of bombing. Since the Nationalists were flying planes given them by the Americans, the Chinese Communists claimed the United States had a part in the sinking.

By mid-April most of the new Nationalist navy had gone over to the Communists, taking with them some fifty vessels supplied by Britain and the United States. The Communists were pleased to have the defections but they did not fail to make propaganda of the source of the weaponry. And, in the course of events, the United States became the *bete noire,* although in fact the American naval presence was far more restrained than the British. The Royal Navy maintained ships along the Yangtze during these difficult times, and when the end came four British warships had to run a gauntlet of Chinese Communist artillery fire to escape the narrows of that river.

So in the end, it could be said that the Americans really did not do much for the Chinese Nationalists to help them secure a navy or to use American naval forces to help the Nationalists in their struggle against the Communists. They did, however, do just enough to build up a residue of animosity in Peking, and thus to set the stage for the far more serious problem that would materialize in 1951.

29

Retreat in Korea

~~~~~~

IN THE WINTER OF 1945–46, the political pressures in Washington for American withdrawal of troops around the world became so great that Lieutenant General John R. Hodge, commander of the American occupation forces in South Korea, observed that his XXIV Corps, which had distinguished itself in the Philippines and at Okinawa, was no longer an effective fighting force. So many units had been decimated by discharge of troops and lack of replacement that Hodge had no confidence in his ability to hold Seoul against any sort of invasion. Indeed, he said privately, the Americans would be lucky to be able to fight their way south and escape capture. Even as General Hodge was making these gloomy predictions, the Department of State in Washington decided that Korea did not really fall within the American sphere of national interest, so nothing was done to shore up the failing defenses. Those defenses were not helped, either, by the struggle within the armed forces in the late 1940s over a unified Department of Defense. The navy, as many officers had suspected, was neglected in favor of the new air force. The new aircraft carrier *United States* was in construction when in 1949 the Secretary of Defense suspended work. The air force, with its supporters, thought only of war between the United States and the USSR. When the air force chief of staff testified on defense before Congress in 1949, he spoke of "the one possible enemy we may have to face." The air force argued for the *B-36* bomber, which was supposed to have the same capabilities as an aircraft carrier and be far less expensive to produce. When the army got into the discussion, its representatives also looked dimly into the crystal ball. It was extremely doubtful if ever again the United States would engage in large-scale amphibious

251

operations, said General Omar Bradley, chairman of the Joint Chiefs of Staff. Admirals Arthur Radford and Arleigh Burke and General Clifton Cates of the United States Marine Corps all fought the ''big bang'' concept as hard as they could and were joined by almost every senior naval officer, but this quarrel virtually paralyzed defense planning. Secretary of State Dean Acheson chose this unfortunate period to send a message to the world that the United States did not consider either South Korea or Formosa (Taiwan) to be within the American defense perimeter.

By the spring of 1950, most American troops had been withdrawn from South Korea and the Asian mainland. The marines had left China. Acheson's statement told the USSR and the North Korean Peoples' Republic that if they marched south, nothing would happen.

So, on June 25, 1950, at four o'clock in the morning six North Korean infantry divisions supported by tanks, artillery and the North Korean Air Force, began the march into South Korea to unify their country by force. Soon one hundred and fifty thousand North Korean troops crossed the 38th parallel to drive south on Seoul.

At this point the American politicians sat up and took notice. By coincidence—rather because the USSR had been balked repeatedly in the Security Council of the United Nations—the Soviet representative was not in New York when this invasion came before the Council. It was apparent that unless checked, the North Koreans would overrun South Korea. President Truman, assessing American policy, authorized General MacArthur to secure the evacuation of all Americans from the war zone. If necessary, MacArthur was to stop Seoul, the port of Inchon, and the air base at Kimpo from being seized by the North Koreans. Within hours it was apparent that words would not stop the attack. But Soviet negligence in the United Nations Security Council had left one opportunity. The United Nations, pushed by the United States, authorized its member states to repel the armed attack with force, and there was no Soviet member there to veto the action. So General MacArthur was told to use navy and air force planes to bomb the North Korean invaders and blockade the coast, as the representative of the United Nations.

President Truman's brave words about use of a navy force to act would have seemed hollow to the American people had they known the true state of affairs. The total staff of the American naval forces in the entire Far East consisted of Vice Admiral Turner C. Joy and twenty-eight officers in Tokyo. The ships available were one cruiser, four destroyers, six minesweepers, and six attack transports. There was not a carrier in the western Pacific. Admiral Joy could and did order the United States Seventh Fleet to move from the Formosa area up to Okinawa, but that was not going to drive back the North Korean invaders. Since the Seventh Fleet's mission in recent years had been to ''show the flag'' around the Orient, that fleet was weak and scattered. Only

252

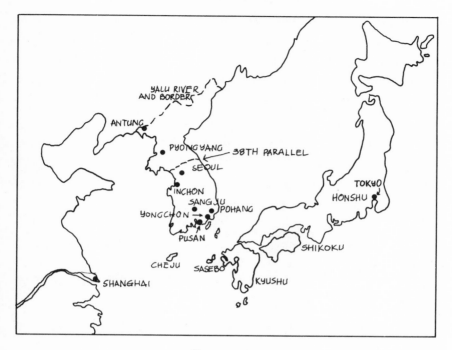

Korea, 1950

one carrier, one cruiser, and eight destroyers were close enough to be called to action. In comparison with the power of that Seventh Fleet even at Leyte Gulf, where it had an entire flotilla of escort carriers, the American weakness was certainly glaring. No responsible American military officer had expected a decision to fight in Korea or elsewhere in Asia, because they knew better than anyone else that the politicians had stripped them of the means to fight. It was a matter of pure good luck that the amphibious force under Rear Admiral James H. Doyle was just then at sea, conducting amphibious training exercises off Japan.

On June 26, Admiral Forrest Sherman, United States Chief of Naval Operations, ordered the Seventh Fleet to Sasebo. The president and his advisors suspected that the North Korean invasion might be just one of several orchestrated by the USSR. They worried lest the Chinese Communists move next against Taiwan. For that there were not enough ships to go around.

The naval situation changed for the better when the British offered three cruisers, a carrier, two destroyers and three frigates, the Australians offered ships, and so did the New Zealanders. A task force was organized, consisting

253

of ships built around the American carrier *Valley Forge* and the British carrier *Triumph*. Early in July, these ships sailed north, and on July 3 they hit the Haeju airfield in North Korea and several railroad bridges and rail lines. Other planes struck the Pyongyang airfield and destroyed several North Korean planes. For the first time the United States Navy was using a jet aircraft, the *F9F2 Panther*. For two days, the jets and propeller craft bombed and strafed transportation targets. Three American planes were destroyed in an operational accident (one bomber bounced into the parking area of *Valley Forge* and hit eight airplanes before it came to a halt). They destroyed eleven aircraft and damaged one, but they lost three aircraft and had nine damaged. In the weeks to come the pilots of the carriers damaged so many North Korean planes that the fifty-four-plane North Korean force never really appeared in the skies.

But on the ground, the North Korean advance was rapid; the South Korean army could not stand up against it. By July 15, the North Koreans had reached Sangju, halfway to the southern port of Pusan. Seven hundred Americans of the army's Twenty-Fourth Division had been flown into Korea from Japan. They did not make much impression. Later three regiments were brought into action, but they could not stop the advance either. They were short of artillery and tanks. They had only the American 2.36-inch bazooka, which had proved ineffective against the German Tiger tanks of World War II. It was even more ineffective against the new Soviet tanks the North Koreans were using.

In the third week of July, it seemed likely that the Americans would be pushed out of Korea altogether, and they certainly would have been, had it not been for aid from the sea. Rear Admiral James H. Doyle brought an amphibious force of six AKA transports and six landing ships to Pohang, seventy miles north of Pusan, carrying the First Cavalry Division. Ten thousand troops landed, two thousand vehicles, and supplies for the force. They were rushed by train from the harbor to the front. The landing was not opposed, so the aircraft carriers were released by the amphibious force, and they made a strike, destroying the North Korean oil refinery at Wonsan.

The carrier planes were used for every conceivable purpose. The Wonsan strike might be called strategic bombing. The planes also were asked to bomb bridges and to deliver close air support along the front to harried American and South Korean troops.

For some time the carrier planes *were* the air force. So badly had American forces in the Far East been stripped that planes had to be sent in from the United States and this took time: it was the last week of July before the first shipment of 145 *P-51* fighters was dispatched from the west coast. Meanwhile the North Koreans were moving more strength down to the south for the "final" assault on the Pusan perimeter. The carrier *Philippine Sea* arrived off

Korea on August 1. The Fifth Air Force brought in planes, too. And then along came the escort carriers *Sicily* and *Badoeng Strait* to augment the force. Little by little the Americans were getting into action. Soon these carriers were conducting strikes on enemy positions in South Korea, and at the same time destroying the enemy's communications lines back into the north. In one month, the Task Force made twenty-four hundred strikes against the enemy and slowed the North Korean advance on Pusan. The carriers and their planes bought precious time for the infantry.

On August 16, the navy came to the rescue of the land forces in another manner. The Third Republic of Korea Division had been cut off by the enemy near Yonghae and was in danger of annihilation. The fleet was asked to evacuate these troops. Rear Admiral C. C. Hartman's destroyers covered the movement from close in and beyond them stood the cruiser *Helena,* delivering naval gunfire on the shore. Four LSTs came into the beach at night, guided by the lights of a jeep on shore. The LSTs beached and the Republic of Korea division began boarding. Before daylight the ships had loaded six thousand troops and twelve hundred civilians and sailed. The next day the Third Republic of Korea Division was landed and back in action.

As September began, the Americans arrived in sufficient force to change the nature of the battle. The First Provisional Marine Brigade and two regiments of the Twenty-Fourth Army Infantry Division launched a counterattack and drove the enemy back across the Naktong river near Yongchon. The North Korean Fourth Division, which had led the attack on Seoul, was almost completely destroyed in this action. The North Korean drive was stopped.

30

The Inchon Landing
and ....

~~~~~~

FOR THE FIRST EIGHTY-TWO DAYS of the Korea war, the United Nations forces were on the defensive. General Hodge's 1946 prediction that he could not stop any force with the means at his disposal had come true, but just in time help arrived, much of it from the navy.

As defenses were shored up around Pusan and the carriers worked over the enemy positions, in Tokyo an amphibious landing was being planned. It had not been an easy struggle for General MacArthur; most senior officers in Washington opposed the move, largely, MacArthur believed, because they neither understood nor believed in amphibious operations. Admiral Sherman objected initially, but on an entirely different ground: feasibility. General MacArthur planned to land at Inchon, drive east and cut off the North Koreans. The trouble was that Inchon harbor had thirty-foot tides. The harbor was surrounded by a fifteen-foot seawall, which had to be scaled immediately after landing. How could any amphibious team overcome such an obstacle?

MacArthur insisted that Inchon must be the place for the landing because it was only fifteen miles from Seoul. The main roads ran through Seoul, and then south. A successful landing would turn the war about completely, but it must be made deep inside enemy-held territory. Another reason Inchon must be the place was that MacArthur was certain the North Koreans would consider Inchon just as "impossible" as did so many highly placed allied officers.

So it was Inchon. The operation began on September 10, 1950. Carrier planes bombed the harbor island of Wolmi with napalm. Gunfire support ships moved up Flying Fish Channel toward the city, encountered a mine

257

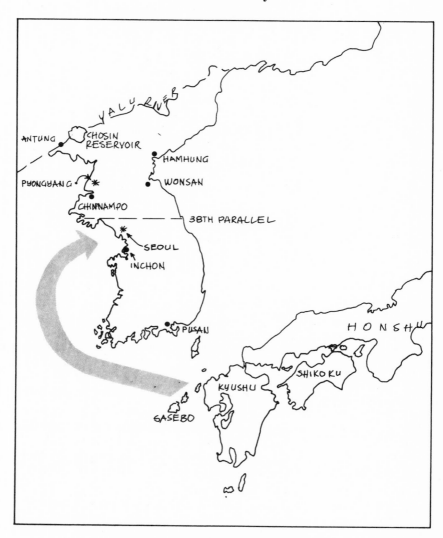

U.S. attack, September 10, 1945

field, and destroyed most of the mines by naval gunfire. The carrier planes continued to attack Wolmi as destroyers anchored behind the island and fired on military targets. Guns on Wolmi fired back and caused a number of casualties on the destroyer *Collett*. The attack on Wolmi continued for two days,

258

then landings were staged on Wolmi on September 15. The carrier planes bombed and strafed the landing beaches, and then the marines went in. By the end of the day Wolmi had been captured and the invasion of Inchon began. Because of the tide the landing craft had to beach just before dark. The landing craft came in, and the marines went up ladders to reach the land. They found they had surprised the enemy. Resistance was light and there were relatively few casualties. On September 16, troops began to advance past the city. That day the ships of the invasion fleet had their first air attack carried out by two Russian-built YAK-3 bombers. The cruiser *Rochester* and destroyer *Jamaica* were strafed and bombed. A few men were hit but the gunners of the destroyer shot down one plane.

The Inchon landing, as General MacArthur had expected, cut off the North Korean army at Pusan and forced that army into a panic retreat through the mountains on the eastern side of the Korean peninsula. It soon became totally disorganized. The Inchon adventure turned the war completely around.

Inchon had another effect. One result of the quarrel between Marine General Howland Smith and Army General Ralph Smith had been a concerted campaign within the Department of Defense to downgrade the Marine Corps. The marines said the army should have only such duties as guarding American diplomatic installations abroad. The army, said the army, would do the land fighting in the future. But the marines once again were called on to undertake the amphibious operations in Inchon harbor, and at Inchon the marines regained all the prestige that had evaporated over the years.

As the marine and army troops of the Eighth Army moved across the peninsula to cut off the North Koreans, the fleet attacked enemy troops along the shore. Carrier planes bombed bridges in the north and struck supply columns. But within a week naval action stopped completely. With the capture of Seoul, the navy ran out of targets.

The North Koreans were routed in their attempt to capture the south. American and Korean troops were stationed along the 38th parallel but they did not cross it because the United Nations had to decide what must be done next. President Syngman Rhee of The Republic of South Korea argued that the United Nations forces ought to move north and destroy the North Korean government, uniting the country under his rule. While the United Nations talked in New York, in Washington President Truman decided that the north should be invaded. General MacArthur made his plans. The Eighth Army was to attack in the west, heading toward Pyongyang, the North Korean capital. The Tenth Corps would stage a new amphibious landing at Wonsan on the east coast and move west to link up with the Eighth Army. The Peking government warned that if the United Nations forces—"the imperialists"—moved north of the 38th parallel, Red China would enter the war, but nobody was listening.

The drive north began. The troops landed in good order, and on October 11, South Korean troops captured Wonsan. Two marine air squadrons were sent north to Wonsan to support the Republic of Korea's advance on the important center of Hamhung. By this time more carriers had come into Korean waters.

On October 29, the Seventh Division landed at Iwon, only seventy-five miles from the Manchurian border. The Republic of Korea troops, meanwhile, were rushing toward the Yalu River, which separates Manchuria from North Korea. The fleet moved to Chinnampo, the port for Pyongyang, and General MacArthur said the war was so nearly over that he expected to be sending troops home for Christmas. Then, on October 16, the Chinese made good their vow to join the war on the side of their North Korean ally. Four armies crossed the Yalu River by bridge; the carrier planes were given a new job: destroy those Yalu bridges. On November 15, the United States Marines moved to the Chosin reservoir, where they expected to link up with the Eighth Army. Instead, they were surrounded at Chosin when thousands of Chinese troops broke through the mountains that separated the marines and the Eighth army. The marines then began a fighting withdrawal through enemy encirclement. Planes of the task force were called on time and again for close air support with napalm and 20-millimeter cannon. The breakout began on December 2. The troops moved back along the narrow road to the coast under an air umbrella of fifty to sixty circling planes. One pilot, Ensign Jesse L. Brown, the first black pilot in the United States Navy, was wounded, made an emergency landing, and was trapped in the wreckage behind the Chinese lines. Lieutenant (jg) Thomas J. Hudner landed alongside, wrecking his plane, and called for a helicopter rescue. He tried to free the wounded pilot but Brown was trapped in the wreckage of his plane. Helicopter pilot Lieutenant Charles Ware came, landed, and helped try to get Brown out, but the ensign died before he could be extricated. The helicopter pilot then flew Hudner to safety.

On December 3, the marines reached the lines of the Eighth Army. By the end of that day came orders that the troops were to be withdrawn to Pusan. Chinese encirclement was prevented by the fleet at Wonsan. On December 11, seven carriers and thirteen ships protected the perimeter as the troops were loaded onto ships. Then began the long war of attrition, in which the carriers played a major role. For example, three carriers, the *Bon Homme Richard, Essex,* and *Antietam* were occupied for several months in attacking rail lines. They operated day and night, and this became the pattern of aerial operation, in the attempt to keep the Communist troops from resupply. During the last days of the Pacific war, the carriers *Enterprise* and *Saratoga* had been converted to ''night carriers'' and this practice was repeated in 1952, as the war dragged on. It was not a very successful effort. In 1952, the Communists strengthened their anti-aircraft defenses. West of Wonsan was an area the pilots called Death Valley, where one attacking plane counted four hundred anti-aircraft bursts.

The navy's work in the Korean War was mostly slow and wearing. In addition to troop support, the Pacific Fleet was given the task of blockading the Korean coast. The blockade was successful, even in cutting off North Korean fishing. The United States worried that the Chinese Communists would invade Taiwan, so the Seventh Fleet was entrusted with patrol of Taiwan waters as well.

By the middle of 1952, the North Koreans and the Chinese flew MIG fighters against American planes, and when the American air forces began a deliberate campaign to knock out power stations in the north, along the Yalu, Communist planes came up in such numbers that the area became known as "MIG Alley." One day an American pilot spotted two hundred MIGS on the airfield at Antung, Manchuria, but since these were in Chinese territory, and the politicians had interdicted the United Nations armies from attacking inside China, the MIGs had to be left alone. On June 23, the carrier pilots showed what could be done in a concentrated attack. They hit a dozen power plants in a two-day action; at the end Pyongyang had no power at all, and industrial plants on both sides of the Yalu river had to stop production. Successful raids were made against Pyongyang, Sindok, and Kilchu, hitting industrial plants. In September, the carriers *Essex, Princeton,* and *Boxer* destroyed the Aoji Oil Refinery. One new development in the carrier strikes was the employment of "drone" bombs, made of pilotless *F6F* (World War II vintage) fighter planes converted to guided missiles directed to the target by control planes.

The success of United States aerial action obviously worried the Communists, for in November, 1952, Russian MIGs entered the war. Four *F9F5 Panther* aircraft were on combat air patrol above the carriers *Oriskany, Essex,* and *Kearsarge,* when they were attacked by seven MIGs. Lieutenant Elmer R. Williams and Lieutenant (jg) David M. Rowlands were sent out to make contact with the incoming planes. Williams sent one MIG into a smoking spiral and Rowlands followed it down. Williams's shells hit another MIG and parts fell off, and then he started a third MIG burning. His plane was hit just then by a shell that knocked out the rudder control. Lieutenant (jg) John D. Middleton joined the fight and shot the MIG off Williams's tail. The pilot bailed out and landed in the sea. Such encounters cost the Americans because the MIGs showed a marked superiority in performance. But before MIG interference could become a major factor in the Korean War, at the end of July, 1953, the war came to an end. It was not a military end, but a political one. The 38th Parallel was reestablished as the demarcation line between the two

261

Koreas, and the fighting stopped. The American fleet went back to Japan, but this time not to be disassembled. The Seventh Fleet was still to be the guardian of the waters around Taiwan to protect Chiang Kai-shek's Republic of China.

31

Vietnam
—The Beginning

~~~~~~~

AFTER THE JAPANESE SURRENDER the returning French discovered a social revolution in Indo-China led by Ho Chi Minh's Viet Minh party. The British navy became involved in actual military operations on the side of the French, but the Americans did not. British involvement came because of occupation responsibilities entrusted to Allied Southeast Asia commander Lord Louis Mountbatten at the end of the Pacific War. For two years, the American navy contribution consisted only of transporting troops out of Indo-China. Early in 1947, the United States State Department notified the Paris government that arms sales to France would not be approved in Washington in "cases which appear to relate to Indo-China." But the American fear of Communism extended to Indo-China, and the State Department indicated that the United States would prefer to see the French deal with leaders other than the avowedly Communist Ho Chi Minh.

Encouraged by Washington, the French established the State of Vietnam, under the former emperor of Annam, Bao Dai, with its capital at Saigon. As usual the interference did not work. Ho Chi Minh continued to operate his own government from Hanoi.

The fall of China to Mao Tse-tung's Communists in 1948 came at a time when Americans were in a frenzy over Communist expansion around the world. In October, 1949, Congress authorized the president to spend up to $75 million at his discretion "in the general area of China." There was a good deal of verbiage in the enabling act about "free countries" and "free peoples." But the meaning was clear: contain Communism. Thus began the

263

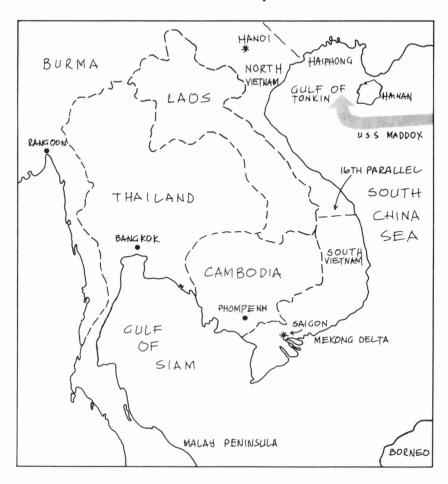

Gulf of Tonkin incident, August 1964

military advisory program that was later to immerse the United States in the Indo-China war.

American concern grew when Mao Tse-tung moved troops down along the Tonkin border of northern Indo-China. Early in 1950, in that fateful speech which told the world that the United States had no stake in Korea, Secretary of State Dean Acheson also wrote off Southeast Asia. The Asian mainland, he said, would have to shift for itself. But within two weeks, the American Joint Chiefs of Staff were asking for $15 million for political and military assistance to be given in Indo-China.

After Red China recognized the Ho government, the United States recognized the "independent" governments of Vietnam, Laos and Cambodia. Soon the Viet Minh launched its first major offensive against the French, and the Indo-China War, which had heretofore consisted of sporadic skirmishes, settled down to attenuated conflict.

Soon, the United States was shipping landing ships and naval aircraft to the French in Indo-China, with the approval of President Truman and the Joint Chiefs of Staff. When the Korean War began, President Truman also increased American aid in Indo-China by sending an American Military Advisory Group to Saigon. The group's arrival on August 3, 1950, signaled the beginning of direct United States involvement in the Indo-China civil war.

From 1950 to 1953, the French fought in Indo-China. They caused thousands of Vietnamese casualties, but Ho's armies persisted, and gradually the tide began to turn in the favor of the Viet Minh. In the summer of 1953, as the Korean War dragged to a close, Washington feared Chinese Communist involvement in the Indo-China struggle, and contingency plans were laid in Washington that would send the Pacific Fleet to Indo-China. By this time the United States Navy was ready. Three years of the Korean War had wiped out all the effects of the uncertain years after 1945. The United States carrier force had been brought up to strength, and the carriers were capable of delivering atomic weapons if necessary. The navy was building new ships, including helicopter carriers. Mine warefare, so much a part of the Korea conflict, had been revolutionized by the United States Navy.

The fleet status after 1953 brought a new difficulty because the United States was not directly involved in war but must maintain a fleet state of "readiness." This was as difficult as it had been in 1941 when "readiness" had been so attenuated that when war came Pearl Harbor was not ready.

Slowly during the next ten years, the American involvement in Vietnam grew. The United States carrier *Langley* was given to the French in 1951. The carrier *Belleau Wood* was transferred to them in the fall of 1953. By the end of that year, the United States had delivered 550 ships to the French in Indo-China, and in the spring of 1954 an American naval force was maintained off the Gulf of Tonkin on a twelve-hour alert, ready to steam to the assistance of the French who had nearly run out of moral and physical resources. The French were then locked in the desperate struggle at Dien Bien Phu. Admiral Arthur Radford, chairman of the Joint Chiefs of Staff, indicated that if the French needed help, 350 carrier aircraft could be employed within two days. He believed that if the French position deteriorated, the United States ought to be prepared to enter the war, and it very nearly happened. For two weeks, the men of the Pacific Fleet's Task Group 70.2 lived in a state of total readiness, expecting to go to war at any moment. The French asked for American direct intervention to save Dien Bien Phu but several congressmen warned the

President to seek the concurrence of America's allies before taking such drastic action. President Eisenhower wrote Prime Minister Churchill, but by the time the talks began Dien Bien Phu was lost to the Viet Minh. Then the decision was made: the United States would not act.

As the French failed in Indo-China, American military aid increased. The United States sent more planes, *F4U*s for the most part. At one point Admiral Robert Carney, United States chief of naval operations, proposed establishment of a Southeast Asia Defense Command with headquarters at Saigon. This move failed only because Britain firmly refused to participate in the Indo-China war. The solution seemed for a time to lie at the conference table, and on July 20, 1954, the French and the Viet Minh signed three agreements, one dividing Vietnam, one establishing Laos, and one establishing Cambodia.

Any hope that the war was over was illusory; almost immediately action began again. The Chinese Communists seemed to be threatening. Cincpac ordered the Seventh Fleet to carry out more vigilant patrols off Formosa. The increased activity brought Chinese reaction. An American patrol plane was attacked by Chinese Communist fighters. Two weeks later a British Air Cathay airliner with eighteen passengers aboard was shot down. On July 26, planes from the carrier *Philippine Sea* were attacked by two Chinese Communist fighters, and the American planes shot both of them down.

By then the United States had four carriers in the western Pacific. Since the Korean armistice attempts had been made in Congress to cut back the number of fleet units, but the navy said there was too much for them to do. The ships of the American fleet were used to transport refugees from North Vietnam to the south. That summer and early fall, the Americans also carried cargo, vehicles, and passengers to South Vietnam. In the end, the Americans and the French transferred eight hundred thousand people from north to south.

By the summer of 1954, during Eisenhower's first term, the Americans had assumed many of France's former responsibilities, especially for the training of the troops of Vietnam. The American military advisory group was increased and a navy was also organized. In March, 1955, the war began again, and soon American ships with Vietnamese crews were fighting in the "riverine operations" in the Mekong delta. In April, 1956, the French moved out the last of their naval forces in the Far East. The political decision was made in Washington that it was important for the South Vietnamese government to survive; and so United States assistance to Vietnam increased, the deep involvement being symbolized at the October 26, 1956, anniversary celebrations of Vietnamese "independence." The United States cruiser *Los Angeles* steamed up the Saigon River to participate.

By this time the United States Navy was overhauling Vietnamese ships at the American naval shipyard at Subic Bay in the Philippines; Vietnamese officers and specialists were trained here; and American naval officers also were training Vietnamese at their own training center in Vietnam.

By 1957, the American military advisory group reported an increase of military activity. Although only seventy-eight American naval and marine personnel were assigned to South Vietnam, it seemed inevitable that there would be more, for in 1958 the Communists in the north were increasing the pressure. Gradually, a little more each year, the United States was sucked into the swirling waters of Vietnam.

32

Vietnam
—Miscalculation

~~~~~~

COMPARED TO KOREA AND VIETNAM the American naval operations of the past had been simple. By the middle of the 1950s, the United States had still not learned that there *were* differences and quarrels within the "Communist camp" and that it was not one camp at all. The implications of the defection in 1948 of Marshall Tito's Yugoslavia from the Soviet world were misunderstood, particularly after the struggle in Korea threw the Soviets, Chinese, and North Koreans together in a move to fend off a "greater danger" in the form of the Western powers. Lost in that period was recognition of a more basic disagreement between the USSR and Red China over the courses of Communist expansion. The Chinese looked with deep suspicion at Soviet designs on areas around the China perimeter.

That is not to say that Soviet expansionism was not real or that Chinese Communist depradations in Southeast Asia did not exist. But America's politicians lumped all such actions together in the "Cold War" and in the need for containment of Communism, so by the middle of the 1950s, the Pacific Fleet was deeply involved in the political aspects of the American containment. In 1957, Admiral Nimitz's old title of Cincpac was revived. Cincpac was no longer primarily a naval commander, but a naval officer (by custom) who was in command of all American forces in the Pacific region. The fleet was only part of his command—to symbolize it, the headquarters moved up the hill from Makalapa to Camp Smith (named for Holland Smith) in back of Halawa Heights.

The late 1950s and early 1960s were a troubled time for the Pacific Fleet. It was held responsible for the safety of Taiwan, which was under constant threat of invasion. And in growing numbers came calls for the use of American ships and protective forces to move Vietnamese troops around in the war zone.

At first, Ho Chi Minh's strategy was to let internal forces disrupt the Vietnamese economy and social system. This attempt was successful enough so that in 1963, the United States decided that more aggressive action must be taken. The new concept, advocated by political scientists during JFK's presidency, was "measured response" to "limited war." The outcome of the Korean War could be used to prove or disprove this theory, depending on how one regarded the war: as a victory in that it prevented the swallowing of South Korea by North Korea, or as a stalemate forced on the military by political forces. The advocates of "measured response" took the former view.

The final commitment of America to Vietnam began in 1964, with the dispatch of General William C. Westmoreland to Saigon to put heart and muscle into the war. General Westmoreland's first encounter on the ground at the airport was symbolic of the future: he met General Huynh Van Cao, a corps commander of the Vietnamese army, whose philosophy was to avoid battle, hide when in danger, and "let the Americans do it." General Westmoreland did not then know that this would be the history of his war.

On Westmoreland's arrival, the war stepped up. In May, a terrorist placed a bomb which blew out the bottom of the *USS Card,* a World War II escort carrier used as a helicopter and aircraft ferry.

In the first years, Westmoreland emphasized supply and training. In Washington, the politicians continued to believe that South Vietnam was a real political entity with a popular base. Even the political chaos that was continually apparent did not seem vital. But in August, 1964, during the presidency of Lyndon Johnson, all that changed. The United States became involved in actual fighting for the first time.

There were many overtones of the past in Vietnam in the early months of 1964. Back in 1940, when Britain was in peril from the Nazi submarines, President Roosevelt had secretly offered assistance to the British in the face of strong American public opinion against involvement in the European war. Officially, American policy was confined to "lend-lease"; actually, in the spring of 1941 American naval forces were engaged in belligerent action against the Germans. In April of that year, the destroyer *Niblack* had an inconclusive encounter with a U-boat in which she dropped three depth charges. When she returned to port her captain was not censured for "interference" but praised for quick action. In July, the battleship *Texas* was nearly torpedoed by a U-boat; in September the destroyer *Greer* was attacked. In October, the USS *Kearny* was torpedoed while trying to protect a British convoy from attack by a U-boat wolf pack. By that time, the United States was in fact at war with Germany.

Vietnam——Miscalculation

So it was in the spring of 1964. American pilots in Vietnam were ordered to fly combat missions against the North Vietnamese and the Viet Cong as part of the program of "advising" the South Vietnam forces. This duplicity was aimed to still complaint at home in the United States about involvement in what many Americans considered to be an impossible morass. It grew worse as Premier Nguyen Khan of South Vietnam began fulminating for an invasion of the north, sure in the assurances from Washington that the Americans would back him all the way. The Americans had been told that South Vietnam was only defending itself. But the fact was, as Air Marshal Nguyen Cao Ky said inadvertently one day, that the South Vietnamese had been attacking the north for three years "by air, land, and sea."

By the first of August, 1964, it was inevitable that the United States would soon become a participant in the Vietnam War. All that was needed was an incident of direct confrontation to spark an explosion.

As part of the gradual buildup, naval involvement had increased considerably by the summer of 1964. The United States carrier *Ticonderoga* was stationed off Da Nang, and although American ships had generally stayed out of North Vietnamese waters, they had invaded these waters on intelligence patrols in 1962, 1963, and in March of 1964. Obviously the North Vietnamese and their Chinese Communist allies were aware of this activity. In fact, the Chinese had begun moving troops down to Hainan Island in the Gulf of Tonkin. Peking had issued new orders in June forbidding foreign ships passage of the fifteen-mile strait between Hainan and the Luichow Peninsula except under the most restrictive conditions.

The Joint Chiefs of Staff decided in July to send an American ship into the Gulf of Tonkin on a new intelligence mission. On July 15, the order went from the Joint Chiefs of Staff to Admiral Ulysses Grant Sharp, Jr., who was then Cincpac—commander of all United States forces in the Pacific (although not those in Vietnam itself). The Joint Chiefs were particularly interested in the North Vietnamese coastal and air defenses. When the order reached Pearl Harbor, it was passed down to Admiral Thomas H. Moorer, then in command of the Pacific Fleet. He gave it to Vice Admiral Roy L. Johnson, commander of the Seventh Fleet, which was on duty near China and Indo-China. Admiral Johnson assigned the duty to Captain John J. Herrick, commander of Destroyer Division 192. Captain Herrick chose to undertake the mission in the destroyer *Maddox*.

And what was that mission specifically? It was to steam into the Gulf of Tonkin, where the *Ticonderoga*'s task group lurked just outside, and into the narrows of the strait, which would bring the *Maddox* within fifteen miles of the Chinese Communist coast and eight miles off the North Vietnam coast. The purpose was to provoke the Chinese Communists and the North Vietnamese to turn on their radar sets so the Americans could measure the frequencies and locate and estimate the power of Chinese and North Vietnamese defenses.

From the military and intelligence points of view, there was nothing particularly unusual about this practice. The intelligence communities of the United States, like those of all other nations, were continually spying on everyone, including their allies. What was unusual was the undertaking of such a mission at this particular time. For several months, the South Vietnamese naval forces had been increasing their sea raids into the north. Indeed, Captain Herrick was cautioned to seek intelligence from Saigon so he would not interfere with any South Vietnamese raids while he was carrying out this mission.

The *Maddox* set out from her station off Japan for what seemed to the crew to be a routine mission. No one aboard knew how great had grown the tensions in Washington and Hanoi. For the first time Washington seemed to realize that the South Vietnamese forces could never win their own war. By this time, of course, the political wisdom in Washington indicated that the war must be won.

The *Maddox* stopped off at Keelung, Taiwan, where it took aboard special electronic spy equipment. Then Captain Herrick moved out to sea. En route, the *Maddox* encountered several South Vietnamese patrol boats just returning from a mission against the north, but Captain Herrick was not on the "need to know" list, so he had not been told these boats had attacked North Vietnamese radar stations with gunfire.

As the American destroyer passed into North Vietnamese waters she was detected; the North Vietnam naval stations along the coast weere excited; the raid of only hours earlier had been the first gunfire raid of the southern forces against the north. The *Maddox* monitors knew their ship was identified as US DD *731* (from the numbers painted on her sides), for that designation was heard all night long as the shore stations tracked the ship.

Early on the morning of August 2, the *Maddox* came to a point near the town of Hon Mat, not far from the place the South Vietnamese had shelled two nights earlier. Captain Herrick was informed of the presence of a number of junks massed in the area. He had been warned that these junks could hold several thousand soldiers, that they could close in on a destroyer (even at the cost of sacrificing a few to collision), and that the troops might try to board and overwhelm the crew. The captain of the *Maddox* ordered the general quarters alarm sounded and the ship moved away skirting the pack of junks. That night the radiomen intercepted a message indicating that the North Vietnamese had, indeed, planned to attack the destroyer.

Captain Herrick sent a message to the Seventh Fleet indicating that he considered it very risky to continue this patrol. He was told to "resume when considered prudent"—in other words, to carry out his orders. So, after a short time, the *Maddox* turned back toward the North Vietnam shore.

In the Red River delta, the *Maddox* sighted a small tanker and three torpedo boats. Captain Herrick paid little attention, until the radiomen had a message: the shore station had ordered the three torpedo boats to attack the *Maddox* to test her reactions.

The PT boats set a course to intercept, at fifty knots. The *Maddox* went to action stations. "This is not a drill," warned the squawkbox. When the range was ninety-eight hundred yards, the *Maddox* opened fire. The PT boats kept coming. The *Maddox* kept shooting at the small targets, and also radioed for air support. The message reached the *Ticonderoga,* which then had three planes in the air, on target practice runs. They headed for the ship.

When the North Vietnamese PT boats reached a point about a mile off the *Maddox,* they began firing .25-millimeter guns. The *Maddox* hit one of the PT boats and it went dead in the water. The other two stopped to give assistance, just as the American jets arrived. The planes attacked the boats with rockets and shells. The North Vietnamese fired back, and one of the pilots announced he was going to have to ditch. Captain Herrick had just decided to go after the PT boats and finish them off, when he had the call from the plane. He broke off the action and headed south to pick up the pilot in case he had to land in the water. But later the pilot discovered that he had not been hit by gunfire and could land on the carrier. By this time the *Maddox* was far from the action and did not return.

When the news of the confrontation reached Washington, it was apparent that an attitude of belligerence had swept over the administration. There was talk about "not running out of places where we have a right to be"—based on the old conception of the three-mile limit as the beginning of territorial waters. The limit might be three miles, but the Chinese Communists and the North Vietnamese did not accept that limit, so it was apparent that if the Americans chose to move into the area, they were seeking confrontation. The secretary of state said he was willing to send the whole Seventh Fleet into the Gulf of Tonkin. It was a fine political show of indignation for an election year, and perhaps the leaders of the Johnson administration did not recognize that the participation of American "advisors" in the Vietnam War meant that America was in the war. They talked that day about the possibility of "retaliatory" action.

On second thought, President Johnson and the others grew queasy enough about the possible interpretation of their activities that they sent a message on the "hotline" to Moscow, saying that the United States did not intend to widen the Vietnam War but insisted on its right to send its ships anywhere in international waters. Strictly speaking, this was a perfectly proper point of view—but hardly one that would guarantee to keep the United States out of the conflict.

Admiral Sharp was already augmenting the naval force in the Vietnam area. The carrier *Kearsarge* was sent to join the *Constellation* and *Ticonder-*

oga. The "freedom-of-the-seas" issue was raised again, and to test it, Admiral Moorer ordered the *Maddox* to adopt a different approach, moving to within eight miles of the Vietnam coast in the daylight hours, then retreat at night, gradually moving northward.

On the night of August 2, the *Maddox* arrived at the point called Yankee Station, where the *Ticonderoga* and other ships lay. She resupplied from a tanker and an ammunition carrier. She also met the destroyer *C. Turner Joy,* which had been on patrol elsewhere in the general area. The two ships were ordered to continue the patrol. The captains were warned that night by the commander of Task Force 77 that the North Vietnamese apparently considered themselves at war with the United States and that the destroyers ought to expect "unprovoked" attack at any time. It was all a matter of what was considered to be provocation; from the North Vietnamese point of view the whole mission was a provocation from the beginning, and that seems to have been how it was envisaged by the United States intelligence community. Only by provoking the North Vietnamese into action could they get the information they wanted—and as for reaction no one seemed to care.

On August 3, another flotilla of South Vietnamese patrol boats attacked a North Vietnamese radar station and a security station, following the route that the American destroyers had taken that day. No one in Washington knew anything about this attack. That day President Johnson issued stern statements to the North Vietnamese about the consequences of further military action against American ships in international waters. Captain Herrick knew about the South Vietnamese attack and he wanted to take his destroyers out of the area, but when he asked, Admiral Sharp insisted that the mission go on, "to demonstrate United States's resolve to assert our legitimate rights in these international waters."

So Captain Herrick realized that he was to "show the flag" no matter the consequences. It was plain that his superiors would not be particularly concerned if he got into a fight because of it.

The watch aboard the United States ships was alert for trouble as they approached the Vietnam coast that night of August 4. The radarmen had a number of contacts. At about nine o'clock, several men at the radar stations were certain they saw a torpedo launched. Sonar men said they tracked it. The *C. Turner Joy* opened fire—no one seemed to know quite what the ship was firing at, but the radar scope indicated that at least two of those "somethings" were sunk. By 11 o'clock the "torpedoes" were coming thick and fast —twenty-two had been reported, although neither vessel had been hit. In the violent maneuvering and shooting, *Maddox* finally found a large clear target and was just about to open fire—when the man at the main gun director realized the ship on which his guns were trained was the *C. Turner Joy.* He did not push the trigger, and the navy was saved the ignominy of sinking one of its own ships in the hysteria of the night.

That narrow escape marked the end of the action. The mission was broken off and the ships steamed swiftly south, sending reports to higher authority. With the first messages, Pearl Harbor went on the alert. Admiral Sharp asked Washington for the power to mount an air strike on North Vietnam. Nobody objected. The carriers *Ticonderoga* and the *Constellation* prepared for action.

As Captain Herrick moved away from the scene, he tried to find out from the crews of the two ships under his command precisely what had happened. By one-thirty in the morning he decided that very little had occurred, that there had been no certain evidence that anything had been fired except the guns of *C. Turner Joy,* and he so reported to Pearl Harbor.

Within a matter of hours, President Johnson had decided to begin bombing North Vietnam in "retaliation." As that word reached Pearl Harbor, Admiral Sharp grew a little more cautious: he was, after all, responsible for the tenor of the messages received in Washington and they did not add up very well with those received at Pearl Harbor from Captain Herrick. Herrick was subjected to sharp quizzing as to whether the force had actually been attacked. He said he could not give any real verification of attack, except for highly conflicting statements from men of the *C. Turner Joy* and the *Maddox.* (Later, under no one knows what pressures, Captain Herrick revised his estimates and concluded that there had been an attack.) The admirals were not in any mood to back down. They had said there had been an attack on the American ships, and they were going to stick with that interpretation.

President Johnson made the decision. Without congressional declaration, he decided to carry the war to the North Vietnamese, and even as the admirals were beginning to have second thoughts and were crossquestioning (by radio) the captains and crews of the destroyers, the planes were flying from the *Ticonderoga* to drop American bombs.

Just as surely as had the bombs at Pearl Harbor announced that Japan was at war with the United States, the American bombs on a minor patrol boat base in North Vietnam announced that the United States was warring on North Vietnam. Thus came the escalation of the American effort in Vietnam. Certainly the evidence secured (subject still in 1980 to the strictures of naval security) indicated that the whole Tonkin Gulf affair was debatable at best and that the president's decision to bomb North Vietnam was based on misinformation and miscalculation. Far more important was the apparently forgotten fact that military men exist to perform military acts and that the standard of their performance is the excellence by which they perform. At the moment that the United States sent its first band of "military advisors" to

South Vietnam, the indications were dangerous. When General Westmoreland and a larger and more important group were sent on, to try to create a national military force for South Vietnam, the commitment to the war became certain. It would have demanded a decision by the president of the United States that the United States must extricate itself from Vietnam to reverse the course. After the Westmoreland mission arrived, everything else was foreordained, barring that presidential act. The military men were told to go in there and fix it so the South Vietnamese could win the war. Immediately they learned that the South Vietnamese forces would never have the morale to do that; and from the outset it was apparent to anyone who had followed the history of the area since 1940 that South Vietnam could be made viable only if some strong power stood by to spoon-feed and protect that government. Admirals and generals are employed to win wars, and that was what they were trying to do in Vietnam. All the vital decisions that first involved America, and then made it impossible for the Americans to win the war, were the decisions of the politicians. The politicians had not learned how to cope with the different philosophy of war that had been engendered on the day that the first atomic bomb was dropped on Hiroshima. The counsels of Clausewitz and Mahan no longer applied in the world of the last half of the twentieth century. Already there had been one lesson: wars cannot be won unless the military is given full authority to prosecute the war to a finish, and in the shadow of atomic holocaust, no politician dared go that far. So the lesson of the 1960s was that none but defensive wars should be begun by major powers, since they could not win through selective action. That was the major miscalculation in the Gulf of Tonkin incident. But even when that incident was subjected to the scrutiny of Congress, within a matter of days after the *Maddox* patrol, the lesson did not seem to be learned by the politicians any more than it had been learned in Korea.

Under those conditions, the fleet would have a role that could never be satisfactory. That was the problem after the summer of 1964.

33

Run Aground

~~~~~~~~~~

FROM THE STANDPOINT OF NATIONAL HEROISM, the Vietnam War proved most unsatisfactory. Not that there was a shortage of individual acts of valor, but there were so many conflicting emotions among Americans that there could be no public support of the war of the sort that creates national heroes. There were no Corregidors. There were no Guadalcanals, where a beleaguered American force turned defeat into victory. There were no victories. The Vietnam War was a dirty little war, filled with endless dangerous and thankless routine for the Pacific Fleet. Or, as one commander put it: it was a logistic war—and who in the public gets excited about that?

Control—that was the key. Everything the Americans did was controlled. The air strikes of the marines and the navy pilots were "controlled." They were interdicted by political decisions from hitting some targets. The navy could have blockaded the North Vietnam port of Haiphong but the politicians decided that this should not be done because it increased the danger of war with China and Soviet Russia, the major suppliers of North Vietnam. The admirals suggested that the United States should set a blockade. They were convinced that it would be as effective against North Vietnam as it had been against the Japanese, who were brought almost to their knees by the American naval and air blockade in 1945. So the navy was given the task of "sealing off" the eleven hundred miles of the irregular coastline of South Vietnam. From the beginning it was an impossible task, as proved by the constant uncovering of Vietcong supply dumps along the coast. The South Vietnam government licensed fifty thousand junks and, from afar, who was to know the character and purpose of a junk putting in toward land? That was to say nothing of supplies coming in through Cambodia and China. Cambodia was at first treated as a neutral, and China was left alone out of respect for the danger of extending the war. There was no way that an American navy blockade could succeed under these conditions.

The navy role developed in two directions: one to limit the Vietcong's supplies and one to supply the South Vietnamese and the growing force of Americans committed to action over the years after 1964.

One result of the Tonkin Gulf incident was the dispatch of regular soldiers of the North Vietnam Army into South Vietnam. It would not be long before the fiction of the war would be over: that the Vietcong were completely independent of North Vietnam and that the South Vietnamese were independent of the big powers—which in the end turned out to be the Americans.

By February, 1965, American carrier planes were ranging into North Vietnam on bombing and strafing missions. On March 8, when American marines went into action at Danang, the United States involvement was complete.

The next month, planes from the carriers *Hancock* and *Ranger* bombed an ammunition depot at Phu Qui. In April, planes from *Coral Sea* and *Midway* bombed and strafed Vietcong elements in South Vietnam. The carrier task force station at the mouth of Tonkin Gulf was retained and another carrier force was placed off South Vietnam on a permanent basis. This was necessary because South Vietnam did not have adequate airfields for bomber operation.

In the summer of 1965, a number of United States surface ships arrived in Vietnam. The *New Jersey,* Admiral Halsey's flagship during the last days of World War II in the Pacific, was brought out of mothballs to make use of those 16-inch guns in bombarding shore targets. This was the sort of naval war it was to be; nothing spectacular, just application of force in the hope that it would stop the infiltration and movement of North Vietnamese troops and supplies to the south.

By the spring of 1965, General Westmoreland was calling for more American troops. He had been in Vietnam long enough to realize that there was no hope of victory if the Vietnamese were to be relied upon. No one seemed to draw the corollary that if this was true, there must be something basically wrong with the South Vietnam social and political structure. General Westmoreland called for a Marine Expeditionary Brigade to come to South Vietnam. Admiral Sharp took an equally hawkish approach, and with presidential blessing the American troop buildup began.

Some opposition voices were raised. General Maxwell D. Taylor, American ambassador to South Vietnam, objected. He said that if the Americans came in, they would be forced to carry the war, and he foresaw nothing but disaster. Retired General James Gavin suggested in *Harper's* magazine that the United States would be mired in Vietnam and the best solution was a political solution. But the active admirals and generals rejected this approach. Fighting was their business; they had been given an opportunity, and they wanted to fight. By 1966, one hundred and twenty five thousand Americans were committed to Vietnam. By 1967, the navy was involved in a new operation: manning the Riverine Force which the United States had created in the Mekong delta, so that army troops could be moved quickly about and engage units of the Vietcong. In 1967, the Riverine Force engaged in five "major actions" and destroyed a thousand Vietcong troops or two hundred bodies per "major action." It was a romantic idea, but very expensive; the Riverine Force string of "victories" added up to nothing, a symbol of the frustration of the American attempts to "win" the Vietnam War.

The navy and the marines conducted a number of amphibious landings during these years. In 1965, the Ninth Marine Expeditionary Brigade was landed at Red Beach in Danang Bay to reinforce defenses of an airfield there. Later marines landed at Chu Lai. By 1967, marines were fighting in many places in South Vietnam. Indicative of the nature of the struggle there was the story of the "Battle of Khe Sanh" which lasted from April, 1967, to April, 1968.

Khe Sanh is located just below the 17th parallel at the extreme northwestern corner of South Vietnam, almost on the Gulf of Tonkin. This was part of the "demilitarized zone," a sanitary belt set up at the Geneva conferences between the French and the North Vietnamese, whose purpose had been to eliminate military activity along the frontiers. But by 1967, both sides were moving into the zone. The purpose of the marines and the troops of the army of Vietnam was to destroy the local guerilla forces in what was called the I Corps tactical zone. As usual in guerilla warfare, the Vietcong fought, disappeared, and then returned. Only by maintaining a large force could the Americans keep control of the area, and "control" was never total. It took a full year to gain control of sixteen hundred square miles. But when that was done in 1967, the change did worry the North Vietnamese enough so they sent regular North Vietnamese troops to wrest control back from the Americans.

The body count, which became the standard measure of military success, looked very good for the marines. By April, 1967, they claimed to have killed 3,492 North Vietnamese troops, while losing only 541 Americans. But on April 24, a marine patrol engaged an enemy force at a hill near the Rao Quan river north of Khe Sanh. Unknowingly the United States patrol had triggered an offensive that was intended to isolate and wipe out the marine force. The first battle involved three hills for eighteen days. At the end, superior American fire power drove the North Vietnamese off the hills with a loss of about a thousand men. Marine losses were 155 killed and 425 wounded.

The battle moved east where the North Vietnamese were trying a frontal assault south through the demilitarized zone. General Westmoreland moved army and marine troops constantly. The fighting was almost constant too; small actions that took a high toll in dead and wounded. The enemy casualties, according to the body count were always high: 1,290 killed at Con Thien in July, 1,117 in October. But so were the American casualties: 159 dead and 345 wounded in July, 340 killed in October. It was deadly but most unspectacular warfare. There were no great drives; there was none of the finality of a marine operation against one of the Pacific islands in World War II or even a surge forward as at the Inchon landings of the Korean War. There seemed to be no end to it.

The navy was called on for support of the marines. Rear Admiral Edwin B. Hoover was charged with bringing ships, men, and military supply through the Pacific Fleet chain. The Seabees came to build runways for aircraft and helicopters, as the fighting continued around Khe Sanh. Early in 1968, the North Vietnamese brought in their 304th Division, one of their best, and launched a new offensive. In January, the battle was suspended as the Communists launched their Tet offensive. The Vietcong was to seize the southern cities, then wait for the North Vietnamese regular armies to come down and consolidate the territory. But the major effect of the Tet offensive was to bring home to millions of Americans the apparently endless nature of the war in which United States forces were so deeply involved in a country far across the sea. If the national reason was hatred of Communism, to many at home the price seemed to be growing far too high.

When the Tet offensive failed, the North Vietnamese returned their attention to the demilitarized zone in the vicinity of the 17th parallel. They surrounded Khe Sanh and attempted to make of it another Dien Bien Phu, hoping to trade further on the growing anti-war sentiment in the United States by creating an American military disaster. In February, as the battle of Khe Sanh raged, the Americans were surrounded but were resupplied by helicopter and *C-130* transport planes. The struggle continued throughout March. In April, reinforcements fought their way through the North Vietnamese lines and lifted the siege. During the long fight United States planes had dropped a hundred thousand tons of bombs on the enemy and one hundred and fifty thousand rounds of artillery fire were expended. Virtually every man on the perimeter was a hero; acts of valor were commonplace during this long, bitter fight. Thousands of North Vietnamese were killed, and several thousand Americans were killed or wounded. The position was held, but in June, 1968, after all that blood, one of General Westmoreland's last actions as commander in Vietnam was to order the razing of the base and withdrawal of American troops south to the Ca Lu area. So what had been accomplished?

Khe Sanh was indicative of the whole Vietnam War venture. In the end, millions of people in the United States became emotionally exhausted by a struggle in which they could see neither sense nor national interest. And in the election of 1972, as in 1968, the Vietnam War was a major issue. Like Korea, it was ended by political decision, the first war America had really ''lost.'' With the evacuation of troops, the enormous fleet operation suddenly came to an end. The Pacific Fleet would now turn to other tasks.

34

Covering
Half the World

~~~~~~~~

IN 1972, even before the Vietnam War ended, the Pacific command was given responsibility for covering more than half the world, from Alaska to the shores of East Africa, an area of more than one hundred million square miles.

By that time the responsibility and activity of the Pacific force had so changed that an Admiral Nimitz would scarcely have recognized Cincpac. The staff had grown to six hundred, with another five hundred civilians and officers assigned to support activity. By 1977, the Cincpac controlled three hundred and twenty thousand military personnel. No longer was Cincpac responsible to the commander in chief of the navy but directly to the Joint Chiefs of Staff. American forces in Korea, Japan, and Taiwan were all responsible directly to Cincpac, and when the American expeditionary force was sent into the Persian Gulf at the time of the Iranian crisis of 1979–80, this, too was a Cincpac responsibility.

Cincpac was responsible at Hawaii for the Pacific Air Forces, which in turn had two commands, the Fifth Air Force in Japan and the Thirteenth Air Force in the Philippines. Besides, the force kept a "nuclear-deterrent" wing at Guam.

The army command at Hawaii was responsible for the Eighth Army in Korea, the United States Army forces in Japan, largely at Okinawa, and the Twenty-Fifth Division at Schofield Barracks, Hawaii.

In 1980, the Fleet Marine Force included two of the Marine Corps's three active divisions with troops scattered about in various stages of readiness for action. The First Marine Brigade and the Marine Aircraft Group 24 at Hawaii were the "mid-Pacific ready force."

And last, of course, came the Pacific Fleet, the granddaddy of the command, with headquarters still located up the hill above the submarine base at Makalapa, where Admiral Nimitz had held forth in those vital years of the Pacific War. The Pacific Fleet had grown to be the world's largest naval command, in size of forces and in area of responsibility, with more than two hundred ships, two thousand planes, and twenty thousand men, manning everything from aircraft carriers to ballistic missile submarines. The fleet itself was so large that it was split in two: the Seventh Fleet operated in the Western Pacific and Indian Ocean; the Third Fleet was responsible for the Eastern Pacific, including the west coast of the United States.

In 1980, the change in the American defense posture was illustrated when the allies of the Pacific held joint maneuvers in Hawaii waters. Naval, air, and ground forces from Canada, New Zealand, Australia, the United States, and Japan combined for war games. It was a long time since that last battle at Okinawa in the Pacific War, and America had since made partners of old allies and enemies alike.

There was no question in anyone's mind but that the only power with the military capability of threatening the United States lines of communication in the Pacific was the USSR. But the Pacific Force was not aligned belligerently against the Soviet Union. Since the days of Vietnam there was no indication of an interest in military activity. Military America as well as civil America seemed to have learned the futility of outside interference in local revolutions. American policy, at least at the moment, encouraged non-American economic and political associations such as The Association of Southeast Asian Nations (ASEAN) without direct American involvement.

With the coming of the Reagan administration in 1981 and the change in general foreign policy to a more nationalistic stance than that of President Carter, there were some indications (El Salvador) that the United States's role in world affairs would again be more positive. Even so, President Reagan's approach was for less aggression than with President Johnson's or President Nixon's.

With the buildup of Soviet forces in the Pacific, the potential for conflict certainly existed. By 1979, it was apparent that the American involvement with the Peoples Republic of China was increasing, although on a defense level it was still minimal. But once again, an old enemy had become a new ally. There was still talk in military circles about "United States interest in limiting Communist inroads" (the myth of monolithic Communism died hard in military circles), but of more serious concern was Soviet expansionism, which had its roots in the old Czarist imperialism in the Pacific of the nineteenth century. In the spring of 1980, the American posture had been complicated by the Iranian crisis and the movement of American and Soviet forces into the Indian Ocean and the Persian Gulf region. In the fall, the Iran-Iraq War demanded constant United States attention. In 1981 there were more bush-fires.

Every morning, the admiral who was Cincpac arose in his mansion down by the submarine base at Pearl Harbor to greet the day with a political and military briefing conducted by his chief of public affairs, whose staff maintained a news watch that would have done credit to *The New York Times*. As he started his day, Cincpac knew precisely what condition the world was in as of that moment—he was far more completely aware of political and economic matters than his predecessors had been. Leaving that command in 1980, Admiral Maurice Weisner had summed it up.

The unique aspect of the Asian/Pacific basin, he said, "is the far-reaching impact which the action of any single nation has on the other nations in the region." For that reason, the possibility of conflict was constant, and as far as the United States was concerned, the answer was the need for forward forces that could go into action immediately to support American commitments and the decisions of American political leaders. The job of Cincpac in 1981 was like that of a demolition expert whose task was to sit constantly on top of a case of unstable nitroglycerin. The Pacific Fleet was not a very comfortable place to be, but that was the sort of world that existed in 1981, and there were many indications that it was going to be that sort of world for a long time to come.

Acknowledgments
and Notes

I AM INDEBTED to Admiral Maurice Weisner and many officers of the staff of the commander in chief of the Pacific for various materials in this book. Particularly helpful were Captain Dale Patterson, then chief public affairs officer of the Pacific Fleet, and Lieutenant Colonel William Zint of the Air Force, public affairs officer of Cincpac. Rear Admiral Lloyd Vasey (United States Navy, retired) was also helpful in steering the author to sources, as was Dr. Dean Allard, chief of the Operational Archives of the United States Navy in Washington. Librarians at the University of Hawaii, the Hawaii State library system, and the Pearl Harbor base library were most accommodating. Dr. Herman Gotlieb of Boston University's Mugar Memorial Library responded generously, as always, to innumerable demands for papers and manuscripts deposited with the library.

I drew heavily on a number of books that I have written about the Pacific, including *Damn the Torpedoes*, the biography of Admiral David Farragut; *Oliver Hazard Perry*; *How They Won the War in the Pacific*; *Blue Skies and Blood*, the story of the battle of the Coral Sea; *The Lonely Ships*, the story of the Asiatic fleet; *Storm Over The Gilberts*; *The Battle of Leyte Gulf*; *The Last Cruise of the Emden*; *The Typhoon that Stopped a War*; *The Carrier War*; *War in the Deep*; *To the Marianas*; *The Men of the Gambier Bay*; and *Destroyers*. I also consulted many other books and manuscripts, as noted in the chapter notes.

1 : Beginnings

Most of the material for this comes from my own unpublished *The End of the Essex*, which was in turn derived from *Damn the Torpedoes*, and various

287

works about the early American navy, including Edgar S. Maclay's *History of the United States Navy from 1775 to 1898*, and Dudley W. Knox's *History of the United States Navy*. I also used A. T. Mahan's *Admiral Farragut* and the Farragut biography written by his son. The adventures of the Americans in the Marquesas are largely forgotten since no attempt was made to follow up on Captain Porter's claim to the territory. Lieutenant Gamble, by the way, was the first marine officer ever to command a warship in battle.

2 : Stirrings

The basic sources for this chapter were Edgar S. Maclay's *History of the United States Navy from 1775 to 1898* and David M. Cooney's *A Chronology of the U.S. Navy, 1775–1965*. Lieutenant Commander Cooney noted that in the spring of 1811, the Americans began to become aware of the potentials of the Pacific, along the American coast, at least. In that year, the American ship *Tonquin* reached Point George on the Columbia River, and Lieutenant Jonathan Thorn established the trading post at Astoria in what is now the state of Oregon. The adventures in the Pacific trade are discussed in various manuscripts at the Mystic Museum in Mystic, Connecticut; although these do not quite fit the scope of this book, the stories of the spice and China trade make very interesting reading.

Another incident involving the navy and Pacific coast history was the landing of Captain James Biddle of the United States sloop of war *Ontario* at Cape Disappointment on the Columbia River in August, 1818, and his claim of that Oregon territory for the United States. The circumnavigation of the earth by an American naval vessel did not occur until 1830, when the USS *Vincennes* sailed around the world. This voyage brought the publicity that interested various merchants in the spice trade, and resulted in the incidents in the Dutch East Indies which caused the United States Navy to take cognizance of the Pacific.

3 : Expanding

The sources of this chapter include Maclay's *History of the United States Navy,* my own *Lonely Ships* (the story of the Asiatic fleet which discusses early American forays into the Pacific), and Cooney's chronology. I also used Harold and Margaret Sprout's *The Rise of American Naval Power, 1776–1918*. This work has a very good capsule history of the changes in the navy when the conversion from sail to steam was made in the later years of the nineteenth century. I dealt very briefly with the serious incident involving American, German, and British warships at Apia, Samoa, in the spring of 1889. I deal with it more fully in *The Typhoon That Stopped a War*. By this time, the navy was determined to have bases in the Pacific, and this determination, passed on to the politicians, was an extremely important matter in the

288

thinking that led to the overthrow of the Hawaiian monarchy and eventual annexation of Hawaii to the United States. For the story of the Perry expedition to Japan, I drew on the detailed study of the expedition written by the Reverend Francis L. Hawkes, published by congressional order of the Thirty-Third Congress, second session. This excellent three-volume work (one of them consisting of paintings prepared for illustration to an unknowing public) is available in many libraries. I also used Edward M. Barrows' *The Great Commodore* and Samuel Eliot Morison's *Old Bruin*, the life of Matthew Calbraith Perry.

4 : "A piece of land at this port, sufficient for a wharf. . . ."

The basic source for this chapter was R. S. Kuykendall's *The Hawaiian Kingdom*, the three-volume authoritative work on the subject. I also used Lorrin Thurston's *Memoirs of the Hawaiian Revolution*, and my own *Davies: The Story of a British American Fortune*, which tells the story of the revolution from a British businessman's point of view. It seems certain that the American maneuvering in Hawaii in the 1870s was finally responsible for the overthrow of the kingdom; without guarantee of American support, the rebels would never have succeeded. Britain refused to become involved; indeed, even loyal British businessmen like Theo H. Davies could see that the economic interests of Hawaii were closely tied to those of the United States. But economic interests and political ones were two different matters. Davies and many others, including such men as Samuel Parker, of American-Hawaiian descent, wanted no part of an American Hawaii. The influence of the navy in all this was more important than most people realize even today, not just because of the presence of various American men of war through the years, but because of the powerful influence of such men as Captain William Reynolds.

5 : Gridley Fired When He Was Ready

In a way, the best accounts of the Spanish-American War in the Pacific were those which appeared very shortly after the end of the war, for they ring of the jingoism of the day. For this chapter, I used G. F. Zaide's *The Philippine Revolution*, W. T. Sexton's *Soldiers in the Sun*, T. M. Kalaw's *The Philippine Revolution*, the Sprouts's *The Rise of American Naval Power*, C. H. Brown's *The Correspondents' War*, H. W. Wilson's *The Downfall of Spain*, and my own *The Lonely Ships*, which itself relied upon many other sources for information about this period.

6 : The Philippine Quagmire

Maclay's *History of the United States Navy* was vital to this chapter. It was written originally before 1893, but in 1901, Appleton brought out a revised edition which dealt thoroughly with the Spanish-American War and the Philippine insurrection, which ended that year. I also used T. M. Kalaw's *The Philippine Revolution* and T. H. Agoncill's *Malolos: The Crisis of the Republic*, published by the Philippines Social Science and Humanities Review.

7 : Into the Suluan Soup

Maclay's *History of the United States Navy* was again important here, as were the various above-mentioned accounts of the insurrection written from the point of view of the Filipinos. I had some background in the nature of the American occupation and the difficulties of the troops from research done many years earlier for *A Gentleman of Broadway*, a biography of Damon Runyon. Few of his contemporaries knew it, but Runyon served in the Spanish-American War and was one of those soldiers jammed into the troop ships and nearly suffocated on the way to Manila. Sexton's *Soldiers in the Sun* also gives the viewpoint of the participants. Zaide's *The Philippine Revolution* tells the story of the capture of Aguinaldo, one of the most remarkable adventures ever undertaken by an American general officer.

8 : The Boxers Didn't Really Want to Box

In the 1960s, I wrote *The Boxer Rebellion*, and this brief recapitulation draws on that source. I also used W. W. Willoughby's *Foreign Rights and Foreign Interests in China* and Maclay's *History of the United States Navy*, which although completely outmoded as a naval history has the virtue of dealing at some length with such incidents. Modern histories, such as those of Knox and Fletcher Pratt, scarcely mention the rebellion in terms of the United States Navy, and properly so, since it was a minor incident in that sense. But it was important in the shaping of the naval attitude toward Asia, and the Asian attitude toward the United States. With the exception of a few "protect-the-property" landings at Canton and other trade ports, the rebellion marked the first time that American troops landed on a continental Asian shore, and the first time that the United States Navy was involved in any sort of cooperative international activity. For *The Boxer Rebellion*, I consulted many sources, including diaries and papers of participants. Rather than relist them here, I refer the reader to the bibliography of that book.

9 : The Great White Fleet

The chapter title is borrowed from Robert A. Hart's *The Great White Fleet, Its Voyage Around the World, 1907–1909*. I also used Edwin A. Falk's *From Perry to Pearl Harbor*, and Gordon O'Gara's *Theodore Roosevelt and the Rise of the Modern American Navy*, and E. B. Potter's *The United States and World Sea Power*. As Hart noted, Teddy Roosevelt and his contemporaries would have found the term "Great White Fleet" meaningless, because

American warships had been painted white since the beginnings of the steel-hull navy. The United States, unskilled in international warfare, had never apparently considered the sort of target the gleaming white hulls would make. A bit later, battleship gray was borrowed from the British (although not precisely the same shade until World War II). The remarkable, and largely forgotten fact of the voyage was the basic reason for its inception: Teddy Roosevelt's worry over a growingly militaristic Japan. The whole concept of Japan as the ultimate Pacific enemy, which was full-blown by 1930, arose in this first decade of the twentieth century. In part, it can be traced back to Japanese dissatisfaction with the role played by the United States in ending the Russo-Japanese War. I dealt with that earlier in *The Russo Japanese War*. But there was more to it than that—to wit, the extreme anti-Japanese feeling that the Americans on the cruise encountered in Australia. As with the Chinese, it was not the movers and shakers of America and Australia who were frightened by the orientals, but the workingmen, who saw in these industrious, intelligent, and efficient people a threat to their own livelihoods. I dealt with this to some extent in *Asians in the West*.

10 : The Cunning Japanese

I used Knox's history of the navy as a basic source for the American naval viewpoint in this period. Also helpful was William Reynolds Braisted's *The United States Navy in the Pacific, 1909–1922*, which tells in considerable detail the virtually unknown story of Admiral George Dewey's enormous influence on American foreign policy in the first quarter of the twentieth century. The behaviour of Japan during World War I is documented in Braisted. I also encountered various other studies of the Japanese activity in this period in doing research for my *The Fall of Tsingtao*, *The Last Cruise of the Emden*, and *Defeat at the Falklands*, the story of Admiral Von Spee and the German East Asia Crusier Squadron in World War I. For the later period (after World War I), I used John H. Maki's valuable collection of key documents in Japanese-American relations, *Conflict and Tension in the Far East*, David H. James's *The Rise and Fall of the Japanese Empire*, and Gerald Wheeler's *Prelude to Pearl Harbor*.

11 : The Wicked Japanese

For this chapter, I again relied on Gerald Wheeler and Knox. The rise of Japanese militarism is documented very well in Takehiko Yoshihashi's *Conspiracy at Mukden*, which gives the background, extending to a period before the Russo-Japanese war. I had learned the young marshal's story (Chang Hsueh-liang) while in China in the mid-1940s. Takehiko Yoshihashi brings together impressive detail about the Mukden incident and some of its aftermaths. I also found Saburo Ienaga's more recent *The Pacific War*, interesting in this regard. Dr. Syngman Rhee told me several tales of the Japanese in the 1920s and 1930s when I was a correspondent in Seoul at the end of World War II. The late James Young, long-time correspondent for International News Service and an editor of the Japan Advertiser in the 1930s, also told me a number of stories that figured in this chapter. So did Hiroyuki Agawa's *The Reluctant Admiral: Yamamoto and the Imperial Navy*.

12 : The Nefarious Japanese

Agawa's biography of Yamamoto was primary for this chapter, as was Samuel Eliot Morison's *The Rising Sun in the Pacific, 1931–April 1942*. I also drew on research I had made in preparation for my own *How They Won the War in the Pacific*, including the action reports of various vessels and commands at the time of the Pearl Harbor attack. The poem illustrating the Japanese pilots' feelings about the attack on the eve of it comes from *The Death of a Navy*, by Andrieu D'Albas.

13 : Debacle at Wake

From Admiral Morison's account of the Japanese attacks on Wake Island (the first attack failed miserably), it seems apparent that if Admiral Halsey had been allowed his way, Wake could have been saved. That, however, is pure hindsight, only valuable because the fumbling actions of the American command at Pearl Harbor and the reluctance of Admirals Fletcher and Brown to risk their carriers by taking them to war indicate a fundamental problem in the fleet in the early days of the war. The politicians could not be called blameless either, for now, nearly four decades after the fact, it seems apparent that Admiral Kimmel, the goat of Pearl Harbor had been chosen wisely as Cincpac for his aggressive qualities and that these were sacrificed needlessly on the altar of an uninformed public opinion. Kimmel was ready to fight and had made the plans and issued the orders for the relief of Wake before the Japanese got there. But he was hamstrung in mid-motion, declared persona non grata by his own government, and the command was thrown into the hands of Admiral Pye, who had neither the imagination nor the aggressiveness of Kimmel. In my studies of various aspects of the Pacific War it becomes ever more clear that many of the problems of the first few months could be ascribed to sheer timidity on the part of otherwise responsible officers. Admiral King, of course, could not give way to his feelings at the expense of destroying the navy's morale, but in the King-Nimitz conference reports of the period it is apparent that this was one of his major concerns. Also, had he been more forceful at the outset, things might have gone much better in the South Pacific. Admiral Frank Jack Fletcher had dillied and dallied in the Wake defense, he did the same at the battle of the Coral Sea, after having made an ineffectual stab at the enemy in the Central Pacific. He deserted the amphibious landing at Guadalcanal, and had it failed, he most certainly would have had to bear the lion's share of responsibility for the disaster. Yet Nimitz, who liked Fletcher, and who was in addition a kindly man, interceded for him time and again until King finally lost patience and transferred Fletcher out to Alaska, out of harm's way, so to speak. But Fletcher was the hero of Midway, one might protest. Not true, the architect of the victory at Midway was Captain Miles Browning,* chief of staff to Admiral Halsey, who was "borrowed" by Admiral Spruance when Halsey fell ill on the eve of battle. It was Browning who shrewdly assessed the Japanese situation on the morning of June 4. Admiral Nagumo, not knowing that the American fleet was out, had launched an early morning strike to soften up Midway. The news of this came over the radio, and Browning realized that the Japanese planes on return to their carriers would foul the flight decks so that they would be a wonderful target—if only the American planes could get there in time. So the victory in fact was Browning's, although he never received the credit he deserved nor the promotion he should have had, because like many another officer, Browning had fallen into Admiral King's bad book for peacetime transgressions that had nothing to do with his fighting ability. I also used the biography of Yamamoto to show the Japanese view at the time.

14 : Confusion in the Coral Sea

The material for this chapter comes from the papers of Admirals Nimitz and Halsey, which I consulted at various times in research for other books. I used the Yamamoto biography to show his activities as commander of the Combined Fleet, and his attitudes as an officer who had opposed the war against the United States up until the last. The story of the battle of the Coral Sea comes from my own *Blue Skies and Blood*, for which I studied all the action reports, including the report of survivors of the oiler *Neosho*, a tale that indicates some of the best and worst qualities of the American naval officers of the period. In 1968, I had a long discussion with Admiral Aubrey Fitch about this battle. He was true to the naval tradition and refused to criticize Fletcher for his failure to turn the tactical command over to himself, an experienced and aggressive airman. Here again, was an illustration of the American problem in the first days of the war. But the Japanese had their troubles too. I had not known, until informed by the Yamamoto biography, that Admiral Nagumo had so poor a reputation among his peers of the Japanese naval establishment or that his naval failure had really caused the Japanese debacle at Midway. Nor had I known that the Midway operation was triggered by the

---

* My friend Robert Sherrod, correspondent, author, and magazine editor, demurs here. Browning was given too much credit, he says. But Browning knew his carriers in 1942 and Spruance did not.

Doolittle raid on Japan that spring. Jimmy Doolittle did not know it either, I believe. I interviewed him a number of times in connection with an abortive book project, and we discussed the Tokyo raid thoroughly, but he never indicated any such information. Also, while it is generally known that the naval intelligence unit at Pearl Harbor had managed to break the Japanese code, the facts of the matter were always very vague until publication in 1979 of W. J. Holmes' *Double-Edged Secrets*, which tells the whole story of the operation of the radio intelligence unit (at least in as much detail as the Office of Naval Intelligence permitted, after holding up publication for a dozen years). For the Coral Sea battle itself, I consulted several Japanese accounts, including that in *Boei Chiyo Baei Senshusho Senso Shitsu Cho Dai Toa Taiyo Senzen Shiso Sho*, the Japanese Self-Defense Agency Training Institute's Military History Room Library of the Pacific War, which has half a dozen volumes on South Pacific operations. It is apparent in these accounts that neither Admiral Nimitz nor Admiral Yamamoto were very well pleased with what had happened at the Coral Sea, but both were bemused by the immediately upcoming operation at Midway.

15 : Turning Point at Midway?

It is odd how very differently two nations can analyze the same basic set of events, but the histories of the Pacific war certainly prove the point. The Japanese have never accepted the theory that Midway was the "turning point." Rather they felt that the long struggle of attrition in the South Pacific turned the war about. Conventional American opinion, on the other hand, holds that until Midway the whole American effort was confused and not very competent, although naval officers would wince at that harsh characterization. Midway *was* important. It prevented the destruction of the American fleet and probably the seizure of Hawaii, for which the planners back in Tokyo were already making ready (according to information discovered in Tokyo in 1980 by John Stephan, a University of Hawaii history professor). Of course the Japanese had contingency plans for all sorts of invasions, including Australia, but because of the large Japanese-descended population of Hawaii and historical interest by Japan in those islands, there was a stronger pull. But Midway was not some point about which the whole war turned. Midway showed many of the American deficiencies, but it did not correct them. The *B-17*s at Midway didn't hit anything at all in their raids on the Japanese fleet, because the army pilots did not know how to bomb ships accurately. The American torpedo bombers were a miserable failure, not because of any lack of gallantry by the pilots, but because the aircraft were obsolete, and the torpedoes did not always explode even if they hit a target. At Midway not one bit of damage was done by the torpedo squadrons of the American carriers, and certainly much of that must be attributed to faulty equipment. It would be many months before the fleet got the new planes it needed and a matter of years before the torpedo problem was finally solved with the manufacture of a new electric torpedo. None of this changed at Midway, and the loss of those four carriers to Japan was not vital, in the sense that she still had more carriers than the Americans did. From a long-range point of view, the Midway battle was important also, because it cost the Japanese hundreds of skilled pilots. Somehow, in the command structure no drastic measures were taken to speed up training to replace these fliers, and that, more than the loss of ships, brought about disaster for Japan.

16 : Carlson's "Foolish" Foray

The title for this chapter comes from the snorting remarks of Marine General Holland M. "Howling Mad" Smith, the architect of the early marine victories in the Central Pacific campaign. After his marines had invaded Tarawa, to meet the most desperate sort of opposition and suffer casualties far greater than anyone had anticipated, Holland Smith discovered that the Japanese had begun the fortification of Betio almost immediately after Colonel Carlson's raid on Makin island. Smith blamed Admiral Nimitz and Admiral Spruance (whose idea the raid was) for the state of readiness of the enemy. And he was contemptuous of the results of the Carlson raid.

It was true that the raid did not produce what it was intended to bring forth. Carlson's big problem was the supply department, and the failure was occasioned by the refusal of a Pearl Harbor supply officer to listen to the marines when they asked for a certain brand of outboard motor for their rubber landing craft. So Carlson's men had difficulty in getting ashore and more trouble in getting back to the submarines. The story of the raid is based on my *Carlson's Raiders* and comes from the operations reports of the Second Raider Battalion, the submarines *Nautilus* and *Argonaut*, and the war diary of Cincpac for the summer of 1942. I also used the library at the United States Naval Academy and consulted several unpublished manuscripts written by midshipmen who had studied the raid in the course of their classes.

17 : Gauntlet At Guadalcanal

As far as Admiral Yamamoto and his successors in command of the Japanese Combined Fleet were concerned, the tide of battle turned against Japan beginning at Guadalcanal. The capture of Australia was one of the alternate operations at the time that the Midway-Aleutians drive was approved by Imperial General Headquarters in Tokyo. When the Midway operation failed to destroy the American fleet, the Japanese decided to go ahead in the south. They rejected the Yamamoto favorite plan to drive through the Middle East and link up with the German Army in the Soviet Union. They also rejected a Kwantung army plan to declare war on the USSR and move upward from

Manchuria. All these were given serious consideration. Otherwise General Yamashita, "the Tiger of Malaya," would not have spent all those years in Manchuria preparing for the expected war against the Soviets. But the drive south made more immediate sense, for it would cut off the threat posed by the American buildup in Australia. The first Japanese failure was the failure to land the invasion army at Port Moresby and secure all of New Guinea. That was stopped at the Coral Sea. The second failure was to hold Guadalcanal, complete the airstrip, and begin the shuttle combing that would soften up Australia for invasion. I first studied the Guadalcanal campaign for *How They Won the War in the Pacific* and later went through the action reports in study for a biography of Admiral Halsey (unmaterialized) and for *Raider Battalion*, since the Raiders played a major role in the Guadalcanal campaign. Guadalcanal was particularly interesting because the campaign marked the almost complete disruption of the Japanese navy's submarine service. From that point on, so much of Japan's effort was put to using naval vessels to supply isolated detachments, that the effectiveness of the submarines was largely lost. In the beginning, the submarines had done very well, particularly against American carriers. *Saratoga* was put out of action twice for many months, and *Wasp* and *Yorktown* were lost. But after the Guadalcanal campaign the Japanese submarine service lost its drive. Perhaps this would not have occurred had Admiral Yamamoto not been "assassinated" by the Americans. The term is just, I think, for there was no accident of war involved. A trap was set for the admiral after specific approval from Admiral Nimitz, based on his belief that Yamamoto was the most effective naval person in Japan and would never be adequately replaced. As events showed, Nimitz was quite right. Guadalcanal was important, too, because here the United States Navy sorted out its admirals and other senior officers. Many a career was made or broken at Guadalcanal, one or two of them unjustly so. The attenuated naval battle was also remarkable because it showed the tactical superiority of the Japanese navy over the Americans at that time, particularly in night fighting. The Americans were really saved at Guadalcanal by the shipyards in the United States, which were beginning to turn out the products that had been hastily begun a year earlier. Before Guadalcanal the Americans suffered from physical inferiority in the matter of ships and planes, and during the first weeks of the battle the Japanese had superiority in the air as well, with the Zero fighter still looming as the most effective aircraft in the Pacific. That all changed with the coming of the *P-38* and the *F6F*, each of which had characteristics superior to the Zero.

18 : The Solomons Slog-Along

Some of the information about Admiral Halsey and his method of command comes from a series of interviews with Admiral Arleigh Burke, who gained his nickname "Thirty-One Knot-Burke" from his exploits as a destroyer squadron commander in the Guadalcanal campaign. The material about Admiral Richmond Kelly Turner comes from Admiral George Dyer's extensive biography *The Amphibians Came to Conquer* and from materials lent me by Admiral Dyer. I also used the excellent account of the air war, *Cactus Air Force* by Thomas G. Miller, Jr. and *The Reluctant Admiral*, as well as the Japanese Self-Defense Agency's *Nanto Homen Kaigun Chikusen Ga Shima Tesshu* (Southeast District Navy Operations, Guadalcanal Island, Until Withdrawal), volume 2, and the United States Marine Corps official *History of the U.S. Marine Corps Operations in World War II, Pearl Harbor to Guadalcanal*, by Hough, Ludwig, and Shaw.

19 : The Carlson Comeuppance

The material about the Aleutians campaign comes from my *How They Won the War in the Pacific*. The story of the invasion of the Gilberts is told in my *Storm Over the Gilberts,* and the research materials are cited in that book's bibliography. The most complete account of the tide difficulties the invasion force faced is contained in Admiral Dyer's *The Amphibians Came to Conquer*.

20 : Torpedo Junction

The story of the American torpedoes has been told a number of times, first by Admiral Charles Lockwood himself in his writings about the Pacific War. I have told it in *War in the Deep, From the Turtle to the Nautilus*, and *How They Won the War in the Pacific*. I continue to be amazed, however, each time I look at the research materials, submarine action reports, ships' logs and the like, that it took so long for the navy to recognize the difficulty and correct it. The captains of the submarines began complaining in the first days of the war in the Philippines because they got "hits" and no sinkings. But the senior officers simply would not believe them, until finally Admiral Lockwood became convinced, and then even he had an uphill battle to get something done. Admiral Christie was one of the most skeptical, and because he was a torpedo expert who had designed the faulty torpedo and commander of the South Pacific submarine force, his words carried great weight. He was, in effect, the biggest fly in the ointment. Nimitz stood back in such matters, and let the experts fight it out. But Admiral Lockwood was not getting very far until Commander Daspit conducted his convincing experiment, which was the most scientific possible. Lockwood needed no more. He took the matter to Nimitz and secured his backing, and when the ordnance experts in Washington balked, Nimitz went into action in his effective way, and the problem was solved. Until it was solved, the submarine effectiveness was about half what it should be, as the events of 1943, 1944, and 1945 indicated.

Notes

21 : The Marshalls Campaign

This chapter was written from research begun in the writing of *How They Won the War in the Pacific*. Rear Admiral Ernest M. Eller, former director of naval history, was assistant gunnery officer on the Cincpac staff for some time, and he told me about the difficulties of bombardment during the Central Pacific operations. I also used action reports and other documents from the navy's Operational Archives, and the Marine Corps history's *Central Pacific Drive*, volume 3, by Shaw, Nalty, and Turnbladh. The story of Japanese submarine activity is well told in Zenji Orita's *I-Boat Captain*. I also used research materials compiled for my *To the Marianas*, which deals with the Marshalls invasion in part. Admiral John Towers's widow was kind enough to let me use the Towers papers several years ago, and from these I extracted much of the material about the command difficulties in the fleet's air arm.

22 : Into the Empire

All during the first two years of the war, Admiral Nimitz was bemused by Truk, the big Japanese naval base in the Caroline Islands. "The *cojones* of the Japs" he liked to say, and he intended to grab them by these testicles before long. So it came as a great surprise when the Japanese navy abandoned Truk as a naval base and moved back within the empire at the time of the Marshalls operation. Actually, the Japanese army had just begun to realize that the Japanese navy was unable to hold the territory taken in those first euphoric months when staff officers were talking about walking in the streets of Sydney and lolling on the beach at Waikiki. The material for this chapter was largely gathered in the process of writing *How They Won the War in the Pacific* and included Japanese and American records from the Navy's Operational Archives. The study of the battles for the Marianas Islands comes from various sources, the Marine history of the Central Pacific as already cited, Holland Smith's *Coral and Brass*, Admiral George Dyer's biography of Admiral Richmond Kelly Turner, and *Kogun*, the story of the Japanese army in World War II, by Saburo Hayashi. I drew the story of the "Marianas Turkey Shoot"—the fleet action against Admiral Ozawa's Japanese force— from the action reports of the Fifth Fleet during this battle. My conclusions about Admiral Spruance's cautiousness came from several conversations with Rear Admiral Charles Johns Moore, Spruance's friend and chief of staff in the early campaigns until forcibly removed because Admiral King insisted that every "battleship" admiral have an aviator as chief of staff and every "aviator" admiral have a battleship man.

The material about General MacArthur's visit to Pearl Harbor comes from the Nimitz papers and various biographies of MacArthur.

23 : And MacArthur *Did* Return

The material about the summer of 1944 and the various raids by the carriers comes from the action reports of the Third Fleet. The story of the raid on Formosa comes from those action reports as well, and so does that of the battle of Leyte Gulf. I also used other research I gathered for my *The Battle of Leyte Gulf* in this chapter plus research for *The Men of the Gambier Bay*, which was the story of the sinking of an escort carrier after a brief but eventful life.

24 : But it Wasn't Easy. . . .

The story of the desperate gambit of Admiral Ohnishi in establishing the Kamikaze corps was told in *Divine Wind*, the story of the Kamikazes. Halsey's activities are detailed in the operations reports and action reports of the American and Japanese navies.

25 : The Desperate Days of Iwo Jima

The Iwo Jima story comes from *Coral and Brass*, the Dyer biography of Kelly Turner, and E. P. Forrestel's *Admiral Raymond A. Spruance*. The action reports of various commands provided some detail. I used Samuel Eliot Morison's *Victory in the Pacific* for some detail and Allen R. Mathews *The Assault* for the feel of the Iwo Jima land fighting by the marines. The sad end to Holland Smith's active career was related to me by Admiral Harry Hill in a series of interviews in 1968. The fate of the Japanese was described in *Kogun,* the Japanese army story.

26 : Assassins at Okinawa

So many events occurred in the spring of 1945, that many Americans were unaware of the seriousness and implications of the changed Pacific war of that year. When the Americans reached Saipan, the invasion brought about the fall of the Tojo government. When it became apparent that the Philippines could not be held, the Japanese were already planning for the reaction they would make to invasion of their homeland. Iwo Jima confirmed the seriousness of the situation, and then came the invasion of Okinawa, which was regarded in Tokyo as part of Japan proper. Here, the Japanese hoped to make a stand that would so injure the Americans that they would be forced to bring about an "honorable" peace. The Ohnishi concept of suicide forces was carried to its highest degree here. Literally thousands of young men were trained to make one-way flights and give their lives for Japan. Some accepted the responibility gladly and some fearfully, but by the time that the troops came to Okinawa, the Kamikaze force was ready. The damage done to the American ships at Okinawa was almost unbelievable. The United States Navy suffered more casualties than in any other action of the war, more ships were sunk and damaged than in any other fight. In the Kamikazes, the Japanese had developed a truly fearsome weapon, and also an extremely cheap one and one quickly produced. One airplane could sink a million-dollar ship, and that was something new. For this chapter, I relied on many conversations with Admiral Harry Hill, who took over from Admiral Kelly Turner as commander of the amphibious forces at Okinawa, and on Hill's oral history, which is in the possession of the navy. I also used *Divine Wind* and Masanori Ito's *The End of the Imperial Japanese Navy*. For the study of American planning I went back to the research I did for *How They Won the War in the Pacific*.

27 : The War Ends

Admiral Halsey was sometimes compared to a bull in a china shop, and he did have a certain bulldog air about him, too. But when it came to the war, he conducted several of the most audacious and effective operations in the Pacific, and not least of these, although little known, was his decimation of the Japanese economy in the summer of 1945. For this story, I used the action reports of the Third Fleet and materials I had collected for the unwritten Halsey biography. The story of the sinking of the *Indianapolis* is an indication of the difficulties of this new war, where communications were not what they had been in the early days. The bombing of Hiroshima and Nagasaki raised some moral issues in America that still remain. But the fact was already shown in the stories of Iwo Jima and Okinawa that if the Americans invaded Japan, as they were preparing to do, the casualties would be enormous, and on balance, President Truman's decision to drop the atomic bomb seems to have been the cheaper route in terms of human life. I had not realized this myself until I read *Enola Gay*, the story of the development and dropping of the atomic bomb, and it came to me that the United States was never quite certain of the results that would be obtained until the Hiroshima bomb was actually dropped. Some worried that the A-bomb might not even explode, and this in turn exploded my personal theory that the president ought to have arranged for a Japanese committee to witness a private explosion somewhere out in the Pacific. But when one studies the attitudes of the Japanese army and navy officers at that moment and the fact that they were dealing through a Soviet Union that had much to gain by entering the war at this stage and absolutely nothing to gain by arranging such an affair, then the difficulties posed by the real situation appear to have been insurmountable for the president. Besides all this, the supply of A-bombs was so limited that to waste one—if the Japanese refused to believe—might have forced the allies to make the landings on Honshu and Kyushu after all.

300

28 : The Wiles of the Communists

I was in China at the end of World War II, when the Seventh Fleet sent elements to Manchuria and Chefoo, and from Shanghai and Peking I followed much of the activity. Later I had opportunity to discuss the postwar operations in China with Admiral Daniel C. Barbey, who was in charge there, and it was perfectly clear that the navy tried its best to remain aloof from the Chinese civil war, but by the terms of the Yalta agreement and other pacts, the United States was bound to treat the Nationalist government as the legitimate government of China. And that was where all the trouble began. Later on I visited Northern Manchuria, held by the Communists, and Dairen and Port Arthur and saw the extent of the stripping that the Russians had undertaken, which went so far as to leave whole factories absolutely vacant down to the bolts in the floor. Oddly enough (if one considered Communism as monolithic) the Russians were not nearly so much interested in helping Mao Tse-tung as they were in retrieving from Japanese possession some of the losses they had suffered from the depredations of Japan's German ally.

The Communists were extremely annoyed by the American movement into Peking and Tsingtao. I visited both places (lived in Peking for a time) and got to know Chou En-lai and a number of the other Communist leaders. They were obdurate in their violent opposition to any American aid to the Nationalists and, of course, the supply of Nationalist forces, which had been going on for five years, and the use of American ships to transport Nationalist armies infuriated them. My personal observations were buttressed by reference to Admiral Barbey's reports and by a Ph.D. thesis written by Lee Stretton Houchins, *American Naval Involvement in the Chinese Civil War*, which coincided with my own observations. One small note tells the tale: if the United States Navy had been wholeheartedly behind the Nationalists, rather than feeling its way in a difficult situation, then there would have been no hesitation in acceding to Chiang Kai-shek's request that the Chinese navy flagship *Chungking* be destroyed by American planes after the captain and crew defected to the Communists in 1948. The United States Navy politely refused.

29 : Retreat in Korea

In the winter of 1945–46, in Seoul's Hanto Hotel Building, Lieutenant General John R. Hodge used to sit back in his swivel chair, smoke his pipe, and talk about the mad political scene in Korea from which he was supposed to construct some order as chief of the United States occupying forces. I was a correspondent there and saw the general nearly every day. Very shortly after the surrender it became apparent to General Hodge that the Russians were not going to be accommodating about securing the unification of Korea. Under the general's orders, he had to maintain a military government, while in the North, the Soviets with much fanfare installed the puppet government of Kim Il Sung and then destroyed all opposition. It seemed apparent to General Hodge, even in the winter of 1945–46, that the North Koreans would eventually march south and try to unify the country by force, and he remarked ruefully even then that if they did so, he could not stop them for more than about twenty minutes.

Later, in 1947 in Washington, I had a long talk at one of those Washington cocktail parties with John Carter Vincent, then a major advisor to the secretary of state on Far Eastern policy, and he told me that the Department of State had written off Korea as outside the American defense perimeter. So the Dean Acheson speech to which I referred in the text was no accident but part of a plan, if a mistaken one. For the story of the events that followed in 1950 and later, I used Cagle and Manson's *The Sea War in Korea* and Harry J. Middleton's *The Compact History of the Korean War*.

30 : The Inchon Landing, and. . . .

Once again for this chapter I used the Middleton book and Cagle and Manson's *The Sea War in Korea*. I also consulted army records in the national archives, which I was using primarily for preparation of my *Airborne*, the history of the American parachute and glider forces. Since these did not particularly concern the Pacific Fleet, the information I extracted for this book was more general.

31 : Vietnam—The Beginning

As a war correspondent in China at the end of the war, I happened to be on the "ground floor" of the Indo-China revolution. I went down to Hanoi in September, 1945, to cover the Japanese surrender and remained to cover the struggle (then largely political) between Ho Chi Minh and the French. At that time Ho had taken over the *Gouvernement Generale* building on Hanoi's main street, across from the Metropole Hotel. The governor's palace, meanwhile, was occupied by General Lu Han of the Chinese Nationalist Armies, while the French were jammed up in what I recall as a middle school in the middle of the city. That was a fair statement of the political situation at the moment.

From the beginning, after interviews with all concerned, I found I could understand the points of view of the Chinese (loot) and the Vietnamese (freedom from colonial rule) but not of the French, who seemed to want to hope that everything was going to be all right and that France could come back and take over the colonial government once again. It was too bad the French in charge (Admiral d'Argenlieu and his aides) did not get to know Ho Chi Minh as well as I did or they would have realized even then that the cause was hopeless. Communist or not, the men and women of the Vietnamese revolution were absolutely determined that colonialism would have to go. At that point, I have always believed, American assistance could have moved Ho Chi Minh from the Communist path, but the fact was that the Americans who came down to Hanoi in the summer and fall of 1945 had neither experience nor good common sense to guide them. The military commander, General Gallagher, had previously been commandant of the United States Military Academy at West Point and seemed to believe he was still dealing with cadets. The political representative who arrived in October, a vice consul, was more concerned with finding himself the best digs in town than in any political reportage. A year later, I happened to be in Saigon on the day that the new "independent-within-the-framework-of-the-French-Union" government was installed, and from the looks on the faces of the crowds and the conversations I had with Vietnamese, neutrals, and a handful of intelligent French business people, it was apparent that the puppet government in the south would never work.

So I was hardly surprised by anything that happened in Indo-China in the 1940s and 1950s, including the French disaster at Dien Bien Phu. It had been obvious all the time: highly motivated revolutionaries who are willing to give their lives will always outmatch professional troops in the long run, and that is what happened in Indo-China. The French used their Foreign Legion, which although very tough was not made up precisely of French patriots. And when the French did employ loyal Frenchmen there were too few of them, and they were fighting far from home for a cause in which many did not believe.

The course of the war seemed simple enough to me, but I left Asia before the United States became entrapped in Vietnam. Sending in supplies and administrators to help the French was the first mistake. The facts are all contained in the excellent historical study *The United States Navy and the Vietnam Conflict* by Hooper, Allard, and Fitzgerald. It is a story of a powerful nation allowing itself to be drawn into a quagmire. The navy's part in this, originally, was quite minor. But the navy was an instrument of American policy, and naval officers, no matter their points of view, had their duty to do.

32 : Vietnam——Miscalculation

America's unfortunate envelopment in the disaster of Vietnam began really in the Eisenhower administration. General Eisenhower had a nice simplistic view about Communism that fit in very well with the American temper of the times. Communism was a Russian invention, designed to serve the Soviet State, and therefore bad, to be resisted everywhere at all costs. From that premise, it was not hard for three successive administrations to persuade themselves that they must supplant the French, when exhaustion and poverty

drove General DeGaulle to extricate France from Vietnam. The coming of
General Westmoreland to Vietnam in 1964 marked the beginning of the complete American involvement. As Westmoreland indicated clearly in *A Soldier
Reports*, he had scarcely stepped off the plane at Saigon before he was con-
fronted by the dreadful reality of Vietnam: the South Vietnam government
was corrupt, inept, and self-serving, and it could not hope to win the civil
war without massive injections of American aid. Within a year Westmoreland
was convinced that he could not do his job unless he could bring in American
troops to fight. And that is what happened. Unfortunately the military was
less than honest with the public, and long before the troops were actually
supposed to be in the field against the Viet Cong and then the North Koreans,
American "advisors" were actually participating in combat. That sort of dis-
honesty was the hallmark of the military in this war, the first war in American
history where large elements of the press and public turned against government policy.

When I began this book, I had several conversations with naval officers
at Pearl Harbor and elsewhere, Rear Admiral Lloyd Vasey in particular, but
I never learned much from any of them about the Vietnam war in which they
were deeply involved. It is still a little too soon to have any historical per-
spective on it, and the records will probably not be declassified for years. The
important record, however, became such a matter of public scandal that it has
been made public—and that is the set of circumstances that brought about
total participation of the Pacific Fleet: the celebrated Tonkin Gulf incident.

I consulted Joseph C. Goulden's *Truth is the First Casualty*, the Westmoreland autobiography, and Anthony Austin's *The President's War*. The
Austin book I found particularly compelling in its verisimilitude. The navy
people involved in that book acted like the navy people who I know have
acted. In this chapter, I also used Vice Admiral Edwin Bickford Hooper's
Mobility, Support, and Endurance, his personal record of the war, from his
vantage point as head of what might be called the "services of supply." The
story tells of the frustrations and enormous effort put forth by the navy at
great cost, to what was more and more a failing action.

33 : Run Aground

In a way, the story of the battle for Khe Sanh tells the whole tale of Americans
in Vietnam. The United States Marines occupied Khe Sanh and fought for it
for a whole year, only in the end to be brought back southward, the base
destroyed, and the whole war on the downgrade. So what had they been
fighting and dying for? The trouble was that nobody seemed to know until
very near the end that no amount of American assistance, barring a total
conflict with North Vietnam and all its allies, was going to win the war for
the South Vietnamese government. In 1973, Washington began to recognize

what had been obvious in Hanoi in 1945. The Pacific Fleet was not responsible for the political decisions, although Admiral Sharp's activities and actions at the time of the Tonkin Gulf affair certainly put him forth as a first-class hawk. But the fleet, as a whole, did its job without complaint and without political involvement. The fleet was as much the victim of the Vietnam War as any other organization.

34 : Covering Half the World

My visits to Pearl Harbor in the past five years have indicated to me that the men who guard the American nation from Camp Smith, where Cincpac holds forth, are more politically aware and more properly cautious than the previous generation of guardians. I based much of my chapter on the post-Vietnam role of the Pacific command on a small orientation booklet issued by the Cincpac public affairs office called *The Pacific Command*. I know a number of officers in Hawaii, active and retired, and have had the same impression from them over the years. The command is extremely security conscious and not very responsive to requests for information, but that is normal; their role is defense, not public relations. What I managed to gather, from discussions and reading of local newspapers and occasional encounters with high officers, is that it is most unlikely that the navy ever again would be involved in anything like the Tonkin Gulf incident that could be misinterpreted and misunderstood in Washington, as the facts of Tonkin Gulf seem to have been. And that highly professional level of activity up on Halawa Heights is an indication that the United States is not likely to back into or be stampeded into a new war by any elements of the Pacific Fleet.

Bibliography

Agawa, Hiroyuki. *The Reluctant Admiral: Yamamoto and the Imperial Navy*. Tokyo: Kondansha International, 1979.

Agoncillo, T. H. *Malolos: The Crisis of the Republic*. Manila: Philippine Social Science and Humanities Review, 1960.

Appleman, R. E.; Burns, J. M.; Gugeler, R. A.; and Stevens, J. *Okinawa: The Last Battle*. Tokyo: Tuttle, 1960.

Asahi, Shimbunm. *The Pacific Rivals*. New York and Tokyo: Weatherhill/Asahi, 1972.

Austin, Anthony. *The President's War: The Story of the Tonkin Gulf Resolution and How the National was Trapped in Vietnam*. Philadelphia: Lippincott, 1971.

Axelbank, Albert. *Black Star Over Japan*. New York : Hill and Wang, 1972.

Barrow, Edward M., *The Great Commodore*. New York: Bobbs Merrill, 1935.

Belote, James and William. *Typhoon of Steel*. New York: Harper and Row, 1970.

Borg, Dorothy, *The United States and the Far Eastern Crisis of 1933–1938*. Cambridge, Mass.: Harvard University Press, 1964.

Braisted, W. R. *United States Navy in the Pacific, 1909–22*. Austin: University of Texas Press, 1971.

Brown, C. H. *The Correspondents' War*. New York: Scribners, 1967.

Bryant, Samuel W. *The Sea and the States*. New York: Crowell, 1967.

Butow, Robert J. C. *Tojo*. Princeton, N.J.: Princeton University Press, 1961.

Bibliography

Cagle, M. W., and Manson, F. A. *The Sea War in Korea*. Annapolis: U.S. Naval Institute, 1957.

Cincpacflt. *Korean Interim Evaluation Reports*, Reels 1–6. Prepared by Scholarly Resources Inc. with the assistance of the U.S. Navy History Division.

Clinard, O. J. *Japan's Influence on American Naval Power, 1897–1917*. Berkeley: University of California Press, 1947

Coffey, Thomas M. *Imperial Tragedy*. New York: World, 1970.

Cooney, David M. *A Chronology of the U.S. Navy, 1775–1965*. New York: Franklin Watts, 1965.

D'Albas, Andrieu. *Death of a Navy*. New York: Devin Adair, 1957.

Davis, Burke. *Get Yamamoto*. New York: Random House, 1969.

Dyer, George. *The Amphibians Came to Conquer: The Story of Admiral Richmond Kelly Turner* 2 vols., Washington: U.S. Government Printing Office, undated.

Feis, Herbert. *The Road to Pearl Harbor*. Princeton, N.J.: Princeton University Press, 1950.

Goulden, Joseph C. *Truth is the First Casualty*. New York: Rand McNally, 1969.

Grew, Joseph C. *Ten Years in Japan*. New York: Simon and Schuster, 1944.

Griswold, A. Whiteny. *The Far Eastern Policy of the United States*. New Haven, Conn.: Yale University Press, 1938.

Hart, Robert A., *The Great White Fleet*. Boston: Little Brown, 1965.

Hattori, Takushio. *Dai Toa Senso Zenshi (The Great History of The Greater East Asia War)*, 4 vols. Tokyo: Matsu, 1953.

Herrick, Walter R. *The American Naval Revolution*. Baton Rouge, La.: Louisiana State University Press, 1966.

Holmes, W. J. *Double-Edged Secrets: U.S. Naval Intelligence Operations in the Pacific During World War II*. Annapolis: U.S. Naval Institute Press, 1979.

Hooper, E. B.; Allard, D. C.; and Fitzgerald, O. P. *The United States Navy and the Vietnam Conflict*. Washington, D.C.: Navy History Division, 1976.

Hooper, Edwin Bickford (Vice Admiral). *Mobility, Support, Endurance: The Story of Naval Operational Logistics in the Vietnam War 1965–68*. Washington, D.C.: Navy History Division, 1972.

Houchins, Lee Stretton. *American Naval Involvement in the Chinese Civil*

War 1945–49. Ann Arbor, Mich.: unpublished Ph.D. thesis duplicated by University Microfilms.

Hoyt, Edwin P. The *Glorious Flattops*. Boston: Atlantic Monthly Press, 1965.

————. *The Last Cruise of the Emden*. New York: Macmillan, 1966.

————. *The Typhoon That Stopped a War*. New York: David McKay, 1968.

————. *Destroyers: Foxes of the Sea*. Boston: Atlantic Monthly Press, 1969.

————. *The American Attitude: The Story of the Making of Foreign Policy in the United States*. New York: Abelard-Schuman, 1970.

————. *How They Won the War in the Pacific*. New York: Weybright and Talley, 1970.

————. *The Battle of Leyte Gulf: The Death Knell of the Japanese Fleet*. New York: Weybright and Talley, 1972.

————. *Asians in the West*. New York: Thomas Nelson, 1974.

————. *Blue Skies and Blood*. New York: Paul Eriksson, 1975.

————. *The Lonely Ships: The Life and Death of the U.S. Fleet*. New York: David McKay, 1976.

————. *War in the Deep: Pacific Submarine Action in World War II*. New York: Putnam's, 1978.

————. *Airborne: The History of the American Parachute Forces*. New York: Stein and Day, 1979.

Ito, Masanori, *The End of the Imperial Japanese Navy*. New York: Norton, 1956.

Ito, Masashi. *The Emperor's Last Soldiers*. New York: Coward-McCann, 1967.

James, David H. *The Rise and Fall of the Japanese Empire*. London: George Allen and Unwin Ltd., 1951.

Japanese Self-Defense Agency. *Nanto Bosen Kaigun Sakusen* (Southeast District Naval Operations). (I used the two volumes covering Guadalcanal of this official Japanese war history.)

Jones, F. C. *Japan's New Order in East Asia: Its Rise and Fall 1937–45*. Cambridge and New York: Oxford University Press, 1954.

Kalaw, T. M. *The Philippine Revolution*. Manila: Manila Book Co., 1915.

Kase, Toshikazu. *Journey to the Missouri*. New Haven, Conn.: Yale University Press, 1950.

Kato, Masuo. *The Lost War*. New York: Knopf, 1946.

Bibliography

Knox, Dudley W. *A History of the United States Navy*. New York: Putnam's, 1948.

Kodama, Yoshio. *I Was Defeated*. Tokyo: Booth and Fukuda, 1951.

Maclay, Edgar S. *A History of the United States Navy*, 3 vols. New York: Appleton, 1902.

Maki, John M. *Conflict and Tension in the Far East: Key Documents, 1894–1960*. Seattle: University of Washington Press, 1961.

Matthews, Allen R. *The Assault* (Iwo Jima). New York: Simon and Schuster, 1947.

Middleton, Harry J. *The Compact History of the Korean War*. New York: Hawthorn Books, 1965.

Miller, Thomas G., Jr. *The Cactus Air Force*. New York: Harper and Row, 1969.

Moore, Frederick. *With Japan's Leaders*. New York: Scribners, 1942.

Morison, Samuel Eliot. *History of United States Naval Operations in World War II*, 13 vols. Boston: Atlantic Monthly Press, 1948–61.

Morris, John. *Traveler From Tokyo*. New York: Sheridan House, 1944.

Okumiya, Masatake, and Jiro, Horikoshi (with Martin Caidin). *Zero: The Inside Story of Japan's Air War in the Pacific*. New York: Ballantine, 1956.

Orita, Zenji, and Harrington, Joseph D. *I-Boat Captain*. Canoga Park, Calif.: Major Books, 1976.

Rees, David. *Korea: The Limited War*. London: Macmillan, 1964.

Saburo, Hayashi, *Kogun: The Japanese Army in the Pacific War*. Quantico, Va.: The Marine Corps Association, 1959.

Saburo, Ienaga. *The Pacific War*. New York: Pantheon Books, 1978.

Sexton, W. T. *Soldiers in the Sun*. Harrisburg, Pa.: The Military Service Publishing Co., 1939.

Shore, Moyers S., II. *The Battle for Khe Sanh*. Washington, D.C.: U.S. Marine Corps, 1969.

Sprout, Harold and Margaret. *The Rise of American Naval Power, 1776–1918*. Princeton, N.J.: Princeton University Press, 1939.

Tolischus, Otto, *Tokyo Record*. New York: Reynal and Hitchcock, 1943.

Tomes, Robert. *The Americans in Japan: An Abridgement of the Government Narrative of the U.S. Expedition to Japan*. New York: Appleton, 1857. (This is a short version of the three-volume official document.)

Bibliography

U.S. Marine Corps. *History of U.S. Marine Corps Operations in World War II*. Washington, D.C.: U.S. Marine Corps, 1966.

Westmoreland, William C. (General) *A Soldier Reports*. New York: Doubleday, 1976.

Wheeler, Gerald E. *Prelude to Pearl Harbor*. Columbia, Mo.: University of Missouri Press, 1963.

Willoughby, Westel W. *Japan's Case Examined*. Baltimore: Johns Hopkins Press, 1940.

Wilson, H. W. *The Downfall of Spain*. New York: Burt Franklin, 1900.

Winton, John. *The Forgotten Fleet: The British Navy in the Pacific, 1944–45*. New York: Coward McCann, 1970.

Yoshihashi, Takehiko. *Conspiracy at Mukden*. New Haven, Conn.: Yale University Press, 1963.

Zaide, G. F. *Philippine History and Civilization*. Manila: Philippine Associated Publishers, 1939.

———. *The Philippine Revolution*. Manila: Modern Book Co., 1954.

Index

313

Index

Index

Index

316

Index

Index

Index

319

Index

Index

321

Index

Index

The Author

Edwin P. Hoyt has been aware of the special place of the Pacific Ocean in American destiny since his boyhood in Oregon. He has traveled the length and breadth of the Pacific in war and peace and has written for newspapers, magazines, and the book trade on subjects political, military, and economic in that area. He is a graduate of the University of Oregon and served during World War II, first in the U.S. Army Air Corps, then with the United States Office of War Information in India, Burma, and China and finally as a war correspondent in China. After the war he traveled the Pacific and other areas as a foreign correspondent. Later he edited and published newspapers and magazines and was employed for a time by CBS News and American Heritage Publishing Company. In recent years he had lived in Hawaii, where he fishes the Pacific, and writes about Pacific affairs for the *Far Eastern Economic Review*, the *Times* of London, and writes books, many of them dealing with naval history. He is married, the father of three children, and the grandfather of three.